INTRODUCTION

I am often asked, "Who is the most important person you've ever interviewed?" I've been blessed to interview many world leaders, celebrities, and other notables; however, the most important person I've ever sat down with is not one of them, but rather my own dad.

This is that story. It is a story of war, a story of courage, and a story of a daughter finally getting to know her father.

I should also say that this journey has proved to be the most difficult challenge and "get" of my career. Even though I've wondered about my dad's past and had many questions about it since I was a young girl, it took a lifetime to obtain the answers. It came down to intensive months of asking, searching, and reasking my dad in order to get him to sit down with me and share this story.

Rita Cosby

**Praise for a daughter's touching homage
to her hero father**

QUIET HERO

"A beautiful tribute to the strength of the human spirit."

—Dr. Henry Kissinger, former secretary of state

"This is an incredible story of survival and sheer courage."

—Gen. Tommy Franks, U.S. Army (Ret.),
former commander, U.S. Central Command

"Touching and moving. . . . All true lovers of freedom need to read *Quiet Hero*."

—Dick Morris, political commentator and author of
2010: Take Back America

"One of Poland's great treasures has now been found. Richard Cosby and his Resistance comrades are true heroes in our historic fight for freedom. Without their courage, Solidarity would never have won its final batle."

—Lech Walesa, former president of Poland

"A must-read for all families. . . . *Quiet Hero* is an intensely captivating and inspiring story of a daughter finally getting to know her father. Reading it reminds me of my first visit to Poland in 1964 with my parents. . . . Rita's book captures the passion of her Polish heritage with verve and love."

—Kathleen Kennedy Townsend, former lieutenant governor of Maryland,
daughter of Robert F. Kennedy

"Rita Cosby's compelling book captures an important part of history. In its intimately personal way, *Quiet Hero* honors those, like her father, who fought valiently and often anonymously against true evil."

—David Harris, Executive Director, American Jewish Committee

Quiet Hero has been featured on the *Today* show, *Good Morning America, Oprah & Friends, The O'Reilly Factor, Inside Edition, Extra, Nancy Grace*, TBN, and other national media. It is also available as an eBook.

QUIET HERO

Secrets

from

My Father's Past

Rita Cosby

THRESHOLD EDITIONS

NEW YORK LONDON TORONTO SYDNEY

Threshold Editions
A Division of Simon & Schuster, Inc.
1230 Avenue of the Americas
New York, NY 10020

First Threshold Editions trade paperback edition May 2011

THRESHOLD EDITIONS and colophon are trademarks of Simon & Schuster, Inc.

For information about special discounts for bulk purchases,
please contact Simon & Schuster Special Sales at
1-866-506-1949 or business@simonandschuster.com.

The Simon & Schuster Speakers Bureau can bring authors to your live event.
For more information or to book an event contact the Simon & Schuster Speakers Bureau
at 1-866-248-3049 or visit our website at www.simonspeakers.com.

Designed by Ruth Lee-Mui

Manufactured in the United States of America

1   3   5   7   9   10   8   6   4   2

ISBN 978-1-4391-6550-8
ISBN 978-1-4391-6551-5 (pbk)
ISBN 978-1-4391-6561-4 (ebook)

For my determined and valiant father,
and in tribute to all who have served
so that others may live free

1

SUITCASE OF SECRETS

*M*y dad wasn't with us the day my brother Alan and I scattered our mother's ashes into the ocean off Connecticut. Nor had he been there for the church service in her hometown. In fact, though Mom loved him until the day she died, Dad continued to keep his distance from us during her extended illness, unable to show tears or express any emotions, which not only infuriated me, it hurt me to my core. As we said our prayers and scattered her ashes under a clear blue sky that September 25—her birthday—I couldn't help but think of my father. I was still angry with him. I couldn't let it go. I felt as if he had abandoned us years before.

On Christmas Eve 1983, Dad told us he was leaving. No matter how much time passes, it is one of those raw memories that still breaks my heart every time I think about it. My mother had already made the preparations for our traditional Christmas Eve dinner of ham and cheesecake, the tree was decorated in my mom's red and white Danish flags, and in our annual tradition, rather than buying a gift for my dad, I had written something for him.

For our holiday gifts, since our youth, Dad always insisted we build, draw, paint, or write something ourselves, rather than giving store-bought presents. One year, I wrote a Christmas play and asked him to perform all the parts. Another, I remember making a beaded necklace for my mother. My dad taught us early on that material things were only temporary. Yet no matter how brilliant our ideas might have been as young children, he always challenged us by saying, "You can come up with something better than that."

Sadly, the Christmas I remember most is the Christmas he arrived home from an extended work trip in Michigan with a gift that none of us wanted.

I was downstairs putting on my makeup in our one tiny bathroom, pleased our family was going to have a nice Christmas together. I overheard my mom and dad having a serious, rather heated, conversation in the adjacent living room. I heard him say that he wasn't happy and wanted to "move on." At first I thought he was talking about his work. He wasn't. He wanted to move on . . . from us.

After he presented my mother with the news that their marriage was finished, he came to the bathroom door and said he needed to talk to me about something. He told me simply that he was turning sixty and had decided he was no longer in love with my mother—more specifically, that he'd "found another woman attractive." For a moment I stared at his reflection in the bathroom mirror, unable to look him in the eye, then I burst into tears of disbelief.

"Why?" I asked. "*Why*?!"

My dad was fairly clinical about it, explaining that he was no longer "happy" and that he'd waited as long as he could. "I'm still young enough," he said in his suddenly grating Polish accent. "If I am going to make any change, I've got to do it now or never."

Subconsciously, I suppose I knew that my parents had drifted apart. They had moved into different bedrooms—my mother's room was downstairs, my father's upstairs—but I knew other relatives who had separate rooms. I thought it was a European thing.

It wasn't. Dad was planning on asking his civil engineering company for a transfer to another assignment. He and *Judy* were hoping to relocate to Washington, D.C. "I'm moving on," he said coldly. "I've made my decision."

"Why are you doing this?" I screamed, fighting desperately to keep my family together. "How can you just walk in and do this?"

"Rita," he said, "life is too short not to be happy." Then he turned and walked out of the bathroom.

Christmas was ruined, and truthfully, I don't think my mother ever got over the abrupt end of their marriage. That night I heard her crying in her bedroom, and I went in to check on her. She was visibly shaking and stunned. They had been married for thirty-two years. She told me she had come to terms with the distance that had crept into their relationship, and that she certainly never imagined herself as a divorced woman. "I know we haven't been happy for a while," she said as I gently stroked her hair. "But I never thought it would be over. We've been through so much together."

Divorce is a terrible thing. It really wrecked my mother. It was hard on my brother and me as well. It confused me to realize that my own father was able to so easily compartmentalize his emotions and love for his own family. And it made me grow up very fast. Though Dad promised me, "I'm not going to divorce the family; I'll still be your father, and make sure you and Alan are taken care of," we felt he didn't. His new wife was much younger than my mother, and she and my dad quickly had a child together. When it came time to pay for my college education, he told me he had other commitments. I fought with him and reminded him of the promise he'd made in the bathroom that night to take care of me.

"I have a new family to take care of now," he said.

"You have to take care of your old family first," I told him.

After my father walked out that Christmas, my mother never even dated again. She said she was all right, putting the best face on things, but I know she was deeply hurt by the fact that my dad was able to instantly and so easily sever all ties, to up and leave and then so quickly partition off those years of his life with her as though they never happened, as if she'd never existed.

All I could say was, "We'll get through this."

It was a phrase I'd repeat to her years later on the horrible afternoon I got her grim diagnosis.

I was hit with the news my mother was terminally ill on an otherwise beautiful day. Before that, everything had been going right. When I received the call, the call every child dreads but never thinks she'll actually get, I was moving into my new high-rise Manhattan apartment. After years of living out of boxes, chasing my dream of being a network newscaster, I had finally landed my own show on Fox News. I was thrilled to be making the career move from senior correspondent to network anchor, but my real happiness came from the physical move from Washington, D.C., to New York City, a relocation that, after nearly twenty years, had me again living near my mother's Connecticut home.

One of the most difficult things about being a television journalist is the amount of time spent apart from loved ones. Though both my parents taught me to follow the news and to be interested in world events, my mother had been hit hardest by my decision to actually move away after college and pursue stories around the globe. My frequent travel left her living alone for what should have been the golden years of her life, as my dad had already set off to chase a new story of his own.

Shortly after my dad announced he was leaving, my mother went back to work full time as a salesclerk at Siladis Pharmacy, and had held her nine-to-five job ever since. I spent those years working my way up the journalistic ladder, making my hard-fought way back to New York.

It was a gorgeous day when I moved into my swanky new Manhattan address, and I was excited to settle into my new apartment and my new hosting job at Fox. Two friends were with me, helping pick spots for my furniture and the endless parade of boxes the movers were bringing in. The whole day felt like a great reward—a new position, a new apartment, and a chance to see my mother more.

All at once the day's Technicolor happiness went gray.

The phone rang. It was my brother, Alan. After months of encouraging her, we had finally convinced my mother to see a doctor about her troublesome back pain. As was her nature, she had steadfastly endured it, working on her feet as a salesclerk at the pharmacy and taking her daily five-mile walk with her beloved dog, Hippi. She thought it was simply a pinched nerve that would work itself out.

"Cancer," my brother said. It was a word we'd never once spoken. A word I never imagined I'd hear. "A tumor," he said again, "and it looks really bad." I couldn't speak, couldn't breathe. My friends came over and put their hands on my back, and my brother handed the phone to my mother's doctor.

"Where is the tumor?" I asked the doctor, barely holding myself together, trying to keep the panic that was creeping into my voice in check.

"It's not one tumor, Rita," the doctor said. "They're everywhere. It's like a checkerboard, there are so many of them."

"How bad is it?" I asked, trying to fight off the obvious.

"Very bad. Your mother could die soon." I doubled over and cried, right there in the center of my brand-new living room, surrounded by unopened boxes. My two friends, who both happen to be doctors, hugged me tightly. One of them grabbed the phone and began talking quickly to the doctor on the other end, rattling off medical terms, asking for cell counts and prognoses. Suddenly my friends, who had only signed on to help design the apartment, were helping redesign my life.

When the phone was handed back to me, my mother was on the other end. I didn't know what she'd been told, so I did my best to keep my voice steady and to pretend that everything was all right.

"Hi, Mom!" I said, with a put-on cheerful lilt. "How are you? I want you to know that we're going to get through this. I promise you. I love you and whatever this is, we're going to fight it as a family. Whatever we need to do, Alan and I will be there with you through it all." I took a deep breath and tried to picture her there with the doctor. "I love you," I said again.

I kept hoping that the prognosis was wrong. Her doctor, a general practitioner, was not a cancer specialist, and I was positive a second opinion would prove that everything was all right. Or, if it was cancer, it wouldn't be as severe as we'd been told; a real expert could figure things out and put it all in perspective. Maybe we'd caught it early enough that it could still be cured.

By the next morning, we'd been in touch with one of the best cancer specialists in the world, the incredibly kind Dr. David Kelsen, Chief of Gastrointestinal Oncology at Memorial Sloan-Kettering Cancer Center. He examined my mother, and when I met with him to hear what he'd found, any hopeful fantasies I'd had about her situation quickly evaporated.

"I'm amazed that your mother can even walk," he said. "The pain must be crippling."

I asked him to explain the details of what was happening to her. He told me that her back pain was stemming from a severe tumor entwined around the base of her neck and her spine. When he told her she'd need immediate chemotherapy and radiation, she responded that all she needed was a couple of Tylenol and a little Bengay, thank-you-very-much. "But," he said quietly to me as we stood away from her in the hallway, "the fact is, she's going to be paralyzed soon if we don't stop the growth of this tumor. It could be any day now." He told me that his own mother, whose cancer hadn't been as advanced, had died soon after her own diagnosis. *Oh, my God,* I thought to myself, *what hope is there if one of the top cancer doctors at one of the top cancer hospitals in the world says my mom's prognosis is worse than that of his own mother, whom he couldn't save?*

"How long does she have?" I asked.

"Maybe as little as a month."

I stared at him; the weight of his words crushed me. I felt the familiar feeling of responsibility come surging back, the duty I'd felt for my mother ever since my father left us. I was the mother again. When I look back on that terrible moment, I find solace in the memory of being tasked with tending to the person I cared about most in the world.

"Should I tell her or should you?" Dr. Kelsen asked.

I thought it would be better if Alan and I told her. She should hear it from people she loved. When my brother and I spoke to her, she was just as stalwart as always, repeating the Tylenol and Ben-gay solution. I didn't have the heart to speak with such terrible specificity, to tell her that she might only have a month. Foretold death is a tale no one should have to hear. Instead I told her, "You may not have a lot of time," adding optimistically that "some people survive a month and some people beat all the odds and survive for years. We just have to be aggressive." We tried to convince her and ourselves that she would be the exception, the one who beat the odds.

I was haunted, though, by Dr. Kelsen's inability to save his own mother. The thought came to mind often and I tried to push it aside, tell myself not to think it, to stay upbeat for her sake. The only thing worse than what we were telling her would be her seeing us upset. Throughout the process, she remained as selfless as always, worrying not about herself, but rather about Alan, me, and Hippi. The day we told her the bad news, all she wanted to know was who was going to take care of Hippi. "He looks forward to our daily walks," she said sweetly. Little did she know she was never going to walk Hippi again.

She moved into my new apartment, which for months remained full of boxes I hadn't gotten around to unpacking. She looked at it as a getaway for her, a vacation, and she was excited to be able to spend time with her daughter. For a while—except for the hospital bed and the wheelchair—it *was* like a vacation. We would go to outdoor cafés and talk in ways that we never had before. I remember those talks as some of the best conversations I ever had with her. She talked about how proud she was of my brother and me, and we reminisced about the fabulous African safari that the two of us had recently taken together. She also talked about my dad, and despite their painful divorce, she still spoke of him lovingly and remembered their romance fondly. Even after what we viewed as his devastating and sudden good-bye, he was still, she said, her hero.

She had met him shortly after World War II while working as an au pair for a wealthy Danish industrialist in London. My dad was employed by the man as well, and was dating the family's cook, a Danish woman like my mother. He and my mother first started talking to each other at a party, and he quickly left the cook for the pretty au pair. My mom lit up when talking about my dad. She still blushed at his handsomeness. She told me how smart he was, how hard he'd worked to learn English. She noted almost as a postscript how heroic he was for what he'd experienced during the war, though she really didn't know much specifically about what he'd gone through, even then. I'm sure I now know more about my dad's life than she ever did.

I now see that his life has really been a fusion of three lives: prewar, postwar, and post-us. What I never knew was that the life he lived during the war is the one that he tried to forget. What I would discover is that the life he tried to forget is the one he remembers every day . . . the one that made him who he really is.

As my mother's control over her memory continued to fluctuate and her condition deteriorated, Alan and I began to realize how little time she really had. Soon it became clear that she had only a week left, maybe even just a few days. We had no way of really knowing, and it tore us up inside. It was both sad and terrifying to see someone we loved so much slowly die in front of us. It was such a stressful time, and I needed a caring, loving father whose regard for his children outweighed all else. Instead, I felt there was a total disconnect from my father and his emotions, so much so it not only pained me to talk to him in that period, but it made me question who he was and what happened to his soul. After we spoke by phone about my mother's condition, I hung up, and my anger turned to wailing cries.

The cancer had spread to her brain. It was something we'd been warned to expect, but that knowledge didn't make it any easier. One day, near the end, when I entered her room, she looked up at me at the care facility in Connecticut, and I knew right away that something had changed.

"You're such a pretty girl," she said to me as if I were a stranger. "Who are you visiting?"

For a moment, words caught in my throat, and I was unable to speak for fear of breaking into sobs. After a while, I mustered the ability to say, "I'm here to see you! You're my mother."

"Oh, really?" she replied. "You're so beautiful."

I tried to give her a strong smile. "You're so beautiful, too."

I left that day feeling at sea, as if I had been completely cut adrift. I had no idea what to do. I remember taking the train back into New York City, crying all the way, bent forward in my seat, unable to stop the tears, thinking, "I've lost my mother." It seemed impossible that she could ever come back from this, but somehow she did. Although some hours were better than others, she rallied. When I saw her again a day or so later, I was terrified that she would greet me with the same blank look she'd given me during my previous visit. She didn't remember the last time I'd been there, but she did remember me, her daughter. I was overjoyed. At the time, this seemed like enough of a victory.

Days later, I was preparing to do my Sunday night show and I received a phone call from one of her nurses. This was not out of the ordinary—in the past few weeks, I'd gotten to know all of the amazing nurses who attended to my mother. But this time, the news was especially grave.

"Your mother is slipping," the nurse said. "She's going to die soon."

I couldn't breathe. I was minutes from going on the air. After a long silence, I finally found words and said, "I'll get someone else to do the show. I'll see if Geraldo can fill in."

"No," the nurse said, "do the show. Your mother is here right now, pointing to the television. But I think this will be the last show your mother will see. Make sure it's a good one."

The entire show was a blur. The only thing running through my head as I read off the news of the world was "my mother is watching and she is dying." One of my producers called the hospital during every commercial break, and updated me through my earpiece. "Your mother is still watching. The nurse says she's staring at the TV and smiling from her bed."

Immediately after we finished the show, I had a car ready to take me to her bedside. When I arrived, the nurse was waiting for me. "Your mother is a fighter," she informed me. "She's not going to die tonight, but just know she's going to die soon."

My mom was sitting up in bed when I entered the room. I asked her if she'd seen my program. She beamed, her cheeks still rosy with life. "You should get some rest," she told me, "you look tired."

My eyes filled with tears. I said, "I love you, Mom."

She replied, "I love you more."

It was the last thing I'd hear her say. Sometime that night she began to slip, and two days later she passed away.

Shortly after Mom died, Alan and I boxed up our mother's belongings and put them all in storage. We decided to wait for a while before we tackled the process of going through the precious memories that were tucked away inside that unit. Neither of us was able to deal with the painful realization that our mother was truly gone. More than six years passed before I felt ready to delve into those relics.

One fall weekend, I decided the time was right at last. I arrived at the storage facility feeling confident. I felt that I had come to terms with my mother's death, and that time would have made this process less painful. But I was wrong—going through her old things was like reliving the pain of her illness all over again, like death by a thousand paper cuts. Pain that has been packed away, I discovered, is still astonishingly potent when reopened.

I found myself surrounded by bits and pieces of her life, tasked with making the difficult decisions about what would stay and what would go. Each item I pulled from the containers ignited a new set of long-dormant emotions in me. I agonized over every little thing: clothing, letters, childhood toys. Without my mother here, even the tiniest keepsake took on a profound meaning, a memory I didn't want to let go of. I had been sitting on the floor of that metal cage for a long time, fruitlessly trying to arrange the stuff into "keep" and "give away," when I stumbled upon an old, tan suitcase I had never seen before.

Inside were artifacts from another time, pieces of a life I'd never known. The case was full of my father's memories—particularly remnants from the war. A worn Polish Resistance armband. Rusted tags with a prisoner number and the word "Stalag IV B." And an ex-POW identity card, emblazoned with the name *Ryszard Kossobudzki*.

I had lost my mother, and now I'd found pieces of a father I had never known. One thing I learned through my mother's illness was that time is precious and fleeting. But why does it so often take adversity to connect with the ones we love? My mother was gone, and I still felt a deep and abject emptiness. Although he really wasn't a part of my life anymore, my dad was still here. As I gazed into the suitcase at disconnected memories that only my father could bring clarity to, I couldn't help but think that these relics could somehow bring clarity to our disconnected relationship and help mend my broken heart. How could I break down the wall that separated my father and me? How could I muster the courage to get to know him before it was too late?

I've spoken with and investigated some of the most notable and notorious people on the planet, from Pope John Paul II to the Son of Sam, but standing there in the storage unit, confounded by these relics of my father's life, I realized I had never really focused my investigative skills on my own past. What had happened to my father on his way to America? What kind of horrors had he endured? Why was he still a mystery to me? Who *was* Ryszard Kossobudzki?

2

SILENT SCARS

*E*very scar has a story. Mine was written across my knee in eighth grade during an accidental skirmish with a porcelain lotion bottle. My father's scars were etched on his body when he was of a similar age, but under much different circumstances.

I first noticed my dad's scars when I was eight years old during our annual family camping trip to Mount Desert Island in Maine. "Noticed" is not quite the right word, as his scars, dashed about his body like cracks in dried mud, are hard to miss. Rather, it was while camping that I first consciously comprehended that a scar was an indication that something bad had happened, something we weren't supposed to talk about.

Camping was my family's vacation tradition and remains one of my happiest and most vivid childhood memories. We made the eight-hour trip from our driveway in Old Greenwich, Connecticut, to our regular campsite at Somes Sound View Campground in Maine so many times that every part of it became a ritual. Each summer, shortly after my dad got home for his annual two weeks off, he and my mother would load up our old white Chrysler station wagon and we'd take off for the coast for two weeks of adventure. The "American-made" Chrysler was a family fixture—its influence on my life extends far beyond our excursions to the campground. Later on, it would become my first car.

I never remember it being new. My father said it had "character." What it had was a lot of rust, more than a few dents, and an engine that rumbled like a freight train. It seemed like it had always been beaten up, but by the time I inherited it, it was known around town as "The Bomb." My friends gave it the nickname as a tribute to a popular lyric of the time—"You dropped a bomb on me"—and because of the hole it had in the passenger-side floor. It began as aged white, but after I had driven it for a year or so, it had attained its share of war wounds, including a yellow-parking-barrier stripe down one side and a fire-hydrant-red stripe down the other. An excited teenage girl with a wagon full of equally excited teenage friends does not, honestly, make for a very good driver.

Though most of my friends had more expensive cars with German pedigrees, everyone loved to ride in The Bomb. In fact, it became a popular Greenwich fixture. It was so big that half the neighborhood could fit inside, making it a favorite party spot. It was a club no matter where it was, even when its broken gas gauge left us stranded on the side of the road. Several friends still recall that once while we were driving, something large and dark fell out of the engine and began smoldering in the road. But since The Bomb still kept going, so did we. The car eventually got so bad that my mother drove it to the dump and called a cab to take her home.

My family was certainly a little bit unusual living amongst the white picket fences and storied wealth of Greenwich. Everyone knew my folks were from a different country, even if they didn't know which one. You could tell from their heavy accents that the Cosbys, Richard and Adda on Halsey Drive, were from "somewhere else."

There is a distinctive melody to the way the Polish people sound, accenting words Americans typically don't. While my dad spent time actively working to lose his accent, my Danish mother defiantly refused to let go of hers. She never got the hang of the English "th" no matter how many times I demonstrated the correct placement of the tongue beneath the front teeth.

Regardless of intentions, my parents' heavy accents remained with them throughout their lives, putting me often in the role of translator. I would dutifully explain to perplexed friends and puzzled store cashiers what exactly it was my parents were saying. Growing up, it was admittedly embarrassing for a young girl facing the harsh judgments of her peers, but today, I'd be overjoyed if I could hear my mother say "tink" or "tank you" just one more time.

Even though they stood out amid the Connecticut Yankees, Richard and Adda quickly became well liked around the neighborhood. My father was the handsome, dark-haired European, often spotted running the streets of Greenwich. Tall and thin, with high cheekbones and chiseled features, he was very fit. Every morning, whether he was at home in Greenwich or away working on engineering projects, he'd wake up at six o'clock and go for a run. It always amazed me that he remained committed to doing so even in pouring rain or a half-foot of snow on the ground.

My father enjoyed the outdoors. Whether coming back from a run or doing yard work, he was always willing to strike up lively conversations with the neighbors. My mother became a neighborhood fixture in her own way thanks to her daily walks with a revered series of dogs. She'd zip down the street, a streak of short-cropped blonde hair, greeting neighbors with a wave and a smile as her sneakers trekked quickly behind her furry friend. In the early days, we always had German shepherds, starting with Nicky, my dad's favorite. In later years, we had smaller, more lap-friendly dogs. My favorite was Lucky the Shetland sheepdog, who loved my room most, falling asleep many nights to the ticking of my little red leather alarm clock. (One day, for reasons we never understood, Lucky ate the clock.)

My parents always lived modestly. Our furniture wasn't fancy, our décor was very simple, with European accents. My father never had an expensive suit, nor my mom a costly dress. Neither of my parents ever wore anything flashy, reluctant to draw attention to themselves. My dad's favorite things to wear were T-shirts with slogans like "USA" or "Marine Corps Marathon." Dad liked old clothes and old shoes and always told me, "New clothes make me feel uncomfortable." Even at his busiest time at work, he never had more than three suits, always purchased at modest prices from places like JC Penney. Whenever I commented about the holes in his clothes, especially the T-shirts he'd run in, he'd say, "They really worked hard for me." Even the clothes had to live up to his expectations.

The only new item he'd allow in his wardrobe was a pair of New Balance running shoes every six months, bought loyally from the same sports store in Old Greenwich. Running shoes were his only splurge.

My parents never sprang for luxuries. Thinking about it now, I believe that their frugality taught me a lot of basic values, but as a young girl in a community of bankers' and advertising execs' children, I found my dad's insistence on living modestly exasperating.

Our yard, however, was a popular spot thanks to its size and my dad's love of the outdoors. In the summer, kids would come over to play on the rope ladder Dad built or to shoot some baskets in the hoop he'd put up on a tree. My dad would come out and judge our performance. He'd score our flips off the rope ladder, and even my friends knew to wait until he wasn't around to horse around on it or they'd leave feeling as if they'd trained for the Olympics. Most fun days with Dad in the backyard left me with skinned knees and huge calluses on my hands. My dad would tell me they were "signs of a successful day. Success at anything takes hard work."

Dad also managed to keep a garden growing even when work kept him away for weeks at a time. He'd plant it during a quick weekend trip home in May, tend to it on his two-week vacation in July, and otherwise leave my mom in charge of weeding, pruning, and watering. It always grew. For winter, Dad would create an ice-skating rink in the backyard out of snow and a water hose. It was a popular neighborhood attraction, and I used to charge kids a quarter to come skate. I consider it my first "job."

My dad also thought I should join the Girl Scouts, and I began early on as a Brownie. At the time I didn't give much thought to it, but as I delved deeper into his history, I began to realize that my father's insistence that I join the Scouts might have had something to do with the events of his own youth in Poland. Even though he always spoke of Poland as the forbidden land and said that he would never go back there because it was like "hell on earth," he did mention that he was in something similar to the Scouts in Poland and considered it the best part of his childhood. I knew that being a Scout was something my dad honored. I kept my uniform neatly pressed and proudly displayed my many badges, consumed with checking off the activities to earn them. "Sewing" must have seemed silly to my dad when his Scouting experience had trained him to stay alive. I was, however, a particularly talented cookie salesperson, specializing in Samoas and Thin Mints. My sales strategy consisted of a charm offensive, and I often moved more boxes than anyone else in my troop.

However, we never kept the cookies in our own house. My mother, always concerned with our well-being, liked us to eat nutritiously, even if she wasn't the world's greatest cook. Every summer before we left for our family camping trip, she would pack healthy snacks for the ride: apples and turkey sandwiches on rye. And as we made our way up the coast, my brother and I would always get restless. I'd pass the time playing cards and answering geography questions as we passed various highway signs. My father always quizzed me about cities in New England and would often throw in locations in Europe to test my international skills. We'd also listen to whichever station en route was playing the classics, my dad's favorites. He loved listening to the easily identifiable songs sung by the likes of Frank Sinatra, Nat King Cole, and Dean Martin. Looking back, I suppose those singers served as great English tutors for my parents, a virtual Berlitz songbook of standard American English. Our drive would often be interrupted by the frightening metallic creak of the old seventeen-foot aluminum Grumman canoe peeling loose from the roof of the car, punctuated by my father huffing, pulling the car over to the side of the highway, and tightening the ropes across the old boat.

The excitement was palpable when we pulled into Bar Harbor, Maine, and soon headed through the gates into Somes Sound View Campground by the Atlantic Ocean. My brother and I couldn't wait to get out of the car, and neither could Nicky, who would immediately set out to meet and greet the other inhabitants of the campground. It was the early years of Somes's designation as a campground and it was therefore rather primitive, but it was an ideal vacation spot—surrounded by forest and mountains, yet also right next to the ocean. It had the picture-perfect place to pitch a tent.

Every year, we'd arrive at the same campsite and we'd all help my father unload the car—sleeping bags, the camp stove, Coleman lanterns, a big, sturdy, cooler, and of course, the tent. Our tent wasn't in much better shape than the car. It was itself a family heirloom—just as much a part of our Somes ritual as the drive and the music. It was very old, and had been patched so many times that it had begun to resemble a quilt stretched over the frame of the poles. Inside we'd set up house: our sleeping bags on cots, a place to leave our shoes, and a spot for the dog. We slept lengthwise in the tent, with Nicky right inside the zippered door. Nicky hated the darkness and was the first in the tent every night.

When night fell, my mom would spritz the crisp air with insect repellent and we'd bring out our lanterns to cook dinner and roast marshmallows at a campfire. My dad would include my brother and me in all camping tasks, teaching us how to build a fire, put up the tent, and find food—everything about how to survive in the woods. He'd craft us walking sticks and we'd go for long, steep, treacherous hikes. Dad knew all the different plants and would point out the ones to avoid and the ones that were edible. If we were hiking to the top of a mountain and wanted to take a break, he'd say "gotta keep going all the way to the top." Skinned knees and scratched arms were no excuse.

He taught Alan to fish, and almost every day the two of them would set out for the water returning in the evening with a fish to fry over the campfire. Later, I would also be dragged along, and taught to hunt for bait. My dad always said, "It doesn't make sense to buy worms when all we have to do is lift some stones." I'd wield the old fishing pole, gingerly dangling its rudimentary hook into the ocean. Catching a fish mortified me. I found it traumatic looking into its glassy eyeballs as my father put the flapping creature in the bottom of the canoe and on occasion in a plastic bucket when we had one. Later, Dad would filet the fish with the same knife he used to peel fruit, jabbing slices of apple and not hesitating to take a bite right off the blade.

Dad would often take us canoeing, even on the occasional weekends he was home in Greenwich. He'd drag the rickety old metal boat out into the river and beckon for us to hop in behind him. He taught us how to handle the canoe and use the anchor, which was shaped like a disk. On hot days he would climb out and swim beside us, sometimes disappearing under the surface only to pop back up and upend the canoe, sending Alan and me laughing and shrieking into the water. The only thing that could keep him out of the water was a serious lightning storm, and even then, the bolts would have to be striking all around for him to quit. I have a clear memory of one winter afternoon when we took a family walk along the river. Lucky, the Shetland sheepdog, was with us, and as he tried to climb the riverbank, he slipped and fell into the frigid, fast-moving water. Frantically, he splashed about, desperately trying to keep his head above the surface.

"Swim to me!" my father shouted at Lucky, but the dog was too frightened and disoriented to obey. In an instant, my dad simultaneously pulled his shoes off and jumped into the river, his powerful arms throwing up sheets of water as he raced toward the dog. He quickly towed Lucky back to shore. My father never made a big deal about it. But I remember it vividly. The brief but harrowing experience made me keenly aware that he could save me if I needed saving. A shivering Lucky, however, was scarred for life, and never went in the water again.

My father was indeed rugged. After the divorce, my mother told me she always loved knowing that he could protect her and take care of the family. She never worried about anything bad happening when he was around. But I realized that my father's vacation activities were all dedicated to teaching us how to do things that he felt might help us get through life, just in case he wasn't there when we needed him.

Dad also taught me never to take no for an answer. He and my mom always told the story of the time we were camping in upstate New York when I was little more than two years old. I developed a dangerously high fever, and Dad marched through the thick forest at night, with me in his arms, my brother and Mom in tow, with only a small, flickering storm lamp to guide us to our car. When we arrived at a nearby doctor's office in the middle of the night, the doctor said, "Office hours are over, we are closed." Dad said, "Then give me the address of a real doctor who'll save my daughter." The doctor opened his doors and took care of me.

Though I know my dad cared about me, he was by his own admission absent more than he was present. He had little involvement in my life. My closest high school friends barely knew him. I don't remember him ever giving me advice about boys. Besides my wonderful love of more than ten years, Tomaczek, I can't recall him ever meeting any of my boyfriends. Even when Dad was home with us, he often seemed far away. He wasn't overtly affectionate. I never remember him saying "I love you," and hugs were few and far between.

Even though he had a great sense of humor and could be gregarious when he wanted to be, he also had a short fuse, and always seemed to be carrying around a weight of anger and frustration.

While we were camping, my brother and Dad often went out on expeditions of their own, and my mother and I stayed at the campsite, or went out to gather blueberries, filling large paper cups with the sweet wild fruit. I also spent a lot of time along the craggy coastline, wandering up and down the water's edge collecting artifacts and shells and other castoffs from the sea. It was on that shoreline that I first learned the cruel lesson of life and death. Starfish were a favorite of mine. They seemed so beautiful, these rubbery little stars clinging to the rocks under the water. Once I pulled one out of the ocean, lifting its five legs carefully off the rock it had attached itself to. I wanted to keep it, so I brought it out onto the rocks and watched as it dried in the sun. My mother was horrified when she saw what I'd done.

"It was a living thing!" she said. "You killed it." My mother valued the life of every plant and animal she happened across. Whenever she found a spider in the house she would carefully coax it onto some other surface, and then dart outside to find a suitable shrub or a vacant spot of dirt. She'd set each thing free and wish it well. When she saw the sun-crisped starfish, she couldn't believe that I could be so careless with an animal's life. But my father defended me.

"All things have to die," he said, brusquely. "It's part of life. Some survive and some don't. Sometimes it's the strong and sometimes it's luck, but some make it and some don't. That's life. And Rita needs to understand that." I vividly remember his words to this day, as they seemed like heavy words for a dried-out starfish.

•   •   •

In his own life, my father was always careful to take good care of himself. He was passionate about his health, and an avid runner, jogging ten, fifteen, or twenty miles at a time. At his encouragement, I became an athlete too, but I was more interested in ballet, or team sports, such as tennis and gymnastics—things that involved teamwork and interaction with others. He was always prodding me to be faster, stronger, better, saying those were important qualities for life.

Even though he often wanted me to run with him, running was too quiet for me, too solitary. But not for my father, who seemed to thrive on the isolation it allowed him. It was almost an addiction. When we went camping he adhered to his strict regimen, running every day, sometimes twice. And it was when he was returning from one of these runs that his scars finally became, for a young girl, profoundly intriguing and impossible to ignore. That day they became a question that could no longer go unasked.

It was a hot day, and the midday sun was beating down on us. He came back to the campsite breathing hard and drenched with sweat, and pulled off his white T-shirt. As he peeled off the wet shirt, my eyes locked on the large scar on his right shoulder: a messy, painful-looking hole surrounded by ragged, discolored marks. My eyes jumped to the various other parts of his body and its strangely punctured and puckered skin: a hole near his right wrist, a hole in his left forearm, a crisscross of slashes up and down his legs. It was my sudden realization that my dad's skin was unlike other people's skin. It's a vivid snapshot, indelibly etched into my memory. I remember being immediately overcome by the feeling that there was something strange about it. It looked wrong. I wondered if someone had shot him in a fight or cut him with something, and the curiosity of an eight-year-old girl could not let it go.

That afternoon, when my father was out fishing with Alan, I

finally broached the subject with my mom. She was sitting outside by the tent, soaking up the bright Maine sun. I walked over and, as nonchalantly as I could, asked, "Was Dad in a fight?"

My mother suddenly looked up. She was agitated, noticeably uncomfortable, caught off guard by my bold question. She answered me simply, "Your dad went through some tough times when he was growing up." She then added with finality, "We don't talk about it."

That was the end of the conversation.

And for thirty-five years I did not mention his scars again. But the subject had begun to bother me. After spending my career asking tough questions of the world's newsmakers, it felt odd being scared to ask my dad the most basic questions about his past. And with the memorabilia I'd unearthed from my mother's house, I had more questions than ever.

Determined to decipher my dad's past and finally uncover his secrets, I packed a suitcase and boarded a train to Alexandria, Virginia, the town outside Washington, D.C., where he now lives with his wife, Judy, whom I've always liked, and their son, Eric, my kind and hardworking half-brother.

I made myself comfortable as the train headed south, surrounded by my initial arsenal of books on Poland and World War II history. The rhythmic click-clack of the train moving over the rails lulled me into personal reflection. While covering stories I've been threatened, detained, and even shot at, but I've never been injured. In fact, the only physical wound I've ever sustained is the scar that runs across my left knee. I quickly looked down at my knee, as I sometimes do, as if checking to see if my scar is still there.

Scars are interesting things. They are with us for life, quiet statements of our experiences that don't go away. Sometimes they are badges of honor, but more often, they are tales of careless "shouldn't-haves." Every time I tell the story of how I got my one and only scar, I squirm a bit, remembering the pain. I also think of my father—of what he said and what he didn't say.

My own scar is the result of a "shouldn't-have." One morning, in eighth grade, in an effort to be stronger, I was practicing gymnastics on my bed, diligently doing handstands using the wall as a spot. Things were going well until I attempted a one-armed pushup. I toppled sideways, falling onto my nightstand and knocking over a glass container of lotion. The bottle fell and shattered into a minefield of jagged pieces, and my knee came down directly atop the largest of them.

My scream brought my mother running. Blood gushed from a gash in my leg. The cut was long and deep. When my mother saw it, she became just as hysterical as I was. My father was away, so it was up to her to deal with the crisis. She grabbed a towel and wrapped it around my leg, trying to stop the stream of blood. It was unbelievably painful as she helped me into the Chrysler, and I was teenage-girl dramatic. I shivered with fear in the backseat of the car, but as my mother instructed, I kept pressure on the cut and tried to keep my leg straight. When we arrived at the hospital, I was immediately rushed to the emergency room, where I promptly cried to the doctor, "Will you be able to save my leg?" It seemed so dire; certainly, it was the worst wound I'd ever seen. The doctor laughed and said he thought it would not require amputation. As hard as I tried, I couldn't stop the tears as he stitched my split flesh back together.

I left Greenwich Hospital with a lollipop in my mouth and my knee in a brace, a brace I was shackled in for two months. At first it seemed like a terrible handicap, but when I figured out that I could parlay this misfortune into extra attention from cute guys at school, I completely took advantage of it. The injury forced me to stay off my leg as much as I could. On a positive note, running was definitely out. On the negative side, I knew I would end up with some kind of scar. I was secretly sure, however, that it would impress my father. When he returned from his business trip, I called him quickly to the living room. I was eager to show him my wound, to show him that I, too, finally had a scar of my own.

I remember the morbid fascination I felt as I peeled off the bandages, excitedly anticipating his empathy for my new badge of honor. When I lifted off the gauze, the scar was very apparent; a jagged red line with stitch marks at its edges. It still had the moist plumpness of a fresh wound. I looked to my father for his reaction, hoping for compassion and perhaps even some anecdote about the injuries in his own past.

My expectations were quickly squashed. He didn't mention his own scars. He didn't even commiserate.

"Oh, that's nothing," he said, giving me a pat on the back. "Carry on."

3

GOING HOME

The train hissed to a stop at the Kings Street Station in Alexandria, Virginia, jarring me from my introspection. I gathered my things and stepped out onto the platform into the bright June afternoon sunlight, preparing myself for the encounter I was about to have. My father and I hadn't been in close contact for years now. After my mother's death, my already strained relationship with him became even more troubled. Why didn't he comfort me when my mom died? How could he so easily detach himself from the woman he had been married to for thirty-two years? What made it so simple for him to segment his life so perfectly and just move on, start over again? I felt he had forgotten about us. About me. It made me furious . . . and terribly confused, wondering what, if anything, I had done that was so terribly wrong?

I wanted our relationship to be better. I longed to have as warm a connection with my dad as my friends seemed to have with theirs. I had decided to make an attempt at a deeper bond, to somehow break through his tough shell, hoping to find a soft center. Unsure what to expect, but knowing I wanted answers, I climbed into a cab and headed to his house. I had begun looking into his past, and I carried with me a few conversation starters, as well as a few secrets of my own I'd reveal at the right time.

In 1977, my eighth-grade teacher assigned a term paper on World War II. I titled mine "Jews Under Nazi Rule." I still have it, the A– written in red ink prominently on the title page. The paper was one of the first times I exercised the research skills that would eventually come to serve me in my career as a journalist. (After all these years, that minus after the A still bothers me.)

World War II was discussed often around my family dinner table. My parents would talk about Hitler's horrible hatred, the British and U.S. forces, and how the Jews suffered during the war. Not the usual dinner table talk for a family in Greenwich in the 1970s. Having grown up in Europe, my parents knew a lot about the war. My dad always discussed how the United States had saved the world from a great evil, how, if it weren't for the Americans stepping in, Europe and the world would have been a different place. I remember cooking hot dogs over a campfire one July 4 and Dad saying, "The world owes America a debt of gratitude. I am lucky to now be an American." Little did I know that America had in fact saved his life.

There was never a mention of my dad's involvement in the war, but there was mention of my mom's. She recounted how she was rushed into air raid shelters as a little girl in Denmark. She always thought that the king of Denmark was very heroic for publicly defying Hitler in World War II. And she was very proud that the Danish underground had saved virtually all their Jewish residents by covertly sending them on boats to nearby Sweden.

I had no idea that my dad's discussions were not taken from the history books he liked to read, but rather from his own memories, or that he had at one point lived about two hundred yards from Warsaw's Jewish ghetto. I realize now that those casual dinner table conversations were my mom's way of trying to finally draw out the details of what her husband had seen and done.

Knowing only that my dad had been a young man in Poland during the war, I thought he'd be a great primary source for my eighth-grade "Jews Under Nazi Rule" term paper, and the window into his past would have been extra credit for me. One evening, we sat down at the dining table, and I began interviewing him, taking notes on my pad of paper as I had seen reporters do while talking to notable people. For every question I asked, he asked me two back, testing to see if I had done my homework on the subject. I wanted to hear his personal stories, to get an insider's account of what had really gone on during the Nazi occupation, but my father obviously didn't want to talk about that. He wanted to know what I knew.

"Adolf Hitler was an ignorant, vulgar, and unsuccessful house-painter," I remember proudly telling him. I had gleaned those biographical tidbits from reading part of Winston Churchill's book *The Gathering Storm*.

I don't know what I expected my father to tell me about his experiences, but in retrospect, I see that he revealed very little. He said he had grown up in Warsaw, a city that became a center of conflict at the beginning of the war. He talked about how Poland's Jewish population suffered tremendously at the hands of the Nazis, and mentioned that some brave Poles had organized to resist the invading fascists. He said that unspeakable horrors had occurred in the Jewish ghetto. He didn't say that they had happened right outside his front door.

His input helped me organize my research project, but I sensed that I was only scratching the surface of what he'd seen, what he knew. It was, after all, my first interview, and I didn't yet know the Barbara Walters trick of asking a question and letting it float around in silence until it's answered. It's torture for the interviewee. But, one thing is certain: If I had known then what I know now about my father's early life in Poland, my teacher would have given me an A+.

As the cab weaved through Alexandria's streets toward my dad's house, I pulled the report from my bag and leafed through it, yellowing sheets of wide-ruled notebook paper bound in a black folder with a stark, large, hand-drawn swastika on the cover, and my own careful, oversized eighth-grade cursive writing filling each page. I tried to imagine how much more meaningful and different the essay and my own life could have been if my father had opened up earlier and revealed the truth.

The driver pulled onto my dad's road. The area he and Judy had picked to live in was developed during the 1970s when builders began purchasing lots and putting up homes for the area's many military families who wanted quality homes at fair prices. The Army's Fort Belvoir as well as a Coast Guard installation are both close by, and the area is a short drive or quick Metro ride to the Pentagon.

The cab stopped in front of my father's house. After paying, I stepped out onto his driveway. The house is small and unassuming, a modest brick dwelling surrounded by houses of similar style and size. I climbed the concrete stairs slowly and knocked on the metal screen door. After a moment, I see my father through the glass. My first impression is that he looks older—still in great shape for an eighty-four-year-old, but older. His chiseled good looks and strong European features are still evident, but his hair has thinned and whitened. He opens the door.

"Rita," he says, his accent as apparent as it's always been. He holds the door for me, which saves him the awkwardness of a perfunctory hug. He leads me into the house where he has lived since remarrying. The house seems smaller from the inside than it looked from the outside. It has been a while since I've been there. The mumbling hum of a television spills out from the living room. My father offers me a chair in the kitchen. I have gone maybe three feet into his house.

"Would you like some juice?" he asks.

"No, thanks." I reply.

"I blend it myself," he says proudly. "My special recipe. It's half cranberry and half grape juice."

"No thanks," I say. My dad doesn't know that I've never liked grape juice. The table in front of me is stacked high with piles of papers and envelopes, bills and circulars. My father puts his glass of home brew on the table and sits down next to me.

"Okay," he says, matter-of-factly. "What do you want to know?" He smiles, his glasses slipping a bit down his nose. He's definitely looking older. I wonder if he thinks the same thing about me. His belly is a bit bigger than it's ever been. When he divorced my mom his waist was "a thirty, half his age." I remember him telling me so. His commitment to fitness had always kept him youthful, but in the past few years his asthma has finally brought his beloved running to a stop. The man I see now looks tired in a way he never has before.

The races he trained for had always seemed to be his greatest joys. For several years he ran in the Boston Marathon. I remember going to watch him, following his progress and cheering him on. I'd stand at the edge of the crowd of spectators to hand him water at the ten-mile mark, Gatorade at the twenty. It always seemed peculiar that he never displayed any of the ribbons or trophies he brought home, instead stashing them in the top drawer of his dresser, even when he won the "seventy and older" division of the Marine Corps Marathon.

He never gave up. It took everything he had to finish his first Boston Marathon. I joined him at the twenty-mile mark, running the last 6.2 miles with him. I could tell the race had taken its toll on him already at that point and begged him to stop and rest for a while. His paleness worried me. "Can't take breaks," he said, huffing on. He crossed the finish line, felt light-headed and collapsed. As a young teenager, I was so scared to see my father suddenly fall, and I rushed to get him help. True to form, he recovered quickly, and even said that experience only made him a better runner, and better prepared for future challenges. He would go on to run a total of thirty-three marathons over the next twenty years, training and running enough to, in his words, "run around the equator two and a half times."

More recently, I've realized that my father's almost obsessive commitment to fitness was more complex than a simple desire to stay in shape. Running and exercise were ways for him to escape, to get away from something else for a few precious hours, and in his younger years, those skills had kept him alive. After he left us that Christmas Eve years ago, I began to think of him as a man constantly on the run, figuratively as well as literally. He was hounded by some part of his past that he never talked about, and it was always nipping at his heels. Now, with my father coming to the finish line of his own life, I've finally gathered the courage to find out what that is.

I pull my eighth-grade paper from my bag and put it on the table in front of him. I slowly push it toward him, looking at his reaction. He does not pick it up, but there is a glimmer of recognition in his eyes. "Why didn't you tell me you were there, Dad?" I ask. "That you experienced this."

He sighs. "Rita," he says, "look at the title. It says 'Jews Under Nazi Rule.' I wasn't a Jew." A dodge.

I push forward. There is no retreat. "Dad, what's your first memory of the war?"

He leans back in his chair, and I see flashes of thought play across his face, as though he is watching a movie in fast-rewind. After a moment, he takes a deep breath, and says, "It was Friday, September 1, 1939. I had just turned thirteen years old. It was the day World War II descended on Warsaw. When the first German air raid came, I was standing in the yard with my father, your grandfather, Konstanty Kossobudzki. We heard them before we saw them. The sky filled with a low rumbling sound, like gravel sliding down a metal chute. Soon, planes were visible in the sky, squadrons and squadrons of bombers. For a moment there was nothing but the sound of engines, and a swarm of planes like birds migrating en masse in the same direction. My father tried to reassure me, saying, 'Look, the Polish air force is flying again!' 'But Dad,' I told him, 'those planes are coming from the west! The Germans are west!'

"As the planes drew closer, my father insisted, 'No, I think they're ours.' After a few more minutes of nothing but the dull drone of the engines, a new sound greeted us. Rumbling concussions, two or three at a time, low and ominous, rolled across the land from the outskirts of town. The sound of bombs falling. The sound of war.

" 'My God,' my father whispered with sudden grave concern. 'Germans.' "

It began with a lie. To justify the invasion of Poland, Hitler had faked a Polish attack on the German border town of Gleiwitz. SS troops dressed in Polish uniforms took over a local radio station and broadcast a phony call to arms against Germany. The staged event was exactly the spark Hitler needed to start his war against my dad's homeland.

Poland was no stranger to conflict. The land that constituted the Second Republic of Poland at the beginning of World War II had been fought over, divided, reunified, and divided again for centuries. In fact, for 123 years of its history, Poland didn't even exist on a map. So Poles were raised to fight for their freedom.

The country had only been reformed and independent again for twenty-one years, after being forged from the ashes of World War I in 1918. When German forces invaded, they advanced into Poland from the west, north, and south, cutting a swath of destruction toward Warsaw. It didn't take long for the United Kingdom and France, Poland's allies, to reciprocate and declare war on the invading Germans. But for the most part the Poles were trapped in the conflict, begging for assistance.

Since the end of World War I, trouble had been brewing. Germany had been in a state of economic and political turmoil. The heavy blows dealt by the Great Depression and the strict terms of the Treaty of Versailles had left the German economy in shambles, and the German people wanted someone to blame. Increasingly, public opinion turned against Germany's ruling Weimar Republic. Right-wing thinkers blamed the regime for the country's woes, describing the signing of the Versailles treaty as a betrayal of the German people. Many of the loudest voices of criticism came from the conservative right, most notably from Germany's ultra-right-wing Nazi Party. It was in this volatile political climate that pressure from the right forced German president Paul von Hindenburg to appoint Adolf Hitler, leader of the Nazi Party, as chancellor. The year was 1933.

In the years that followed, Hitler used Germany's economic woes, his own careful political maneuvering, and a fire at the Reichstag, the building that housed the country's parliament, to dissolve the republic and install himself as the sole leader of a single-party Nazi government. Germany was pushed into a state of nationalist overdrive, and Hitler used the situation as an opportunity to begin his violent agenda of expanding Germany's borders across Europe.

Hitler had strategically chosen that week in early September to start his offensive in order to catch my father's country off guard. Schoolchildren like my dad were returning to their first week in the classroom, and adults were returning to their jobs from vacation. It was a period during which the nation usually fell into a routine, but the Nazi invasion threw everything off balance. Germany unleashed a kind of warfare in Poland that the world had never seen before. The Germans attacked with everything they had—aircraft, tanks, cavalry, infantry, and artillery. Hitler had also decided to disregard the international convention and authorized the killing of civilians, including women and children. The goal of this *blitzkrieg*, or lightning war, was to surprise and terrify. And the Nazis did.

It was the end of everything my dad had known.

Only days later, Edward Rydz-Smigly, the newly appointed commander-in-chief of Poland's armed forces, evacuated Warsaw along with most of the government. They instructed Polish officers to go door-to-door and order all able-bodied men to take up arms and defend the northwestern front of Warsaw at all costs.

"Polish leaders ordered all intelligentsia, like my father, who might be able to play a role in a new government to head toward Romania," my dad tells me as we sit at his kitchen table now, an incredible seventy years after the Nazi offensive began. Despite the passage of seven decades, his memory is lucid and clear.

"My father said we had to go immediately. I said I was staying to fight, but he grabbed me by the ear and said we were going." Many other Poles made the same decision to flee, and the roads that ran out of the city quickly became crowded with women, children, and old men, carrying their lives on their backs. "We didn't own a car, so we loaded the few things we could carry into a horse-drawn cart. My cousin, Yolanda, and her mother joined us. It was incredibly slow going in the cart, but before too long we had left Warsaw behind and began to ride into the countryside.

"After the first long day of traveling we had no other choice but to spend the night at a farm. When my father pulled the cart up to the small house, we knew we'd be expected to pay for room and board, but the farmer wouldn't accept Polish money. 'What's the point?' he asked, nodding in the direction of Warsaw. 'It won't be worth anything in a few days anyway.' With nowhere else to go and nothing else of value, my mother pulled off her wedding ring and gave it to the man to pay for our shelter the first night. My father was visibly shaken, but my mother, ever pragmatic, did the best she could to take it in stride. Watching the exchange, I was struck for the first time with the grim realization that from the moment the bombs started falling over Warsaw, nothing would ever be the same."

While the Kossobudzkis made their way toward the Romanian border, Warsaw endured bombings night and day. Terrifying explosions followed nerve-wracking whistles. The air rumbled constantly with artificial thunder. Streaks of flame poured down from the night sky. Poland didn't have the planes, weapons, or soldiers to withstand the immense German onslaught. Poland's pilots were skilled and courageous, but their planes were obsolete compared to Germany's fighter planes and dive-bombing Stukas. With their government gone and their allies silent, the Poles in Warsaw were all alone, left to fight on as best they could. Then, as if that wasn't bad enough, the Germans launched an all-out air attack, leveling much of the city and starting widespread fires.

With Warsaw smoldering in the background, my dad and his parents continued the slow journey to the border. They became part of a stream of Poles fleeing the Nazis, all of them carrying with them their dearest possessions in wagons, hand trolleys, and assorted luggage. They were pushing, pulling, and dragging their lives with them. Little did the Kossobudzkis know that it was truly all they had left in the world. They continued making their way to Romania, traveling in that sluggish cart about thirty miles each day, and stopping at night to stay with friends of friends, or wherever they could. It seemed as if their escape plan would actually work.

"Then, one afternoon, close to the Romanian border, all hopes of escape were suddenly dashed," my dad explains. "My father had stopped the cart in a small town to pick up supplies. While we were standing in line at the general store, a sudden message came crackling through the radio behind the counter. The announcer was dramatically reporting that the Soviets had now invaded Poland from the east, and were beginning a push toward Warsaw."

It was on September 17, 1939, that one final event sealed Poland's fate. The Russians had arrived. The Soviet army invaded eastern Poland and began to claim anything that hadn't already been taken by the Germans. This had all been prearranged in a secret agreement between the Soviet Union and Germany called the Molotov-Ribbentrop Pact, named after both their foreign ministers. While on the surface the document appeared to be no more than a non-aggression agreement between the Germans and the Russians, a secret protocol was included in the pact that actually divided Poland into western and eastern territories, to be controlled, once the war ended, by Germany and Russia, respectively. Poland was being suffocated on both sides by ferocious armies bent on annexing land; power-hungry regimes ready to break Europe into two new empires . . . and Poland was just the opening play.

News of the Soviet invasion stopped my dad's father in his tracks. "Outside people were shouting in the streets. We heard cries, 'The Soviets are coming!' echoing back and forth across the town's little square. The color drained from my father's face. 'We're not going,' he said.

"I protested. 'We're so close!'

"'We're not going,' my father said again, setting his jaw. 'If I have the choice, I'd rather be under the Germans than the Soviets any day of the week.' " He remembered being forced as a child to attend Russian-controlled schools in Warsaw where they didn't even allow him to learn his native Polish tongue. He had experienced Russian oppression before and didn't want to see it again."

Sitting now in my dad's Virginia kitchen, I asked, "What did you do? What did your mom say?"

"We had no choice," he says. "We obeyed. We packed up the cart and hastily turned around. We made the return trip to Warsaw in a lot less time than it had taken to escape. We were headed against traffic, you might say. On the way back the magnitude and gravity of the events unfolding in Poland became clear to me. Partway through the journey, we passed through an area that had seen fighting between the Polish army and the invading Germans. When the cart crested a hill, we came upon the remains of a battlefield. I stared, unable to speak. Destruction was all you could see. The field was scattered with smashed cavalry units; mutilated bodies of horses and their riders laid out on the grass. Destroyed pieces of artillery reduced to heaps of twisted metal. My father stopped the cart and gestured at the scene.

" 'There,' he said, 'that is the glory of combat. That's what it looks like.' I swallowed hard and looked out at the terrible stillness. My father had been a lifelong pacifist, more interested in books than bullets. He thought things could be solved with nice words. I knew there were no words that could stop the Nazis. Until that moment, in my innocence, I had always associated war with a certain degree of valor and glory. But there, staring out at the obscenity of the scene in the field before me, I got my first glimpse at the true face of war. I would bear witness to far worse in the years to come, but the sight of that ruined battlefield stayed with me for the rest of my life."

My dad sits quietly at his kitchen table, lost in the horrific snapshot from the now-opened diary of his mind. There is no sound but the soft chatter of the television in the other room. I sit there, looking at him. It's the first time I've actually understood how drastically different his childhood was from my own. The worst thing I had ever seen as a thirteen-year-old was in a horror movie I'd snuck into.

"What happened when you got back to your house in Warsaw?" I ask, finally breaking the silence that had settled in the kitchen.

"What house?" he asks.

"Your family's house," I say, not understanding.

"Rita," he says, "there was no house."

4

CHILDHOOD IN RUINS

I'm both amazed and saddened that at eighty-four years old my dad can still picture the destruction of his home so clearly. Unlike anything I experienced in my own sheltered youth, the shock of his family's horse cart coming back into Warsaw and of seeing his hometown in ghostly ruins is something my dad remembers vividly. They arrived a few days after the infamous September 25 air attack that dropped five hundred tons of bombs and seventy-two tons of incendiary bombs, targeting the center of Warsaw. He was thirteen years old.

The city was still smoldering as my dad's family crept along toward their home, weaving their cart through the destruction. The damage was so extensive that it was impossible for the fire brigades to make it to every house. "Warsaw had been reduced to rubble," he says. "Our neighbors who had stayed behind had been instantly buried alive, smothered. Or worse, burned to nothing." A disaster like that must be eternally seared into your memory.

I think of the sheer terror and vulnerability we all felt after those two planes were flown into the World Trade Center, all of us helpless as those poor people trapped inside suffered. The world watched as the Twin Towers crumbled. I think of all the stories I covered during that tragedy, the joy of hearing about the accounts in which fate intervened with kindness—of the woman who was newly pregnant and was late for work due to her morning sickness, of the man from the 104th floor who'd just missed his subway that morning and was running late, of those who had been pulled alive out of the rubble hours later. Survivors often ask themselves "Why me?" and "What if?" I myself was supposed to meet someone across from the Twin Towers that morning and had canceled the night before.

As I sit at my dad's kitchen table, I stare at his face. I see the sadness he's seen. I see the pain of survival. I think of my own childhood and how untroubled it really was. "What did you do?" I ask.

"We began sifting through the wreckage," he says. "Searching for someone, for something, anything that might have survived." I suggest the uplifting stories of finding people alive after the collapse of the World Trade Center, but my dad shakes his head. "No . . . we found our radio."

"Nothing else?" I ask.

My dad's lower lip curls downward a bit. "We tried to pick up the pieces as best we could," he says.

"Where did you go?" I ask.

"Since my parents had very little money left, the only place we had to go was to turn to relatives." This stops me. It is a question that I've never pondered. Where would I go if suddenly my house and belongings were all gone? If Midtown Manhattan vanished, where would I turn? "We went to my mother's cousin's house in another area of Warsaw, but when we arrived we discovered that his building had been half-destroyed by the bombing, too. My father put a cover on the bombed-out part, and we lived there for two weeks." Over the course of the next five years, the family would move five times, avoiding the wreckage of war. But each time, once they settled into their new accommodations, however primitive, things seemed to fall back into a frightening routine.

"Did you see people who were killed in the air raids?" I ask. My dad's face darkens. He had maintained a notable detachment as he described the memory of looking out over that roadside battlefield, the smashed artillery and gnarled carcasses of horses. He remained mostly poker-faced as he spoke of his home being reduced to a jumbled heap of debris. But this question strikes a chord.

"Most of the victims were incinerated, buried, gone without a trace," he tells me. "But not all. A day or two after we got back, I went out to see what I could see. I passed a demolished building, nothing more than a pile of rubble, smoke and dust still rising from the ashes. There, amidst the grays and browns of the collapsed walls and ruined masonry, a misplaced splash of color caught my eye. I edged nearer to the ruins, straining to make out what I was looking at. As I moved closer, the details of the scene became clear and it was suddenly hard for me to breathe. I remember the image as if it were yesterday. A woman lay there in the rubble, the hem of her colorful summer dress blowing gently in the breeze." My father pauses for a moment and looks down at the surface of the table in front of him. He runs his thumbnail along the edge of the table's trim. I picture that same hand sorting through the rubble of what had once been his family's home in Warsaw.

"She was dead," he says quietly. I can see that in his mind he's standing there in front of the ruined house, experiencing this brush with mortality all over again. "As I walked back home that day, I noticed more and more bodies lying in the remains of my ruined neighborhood."

"Maybe some of them were alive," I suggest. My dad looks at me. It is evident by the heavy weight of his eyes that they weren't. "Did you tell anyone?"

"That evening, I told my parents what I'd seen."

"Do you remember what you told them?" I ask.

"There are bodies," he says aloud, in a voice notably younger, as if it were yesterday.

"What did your parents say?"

"They just nodded." He sits for a moment and then a thought spills out as it occurs to him. "That was when the terrible truth sank in. That this was war."

In such times, survival is often about dusting yourself off and moving on. After Warsaw agreed to surrender to the Germans, Polish major general Juliusz Rómmel urged the people of Warsaw in a special proclamation to acknowledge the surrender with dignity and 'accept the entry of the German forces quietly, honorably, and calmly.' It's hard for me to even begin to comprehend hearing such a statement, as I grew up in America. Imagine hearing this today in Atlanta, or Miami, or New York. The thought sends a chill to my core.

However, right before the surrender, General Rómmel did something very significant. He secretly ordered the creation of the first Polish underground movement in WWII, knowing the Poles would need to organize their efforts against the Nazis on many levels.

On October 5, Hitler went to Warsaw by plane, and then his armed convoy made its way to Warsaw's City Center where he watched, one hand held aloft, as a brass band trumpeted the march of his well-heeled battalions. It immediately became clear how different things would be under German occupation.

Under the "New Order," the Nazis confiscated automobiles and printing presses. For a brief period, early in the occupation, the Nazis actually outlawed school above sixth grade, but they soon opened trade schools. They realized the war was going to last longer than even they had predicted, and it became clear they would need a workforce with a certain degree of education to drive their brutal war machine.

My dad returned to school, but the Nazis carefully screened the curriculum. Only certain books could be read in his classrooms. Any information that didn't paint Germany in the best possible light was censored. "One day, I found a fact in a textbook they missed," my dad says, a sly smile spreading across his face. "It stated that the American car manufacturer Ford produced before the war more cars than all European brands put together. I was surprised to find that fact in print. Even information that basic was kept from us." American pride somehow shone through in bombed-out Warsaw.

As the occupation wore on, my dad says he continued to goof off in school, but had a newfound interest: learning German, much to his own father's dismay. "For me," he explains, "German was practical in a way that even Polish wasn't. I believed it was important to be able to know what it was that the Germans around me were talking about, strategically. Besides, its air of illicitness made it appealing. The Germans didn't want young Poles learning too much of the language. The German taught in Polish schools was of the most basic kind, barely enough to read road signs. The Nazis were careful not to allow any 'Germanization' of young Poles."

Not long after the Nazis annexed Poland, they began a process of systematic oppression and ethnic cleansing, part of Hitler's master plan to turn Poland into part of the German state. Hitler intended to reduce the Polish population to a serf class beholden to the Germans who would eventually settle there. He also intended to reduce Poland's vibrant Jewish population to nothing. In 1940, the Warsaw Ghetto was officially established, and Warsaw's sizable Jewish population was rounded up and forced into a closed, segregated part of the city. The Ghetto was divided into two sections, one small and one large. The small section was mostly for workshops, where Jews endured long, arduous days doing forced labor for the Nazi war effort. The large section was where most of the population lived, and conditions there quickly became extremely difficult.

"We could almost see into that district of the city," my father tells me, "but because it was so heavily policed and partitioned off, we never had a good idea of what went on there. We had no idea how horrific conditions there would eventually become. We were so concerned with our own survival. We had to be. The Nazis were brutal and no one was safe."

While the general Polish population was not as actively persecuted as the Jews, times were still hard for all under the occupation. German soldiers treated the Poles like animals, and supplies were stringently rationed. All but the most basic provisions became extremely difficult to obtain, and even the wealthiest families of Warsaw had to struggle to make ends meet. Poles who collaborated with the Nazis were treated better by the Germans, while families that did not were forced to trade on a newly emergent black market for their survival.

I ask my dad if he knew people who operated in the black market.

He smiles. "My mother," he says, "your grandmother, was a brilliant businesswoman on the black market."

"How'd that happen?" I ask. "She could have been killed!"

"My parents had run out of money, and my father refused to work for the Germans. Shortly after the first bleak Christmas of occupation, my mother announced that she was going into the black market business for herself. My father said, 'What?! You don't know anything about it.' And she snapped back at him, 'When I'm hungry, I learn fast.' "

"Where'd she hide her black market goods?"

"My mother and I first sold goods out of suitcases, and then the business grew and she somehow got a license to operate a store. We discovered in that building there was a small back room, a closet really, that had been walled up on one side of the store. My mother had grand plans, and she hired a trustworthy carpenter to break through the brick wall and build a huge wooden cabinet in front of it. You could pull a secret lever inside the cabinet and a door would open, leading you through the cabinet into the secret storeroom. In the front of the store she sold rations, sweets, things like that. But in the back room she kept all the good stuff—oranges, chocolates, and all the wonderful things that the Nazis kept for themselves. She became a real force in the black market, and suddenly we were making more money than we knew what to do with! She threw a party one holiday for our family and some of my father's relatives were in attendance. She brought out a case of oranges from the secret room and they all had tears in their eyes. That's how rare they were."

"How'd your father feel about all this?"

His expression becomes serious again. "My father and I," he says, choosing his words carefully, "did not see eye to eye on a lot of things. He refused to work with the Nazis, of course, but he drew the line at joining the Resistance. At the time, I felt he was far too passive. I thought he was doing a disservice to his country by refusing to fight back. Before the war, he had worked for the state, first as a county supervisor and later on as a consultant for the Polish Treasury Department. This position commanded a high salary, and as a child I suppose I led a pretty privileged life. We had enjoyed all the luxuries that came with a prestigious government job—a comfortable house, a car and chauffeur, and a maid, Mary, who started as an employee but eventually became an honorary member of the family.

"When I was in fifth grade, our prosperity came to an abrupt end. My father was fired from his job and blacklisted from government employment. The current Polish government had lost an important election, and my father was blamed. It was the opinion of his superiors that he should have used his position to switch votes and rig the election. When he refused, he lost his job. My parents didn't talk about the incident with me, but I knew that something had gone wrong. One night I heard them having an argument behind their closed bedroom door. My mother was crying about it and asking what they were going to do. The issue wasn't brought up again, but things changed very quickly, and we were forced to leave our house and move to an apartment in Warsaw."

"But your father had done the right thing," I say. "He didn't rig the election."

"My father was as honest as the day is long. During the occupation, when the Germans ordered all Poles to hand over their radios, my father was going to simply comply, but my mother said, 'Are you crazy? You'll never see that radio again. A German general will enjoy it.' She took the radio and smashed it at his feet.

"My father and I were never close; we disagreed on too many points. He was an intellectual through and through, highly educated and highly academic. He held a master's degree in economics from a Belgian university, at a time when most people in Poland didn't even have high school diplomas. I was always more concerned with sports than school, and my grades were often a point of contention. As a young man I was something of a class clown, making jokes and deliberately underperforming to get a laugh from my peers. My grades were so poor that I had to repeat the sixth grade. In junior high I shocked my father by bringing home a report card that warned I was failing three of my six classes, including Polish! My father was furious, but there was little he could do. I was simply not interested in following in his academic footsteps."

I'm tempted to remind him of all the times he said I wasn't studying hard enough in my youth, and that I was going to do nothing but "mess up" my life. But I think better of it. Instead I ask, "Did you play with other kids when you were a child?"

"I was always something of a wanderer as a boy. Because I was an only child, I was forced to leave the house to find playmates, so I would often spend my afternoons out in the street with friends. When there was no one around to play with I would go exploring on my own, swimming in ponds in the summer and cross-country skiing in the winter. I loved those skis. They made life easier for me. There were no school buses in those days, and the walk from our house on the outskirts of town to the school was a long one. My father would sometimes let me ski to school in the winter, and I had an understanding teacher who would let me store the skis in the back of the classroom for the day. It was one of the few ways I found to get excited about going to school."

"How was life in Warsaw different before the war?" I ask.

"Oh, before the war, I spent a lot of time at the movies, going once a week or so with my mother or by myself whenever I could squeeze some money out of my father. I used to love watching American movies with lots of action and adventure. I most enjoyed stories where the underdog beat the big guy, where the young, brave soldier beat unbelievable odds to ride off into the sunset as the victor." I imagine my father as a young boy, getting swept up in the adventure and derring-do of stars like Errol Flynn, Gary Cooper, and Cary Grant. I smile at the thought of those American images, our heroic characters, carrying him through the ravages of war and beckoning him toward the United States.

"When I was a teenager, my parents enrolled me in a boarding school north of Warsaw, a trade school that specialized in engineering. To keep from incurring the Germans' wrath, the school operated under the pretense that it was a 'highway school,' a program specifically designed to churn out workers to build the German road system. At first I resisted the move, but eventually I came to appreciate the lessons I was learning. For the first time in my life, I truly enjoyed my classes. Engineering fascinated me, and as my grades rose I finally found myself gaining my father's approval. When I finished school, I graduated close to the top of my class, and the seeds for my future as an engineer had been sown."

It wasn't long before Poles began to chafe under the oppressive Nazi occupation. The situation in Poland became deeply frustrating. My dad became increasingly irritated with his own father for refusing to do anything to change it.

"He refused to collaborate with the Germans," my dad says. "That was good. But he wouldn't take any action against them, either. He felt it would keep our family safer if he didn't rock the boat and just did his best to survive." But survival under the Nazi regime would prove difficult. In the view of the infamous SS leader Heinrich Himmler, Germany's minister of the interior and chief of police, "The great German people should consider it as its major task to destroy all Poles." Hitler authorized Hans Frank, his personal lawyer and the man who became head of the new German government in Poland, to exploit the country and loot anything of value, then tear apart its economic, cultural, and political makeup. One of his primary jobs was to kill all people of influence, such as politicians, teachers, priests, artists, and intellectuals. Frank said, "What we have now recognized in Poland to be the elite must be liquidated. We must watch out for the seeds that begin to sprout again, so as to stamp them out again in good time."

My father tells me that early in the war, a friend of his family, a male journalist, wrote some powerful anti-Nazi articles. "He was a beautiful writer," Dad says. "But after those articles came out he was put on the Gestapo's list of undesirable Poles. One day he was picked up and taken to Auschwitz, which is located about two hundred miles from Warsaw and initially was used for imprisoning Polish intellectuals and Resistance fighters. He came back six months later a vegetable. At first, we were all very glad he was released, but then when we saw him, we were stunned. He was a zombie. I remember his wife and his mother crying and crying, and my mother trying to console them. They must have tortured him and deliberately released him as a warning to others. There was no better advertising for German ingenuity and brutality than an intellectual who lost his brain. It really scared my parents and me."

"What did he say they did to him?" I ask.

"He never talked about what he saw or what happened . . . because he never spoke a full sentence again."

The Germans, ironically, issued a "Decree Against Acts of Violence," and a reign of terror descended on Poland. Poles were shot, not only for resisting or fighting Germans, but also for being out after curfew, owning guns, trading on the black market, having underground leaflets in their homes, or failing to report those who did. Even children could be given the death penalty for making anti-German statements, or for exhibiting subversive behavior. Poles lived in daily fear of arrest, torture, and death.

"I heard older boys at school complaining about the unfair restrictions imposed on us by the Gestapo. 'The Germans are issuing all these orders,' a boy said, 'if you spit on the sidewalk, you'll be shot. If you offend a German in the street, you'll be shot.' We were all so frustrated by the unfair regulations and harsh punishments that many of us started looking for ways to subvert the Nazis' authority. I began participating in an informal propaganda campaign, acts of minor sabotage, like sneaking out with my friends and classmates to leave anti-Nazi graffiti in public places around the city. My favorite slogan to write on buildings was 'Hitler is an asshole.' The Germans hated it. After they discovered the new graffiti, they'd immediately come by and cover it in white paint. We, of course, would come back and redraw our masterpiece at least one more time. My favorite symbol to leave behind was a Nazi swastika hanging from a gallows." My heart was pounding, thinking if my dad had been caught, he would have been shot on the spot. "But, boy, did the people of Warsaw get a kick out of our new artwork."

Before the occupation, my dad had gotten involved with an organization similar to the Boy Scouts known as the Young Eagles, which organized camping trips and offered survival training, including map reading, rifle shooting, and even teaching young boys how to swim across ponds at night. With the onset of the occupation, the Young Eagles soon became an important part in the underground fight against the Germans, a kind of paramilitary youth organization. "The Young Eagles transformed the graffiti that my friends and I scrawled on street corners from a series of random acts of rebellion to a full-fledged youth movement. Since I was a good athlete, early on I served as a 'runner,' delivering supplies and messages between Resistance cells." The Young Eagles were absorbed as an arm of the Polish Resistance and became more Guardian Angels than Boy Scouts. This top-secret underground network of young Poles was clandestinely fighting to throw off the Nazi yoke.

"My parents quickly became worried about me," my dad says. "As time passed I became more and more involved with the Young Eagles and spent less and less time at home. My friends and I were out writing anti-Nazi graffiti and helping distribute subversive flyers and newspapers. I was still very young at the time, only fifteen, and many of the boys I'd started spending time with were much older. My mother and father didn't know I'd become involved in the Resistance, and instead I think they just assumed that I'd fallen in with a bad crowd. This was around the time I was enrolled at the trade school, and I think that my steadily rising grades helped a lot to assuage their fears."

As my father's academic record improved, his secret life in the Young Eagles was becoming more involved—and more dangerous. He became a courier for the newly established underground press and was often tasked with the distribution of hundreds of anti-Nazi flyers, a dangerous job that could land him in a concentration camp, or worse, earn him a bullet to the head. He developed his own mass distribution technique. "My friends and I would hop onto the cable cars that ran back and forth around downtown Warsaw, concealing stacks of flyers under our coats. The trams were segregated since the occupation began, with certain cars designated for Polish passengers, the better cars for the Germans. We would seek out crowded Polish cars and slip inside. When the tram reached top speed, we took turns tossing our stacks of flyers out the back windows of the car to the streets outside. The papers flew in every direction, disseminating news and anti-Nazi propaganda to both active and prospective members of the Resistance."

As the occupation dragged on and the Nazis became further entrenched in Poland, anger and frustration with what was happening to the country grew. My dad's childhood home had been erased by the war, and as time passed he found himself longing for ways to put things back together.

"Hitler's fist was closing over our city," my dad says. "And I decided I'd rather die fighting than give in to this evil."

5

INNOCENCE OF YOUTH

$\mathcal{W}$e all have images trapped in our minds, regrets that we can't shake off, but until this conversation I never considered what keeps my father up at night. "Rita," he says, "there is something on my mind, something that happened during this time that I've never gotten over. It haunts me because I'm not sure that I did the job that I could have. And I feel like I might as well tell you about it." His posture changes, and I feel suddenly as though he's about to confess a long-harbored sin, that he's taking this opportunity to release himself from something that might reflect badly on his character. He's always been a man ruled by a code of ethics, bound by duty to do the right thing. I've never questioned that. I've also never heard my father question himself. I momentarily wonder, did my own dad commit some atrocity? Was there a skeleton in his closet about to be unleashed? Could I handle what I was about to hear?

He begins to paint me a picture of a summer afternoon in Nazi-occupied Poland, one of the last days of his youth. "When I was in high school," he says, "I was a member of a swimming club that would often meet on the banks of the Vistula River. Since the Germans had also taken possession of the pools, we Poles were left to swim in the rivers. The club was just as much about socializing as it was about exercise, and my friends and I would often go to talk to the girls that came to swim.

"We would meet on a sandbar not far from a bridge that spanned the river. During the occupation the bridge was an important supply route for Nazi troops, and it was kept under constant surveillance by armed German guards. The swimmers in the river had to be careful not to let the swift current carry them too close to the bridge, because the guards had a license to shoot any trespassing Poles on sight. One warm summer day, I had gone to swim, and I struck up a conversation with a girl I liked. The two of us decided to move downriver a bit, away from the crowd. As we walked, another youngster, a boy from my high school class, asked if he could join us. What I wanted to say was, 'Get lost! I'm with a girl here! I mean, come on, buddy!' but instead I said, 'All right, go ahead,' and the three of us swam together in the shallow water by the sandbar. I wish I had said 'no.'

"The boy decided that he wanted to make an attempt at crossing the river. The current in the middle was strong and dangerous, and I could quickly see that the kid was not a good swimmer. He was fighting against the rushing water, but was being rapidly pushed toward the bridge and the watchful eyes of the Nazi guards who patrolled it. I knew that the guy would either be pulled underwater and drown or be swept to the bridge and shot. So, I left the girl and leaped into action. I ran back toward the sandbar to a pair of elementary school-age kids I'd seen earlier paddling in a kayak. I begged the two boys to give up the boat, explaining that someone was drowning. The kids balked, wasting precious time. I ran back to where I'd left the girl and found her standing there, dumbstruck, staring out at the water toward the desperately splashing boy, who was now dangerously close to the armed Nazis on the bridge.

"I tried to quickly ascertain the distance and the time it would take me to get in the water and save the boy, but it was already too late. By the time I would be able to reach him to pull him to safety, we would both be in range of the Nazi guards' rifles. I was left with no choice but to stand on the shore and watch as the boy continued to drift away, his struggles growing more and more weak, until he disappeared beneath the surface and didn't come back up."

My dad stops. His hand inadvertently crosses his heart.

"The incident was difficult for me in many ways. The instructor who supervised the swimming club began an inquiry into the accident, and the girl who was with me at the time was the only one questioned. She testified that I had stood there and done nothing as the boy drowned! I couldn't believe it. I wasn't given a chance to tell my side of the story. I was furious that my good name could be tarnished by the traumatic event."

I'm struck by how an event like this can have a ripple effect for the rest of our lives. As my dad tells me the story I think of his devoted involvement in the American Red Cross, and how he insisted I learn to swim at a very early age. I have a new perspective on why he volunteered as a lifeguard and swim instructor his whole adult life. Perhaps he thought if he'd been better trained all those years ago, he might have saved the boy and wouldn't be haunted now by the memory.

I feel as if I'm slowly beginning to switch on lights, illuminating rooms of my father's character that I'd never known existed. With just a few questions answered, I'm beginning to assemble the pieces of the puzzle that is my father.

"I was never asked to testify," he says. "I was never given a chance to tell my side of the story until school started. My peers elected me class president, and the gym teacher who had been in charge of the swimming club announced that the vote was not valid. He pointed at me and told my classmates, 'This guy doesn't deserve to be president. He let a boy drown this summer.' So, I stood up and said, 'Wait a minute. I'm going to fight this. I've thought about this a lot. If I had gone after that boy, there would have been two victims instead of one. I will not tolerate being accused of cowardice without being given a chance to explain myself. I'll tell you exactly what happened, present the case, and you can all decide for yourselves.' I went to the blackboard, took the chalk, and drew a diagram of what had happened that day. I showed them the distances, told them about the guard on the bridge, explained the kayakers and the current. Then I said to the class, 'You be the judge.' "

My dad nods once. "No one withdrew his vote." His chin trembles. He's clearly dealing with regret at not being able to save the boy, and perhaps still needs to reassure himself that the class's judgment had been correct. One thing I know for certain about my father is that his sense of duty would not allow him to let an innocent man die if there was any way he could possibly save him.

If I were ever at war, I would want my dad to have my back.

Even though the Allies had declared war on Germany on September 3, 1939, the Poles had virtually been left to sink or swim. The Polish army had been destroyed or dispersed in the Nazi invasion, and the

Allies were not helping those who were still left to stand up to the occupying forces. It fell to the young men and women of Poland, braving incredible adversity and the constant threat of death, to establish the Polish Resistance. The dominant group was called the Armia Krajowa—"AK," translated as the Polish Home Army, to which my father belonged. Their acts of sabotage were carefully and strategically chosen to undermine German authority and move toward reclaiming Polish sovereignty. Outmanned and outgunned in a David versus Goliath fight for their homeland, the Resistance made bombs, assassinated Gestapo agents, derailed trains, blew up bridges, aided Jews in hiding, and printed more than eleven hundred anti-Nazi periodicals.

"My country was in distress, and people were being killed," my dad says. "It was so frustrating, feeling that helpless. I remained active in the Young Eagles, continuing our campaign of anti-Nazi propaganda, but training for more aggressive action. I found myself under the command of a man I came to know as Lieutenant Stan. Now, it's important for you to know that Stan was probably not his real name—when we joined the Resistance, everyone in the unit took on a code name for anonymity. That way if you were caught and tortured by the Nazis, you could not reveal your comrades' real identities because you didn't actually know their real names. In fact, some people picked names that were the opposite of who they were: a tall guy would pick a code name like 'Shorty,' a bald guy would call himself 'Curly.' Others picked names that motivated them for battle. For my own nom de guerre I chose the name 'Rys.' It was a pretty common nickname for people named Ryszard, but I liked it because it had a sort of double meaning—*rys* is also the Polish word for a kind of wildcat, a lynx. It seemed like a good name to go by under the circumstances, when fighting could happen at any time. An aggressive name to keep me safe."

"What was Lieutenant Stan like?" I ask.

"He was a serious, soft-spoken young man. He was a few years older than the other boys and me who ended up under his command, but we quickly became very close."

"What did he look like, Dad?" I ask.

"Oh, you know, he was dark haired, medium build, and he had a nice smile."

"Was he handsome?"

"I suppose, yes. Sort of like Errol Flynn without the mustache."

Under his leadership, the Young Eagles organized themselves, first into camps and then into individual units. Lieutenant Stan became my father's commander, and, more important, something of an older brother. "The two of us didn't know each other for long, but he became a great friend, a great influence. He was the best superior I had during the war, and our unit was one of the best in the Resistance."

Lieutenant Stan announced that the Young Eagles were going to become a part of the Polish Resistance. This meant the possibility of real combat. "Finally," my dad says, "I would be able to really fight the Nazis." It was at this point that my dad revealed a bold move from his youth. The minimum age of enlistment in the Resistance was sixteen, and at the time, he was only fifteen. "I had to lie to gain entrance into the Resistance," he says. "I had been born in 1926, a year too late, so I changed the year of my birth to 1925. From then on, all of my documentation bore that date, all the way up to my naturalization as an American citizen."

I am struck anew by how much I had yet to learn about my father. Until this moment, I hadn't even known his real age. My father continues, "Even my Social Security card bears the false date! I wonder if I could have gotten away with collecting my Social Security a year early?"

"But you didn't retire until you were seventy-six," I remind him. "You missed your chance."

"True." He snickers, "but it would have been interesting to try."

Once the Young Eagles became an official part of the Resistance, my dad stopped being a freelancing dissident and became much more involved in the actual campaign against the Nazis. He continued to distribute antifascist propaganda, but on a much larger scale. "Many of us were also issued forged documentation to keep us safe if we were ever caught or questioned—I had forged papers stating that I worked for the German arms industry. I never knew how exactly the Resistance had them made. There was a special stamp that had to be renewed every month, and every month it happened for me. A young woman, one of the brave underground couriers, would bring it to me. My documents stated that I operated a grinding machine at a factory somewhere in Warsaw, but I never even knew where the factory was.

"For the most part my buddies and I managed to avoid trouble, but once, those fake documents probably saved my life. As I told you, under the occupation all of the streetcars in Warsaw were segregated—certain cars were designated for use by Germans only, and Poles had to ride separately. One evening, I was walking home with a friend of mine, and we saw a streetcar pull into a stop ahead of us. The street seemed to be deserted. If there had been anyone around we never would have tried a stunt like this, but because we were young and foolish and thought we could get away with it, we hopped into an empty 'Germans only' car just as the tram was pulling away.

"We rode along for a few minutes, pleased with ourselves for getting away with flouting the law, but before long we heard sirens and a German police car began to follow the tram. I felt a weight like a lump of lead drop into my stomach. We had our forged documentation on us, but I had a terrible feeling that the Germans would somehow recognize us.

" 'Listen,' I said to my friend, 'they must have seen us get on to the German car! We'd better jump out of this tram and make a run for it, or they'll catch us for sure.' We climbed off the tram as quickly as we could and darted down a side street. As we ran I could hear the police car screech to a stop and the sounds of boots hitting the cobblestones behind us, coming closer and closer. 'Halt!' a voice screamed in German. 'Halt!' We rounded a corner and were faced with a dead end—the side street we'd chosen ran onto the grounds of a factory, and the gates were locked shut in front of us.

" 'There's no place else to go!' my friend said, terrified.

" 'They'll shoot us if we try to run again,' I said. 'Let's just hope our documentation is enough to get us out of this.' The two Nazi policemen approached, cornering us against the iron bars of the locked gate.

" 'What were you doing in the German section?' the lead officer demanded. I tried to start explaining but the words stuck in my mouth—I was scared, and my German wasn't wonderful. I looked desperately to my friend, who I knew was a bit more fluent than I was.

" 'We were in a hurry,' he stuttered, 'it was an accident, we didn't see that the car was for Germans only until we had already gotten on.' The officer demanded we present our papers. We both produced our freshly forged forms and handed them slowly to the officers, both of us praying silently that they would pass muster.

"The first officer looked the papers up and down and handed them off to his partner. Without saying anything else, he walked toward my friend and stopped just a few inches away from him. Slowly and deliberately he raised his leather-gloved hand and slapped my friend hard across the face. The sharp sound echoed down the deserted side street. He did the same to me, bringing his open palm down on my face with incredible force. My eyes watered from the impact of the blow, but my friend and I both kept our mouths shut.

"The second officer handed us our documents. 'Go!' he shouted in our faces, 'Get lost!' I stuffed my papers back into my pocket and motioned for my friend to follow me. We ran out of that alley as quickly as we could, only slowing down once we'd gotten far away from the police car. It was incredibly lucky for us that the police accepted our fake papers. If the documentation hadn't been so good, we would have been sent to a slave labor camp for sure, or shot outright. I definitely wouldn't be here right now. Neither would you."

"Wow," I say. "It's amazing how you had to be constantly vigilant."

"The Nazis tried to control everything we did, and carefully monitored what information got into and out of Poland, drastically restricting the news we received in Warsaw. We only got snippets of information about what was going on in the rest of the world, but it was clear that all of Europe was entering a dark time. The Germans were ruthless, and would torture anyone they caught whom they suspected of involvement with the Resistance. I had a cousin, a girl, who worked as a courier for the underground. She was caught on a mission and tortured horribly. They asked her to give up the names of the people she was working with, but thankfully she was strong and kept her mouth shut. She disappeared after that—I think she was sent to Auschwitz and never came back. When this happened she had no idea I was in the Resistance, and I figured I was probably safe. But that incident taught me a valuable lesson—the less said about the Resistance, the better.

"Some of my friends and their families learned this lesson the hard way. I had a friend, a guy from school who was a few years older than me, who was also involved in the underground. He was a blabbermouth—he used to tell everyone who would listen what a great hero he was in the Resistance. He would tell me all the time about the secret activities he was part of, and he barely even knew me. He didn't know I was also in the Resistance—I was cagier than most, and that is probably why I survived. Remember, not even my parents knew about what I was doing. So, surprise surprise, the Gestapo arrested the guy pretty quickly. My mom told me she heard his mother had to go to Gestapo headquarters and 'drink' with them, but she was a gorgeous, vivacious woman, and I think what she really had to do was have sex with them in order to get her son released. 'Be careful,' my mother warned me, 'this is all around us. This is what happens. Sometimes in life, we have to pay the price.' I decided my mother would never have to pay that price for me."

My dad stops. I sense he's deciding whether to tell me something. "Rita, the thought did cross my mind that if the Gestapo caught me, my mother would buy me out. At one point, my mother presented the idea of having me smuggled out of Poland into Switzerland. I immediately said, 'No!' It was so against every principle we believed in as Poles: Even my father was against it. I knew that if I went to Switzerland, I would have been interred as a laborer, sent to a work camp. More important, there was no way I was going to desert my buddies or my homeland. I said, 'I'd rather die with friends than live with strangers.' "

Ryszard Kossobudzki, or now "Rys," was fiercely loyal to his country, and hated anyone who turned against Poland and helped the Nazis. "One day," he says, "I went over to the home of Ewa, a girl I liked. When she left the room, I found a letter that another suitor wrote to her. Normally I wouldn't pry into someone's business, but it was right there in the open, on the desk, staring at me. When I glanced over and saw a few words I had to read further. The letter said how disappointed this guy was that his family didn't qualify to be full-fledged German, or 'Reichsdeutsche.' They were only allowed to identify themselves to Germans as 'Volksdeutsche,' partial Germans. I dropped the letter, sickened at the thought, and quickly excused myself. I never spoke to Ewa again. I made excuses to my mother about why I didn't want to see her or her family. Here I was, fighting for my country, risking my life. How could someone do this, turn on his own country? I'd respect a German officer more than him, a traitor, a turncoat."

Hitler's vision of world rule included his warped concept of eugenics. He believed that the racial purity of the German people had to be preserved, and to this end he began a horrific campaign of systematic, sanctioned mass murder that resulted in the deaths of millions of people in World War II, including six million Jews. This process culminated with the establishment of massive death camps across Europe, but began with the creation of ghettos, blocked-off areas of cities in which Jews were forced to live.

"Dad?" I ask. "Did you know what was going on with the Jews?"

"We knew that Governor Frank, Hitler's man, had decreed that all Poles hiding Jews would be killed. And of course now we know that sometime during the war Hitler and his men developed a plan known as the 'Final Solution,' which called for the murder of all Jews. All we knew then was that the Jews had been rounded up and confined in 'ghettos,' the poor areas in cities and towns, separated from the outside world by walls and fences.

"One of the largest and most well-known ghettos established during the war was located in Warsaw, not far from where I grew up. In 1942, Hitler ordered the liquidation of the Warsaw Ghetto, and Nazi soldiers began rounding up Jews by the thousands and shipping them off by the trainload to concentration camps. Many were sent to Treblinka, located about sixty miles northeast of Warsaw. Some ended up in Majdanek, on the outskirts of Lublin, Poland, about one hundred miles southeast of Warsaw.

"It was often difficult to know what exactly was going on, even within Poland's borders. During my time in the underground, in spring of 1943, I was ordered to deliver a message to an underground officer in Lublin, located about one hundred miles from Warsaw. The mission was a stone's throw from the Majdanek death camp, but I didn't know what it was at the time.

"My cousin Rita—whom you're named after—lived in Lublin. I traveled there on the pretext of visiting her, concealing the message, which was written, I think, on a piece of toilet paper. It didn't take me long to get there, and my cousin greeted me warmly when I arrived. My plan was to stay with Rita and her family for as long as it took me to get in touch with the underground cell. I had no idea how long that would take. As luck would have it, it didn't take long at all. Rita's mother, my aunt, was dating an underground officer. He was not the man I'd been sent to contact, and at first I was hesitant to let him know I had come on a mission—I was afraid he might turn out to be a Gestapo spy. After a few days I decided I had little choice, so I gathered my courage and confessed to my aunt's boyfriend that I was in the underground, and that I was, in fact, in Lublin on official business.

"I did as instructed and turned over the message to the cell. My mission completed, I decided to spend some time with my cousin before returning to Warsaw. She showed me around Lublin, a place

I hadn't been since before the occupation began. 'The best place in town to get a good view,' she told me, 'is from the top of the church steeple.' We went there together and climbed to the top. The city of Lublin stretched out beneath us. At the edge of town was some kind of camp, and Rita pointed it out to me. It was nondescript from a distance, nothing more than a collection of drab barracks lined up like dominoes. There was a larger building, like a factory, smoke rising from its chimneys. From that distance it was difficult to make out any activity in the camp. It almost looked deserted.

" 'What kind of camp is it?' I asked her. 'Military?'

" 'I'm not sure,' she replied. 'I think it's some kind of isolation camp—I think the Germans keep Jews and underground Poles there.' I made a sketch of it so I could show the Resistance back in Warsaw. As we prepared to descend the tower, the wind shifted and a terrible smell reached us. It's difficult to describe—a pervasive stink of smoke. I had never smelled anything like it before. 'They must be burning garbage,' Cousin Rita said, covering her nose with one hand. I nodded and believed her, not knowing what else it could possibly be. It wasn't until much later that I found out what was really going on at Majdanek. That what we were smelling was the smell of burning flesh."

6

A Minus

*M*y dad sits silently at the table for a moment. All I can think about is the horrifying smell of burning flesh and the deep grief I see in his eyes. I tell him, "Sadly, I smelled it, too, while I was covering the atrocities in Kosovo. It's something I'll never forget. You know I also interviewed Slobodan Milosevic after he was arrested, right?" Milosevic's name, like Adolf Hitler's, has become synonymous with "ethnic cleansing."

"You interviewed that killer?" my father asks.

"I did," I say. "In fact, I got him to sort of apologize. You didn't see the interview?"

"No, I guess I didn't," he says. It is the first time I've broached the subject of his seeming lack of understanding of my career, and of television news in general, for that matter. "Rita, maybe I didn't have cable at the time." That was always his excuse, even though I had offered to get him cable, which he clearly viewed as a luxury. "So, when was it?" he asks.

"I interviewed the former Yugoslav president in 2001, after he was arrested and sent to The Hague to stand trial for war crimes. I kept asking him if he felt like he had anything to apologize for. He blamed all the deaths on 'NATO aggression.' I pressed him, reminding him of the mass graves of civilians. He called them 'individual crimes' and said that many had died in that 'chaos.' But then, after I stuck with the 'are you sorry?' line of questioning, he finally said, 'Of course, all of us are sorry for the death of any person anywhere in the world. Nobody can be happy for the death of any person anywhere.' Though the words couldn't reverse the evil, all the harm done to all those innocent people, I considered it a small success, especially since a few years later he died of a heart attack." This modern-day Hitler's death, like that of his evil predecessor, allowed him to escape formal punishment.

My dad nods. "Men like that never think they are doing wrong. They don't see their evil. Hitler probably went to his grave thinking he was right."

"I read once that Hitler said, 'I do not see why man should not be just as cruel as nature,' " I tell my dad.

"Right," my dad says. "Rationalizing his cruelty as the way of the world. The one thing I think it's important for you to know about the Jews in Warsaw is that, sadly, it wasn't until much later on that we knew what was really going on in those horrific concentration camps. The underground press in Warsaw started printing information about what was happening. They said that the Nazis were murdering Jews, but even then it was considered to be rumors in some circles, just bits of scattered information. It wasn't until much later that I actually discovered the unimaginable truth. That I finally understood the magnitude of what the Nazis had done. It really shook me up. I was sickened at the thought that human beings were capable of doing something like that to other human beings. I saw terrible things during the war, but knowing what went on in those death camps . . ." He pauses and shakes his head in disbelief. "To realize years later that there was such an organized butchery of the Jews boggles the mind.

"We knew they were going after Jews because they were going after us, too. If you were obeying the orders, at first it seemed you could survive. If, in 1944, someone had told me that there were six million Jews being killed, I would have said he was a liar. That would stagger the imagination. It's unthinkable."

"What do you think about people who say the Holocaust didn't happen?"

"They are sick," he says without hesitation. "I know it happened. I saw the aftermath with my own eyes."

"What?" I ask. "What did you see?"

"I personally went into the Jewish Ghetto," he says. "And into the abandoned prison. It was the only building the Germans hadn't bombed or torched. The rest of the ghetto had been leveled. I opened a big gate and marched inside. There were four emaciated young Jewish men cowering in the corner all by themselves. Their bodies visibly shook when I came in—remember, I was wearing a German uniform, so they must have thought I was a Nazi. I immediately pointed to my Polish armband, but they didn't understand. I tried to talk to them in several languages, but they wouldn't move. They were terrorized. I tried desperately for quite some time to get them to come with me, but they wouldn't let me touch them or help them. I finally had to leave them because there were German snipers everywhere. They wouldn't come with me. I wanted to bring them to my unit to help them, but they wouldn't leave. The sadness of their eyes was so haunting, I have always wondered what happened to them.

"Earlier, when the Ghetto was still operating, I remember being at home and suddenly there was a little weak knock on the door, and I opened it to find a little girl. I spotted right away that she was Jewish, but I pretended I didn't know. She had probably snuck out from the nearby ghetto. So I asked, 'What do you want?' and she said, 'Could you spare some bread?' I said, 'Of course! I could spare some bread.' So I found a loaf of bread, cut half, and gave it to her. She said, 'Thank you very much' and quickly vanished. If another child came, I would have done the same. I didn't care what religion a person was. She was a fellow Pole who needed food. Yet for giving bread to a Jew, I could've been shot and brought the wrath of Hitler's henchmen down on my whole family."

"What were the thoughts on Hitler at the beginning?" I ask.

"We thought he was a nut," my dad says. "He was in the news-reels every week. The Polish press made him out to be a laughable figure. The comedians, like Charlie Chaplin, were making fun of him. Early on, we never expected he could bring to the world the evil that he did."

I pick up my eighth-grade paper, "Jews Under Nazi Rule," the one with the A– written in red ink on the title page, and read my dad a line: "Hitler's Start. Adolf Hitler was an ignorant, vulgar, and un-successful housepainter."

"Right!" my dad agrees. "How could someone like that rise to power and do what he did?

"The Jews seemed to never escape Hitler's forces. The Nazis were out to get them. No matter how well hidden they were, it seemed that the Germans were somehow always a step ahead. Near our home in Warsaw there was a nice hotel run by a large group of people who said they were South American. They played South American music, and they all even had passports. One day, the Germans came to move them all 'home.' The Nazis even carried the women's suitcases to the train, making a big show of their hospitality. I later learned that instead of being sent back to South America, all of them were taken to the abandoned center of the ghetto and shot. It turned out that they were really Polish Jews posing as South Americans, thinking that their phony passports would keep them safe. I couldn't believe the performance the Germans had put on right in front of us to trick these poor Jewish people."

"Do you have regrets?" I ask.

"I wish I could have done more," he says. "But I don't think those I associated with in the Polish underground had any real idea of the atrocities that were unfolding."

"Did they not believe the stories of the extermination camps?"

"Who could? It sounded so unreal, impossible that human beings could do that to other humans. The Jews were very optimistic. Like us, they probably never imagined that they'd be put in train cars, sent to an extermination camp, and twenty-four hours later be turned into ash. They probably thought that if somebody got shot in the Ghetto, he was shot for doing something out of line, when he might have actually been shot just for recreation."

"For fun?" I ask.

"I think sometimes the Ghetto became like a shooting preserve for the Hitler Youth. I read much later they'd come to Warsaw and be given a pouch of ammunition and a rifle, and they'd sit on a wall or walk in the street and hunt Jews. Can you believe that? I never saw it myself, but I very well believe it. Sadly, by the time the Jews started believing what was happening at the concentration camps, it was extremely difficult to acquire enough weapons to defend themselves. It was too late."

Though my father seems quick to share his story here, this conversation represents a long process, in which I had to take small steps until he was ready to share all the painful details. In preparation for talking to my dad, I had spent weeks educating myself about World War II and the events that unfolded in my dad's native Poland. During the time of the Kosovo crisis, Dad had done a Fox News interview with me in which he revealed a bit of his history and the terrible treatment of the Jews. He told me that when the Nazis began the destruction of the Ghetto, his family was living in a house close by. My teenaged dad watched in horror as a woman, whose apartment within the confines of the Ghetto faced his house, jumped out of her window engulfed in flames.

"When I saw that woman jumping out of the window, killing herself," my dad had said during the interview, "the whole area was surrounded by strong forces with tanks in every intersection. Even if you wanted to help, there was no way. At the time, when I saw that woman jump, I was, I was . . ." and then he choked up on camera, "I was embarrassed to be alive." My father was visibly shaken and overwhelmed with emotion as was my entire crew. A flood of memories came streaming back into his consciousness. He had nightmares for weeks after that discussion with me, and it would take ten years for me to bring up the subject again.

I tell my dad that I had recently discovered and subsequently interviewed a Jewish Warsaw Ghetto survivor who now lives in Tel Aviv, Israel. Also eighty-four years old, Stan Aronson is one of the very few who survived the Warsaw Ghetto and also fought in the Polish Resistance, and thus was part of two of history's tragedies. I had called him to ask about his remarkable story so that I could share it with my dad.

In 1942, after living in the Ghetto for ten months, he was loaded on a transport to the extermination camp at Treblinka, which began accepting shipments of Jews in late July 1942. Between then and the beginning of October, more than three hundred thousand Jews would be transported in freight trains from the Ghetto in Warsaw to be killed. Stan Aronson, then seventeen years old, would not be one of them.

Though he was loaded onto the train with his parents and many other relatives, he became separated as they boarded because of the sheer numbers of people. "The cattle car was packed," he told me, "I almost couldn't breathe. I didn't think we were going to our death, but I knew I had to get out of there." When the train stopped a little outside Warsaw it was nighttime. He climbed out of a thin window next to the ceiling of the train. "I was a skinny guy then and was able to jump out of the small window."

He said, "No one could imagine this would happen, that anyone could exterminate a whole population. It's unbelievable." His whole family would be wiped out, but rather than running to safety, Stan circled back and took up the fight in Warsaw.

He joined the Polish underground and became part of an elite battalion whose missions included liquidation of Nazi collaborators and German officials. They also attacked the trains that were moving German troops across Poland. "You always think you are going to survive," he told me, but added it was what he felt destined to do. "It was so dangerous. You are at the right moment, at the right time, and you become part of history. Once you are in that situation, you think about the job you have to do, you don't think what will happen to you. If you worry, you are defeated by fear. Anyone who fought in the Uprising was very courageous. There was nowhere to escape."

He wasn't afraid to let his commanding officer know he was Jewish, and others in his small unit began to figure it out as they fought together. "Because of my looks, I blended in: It was hard to tell I was Jewish. I had light brown hair, blue eyes, so I didn't look particularly Jewish." But once they began fighting together, others in his small unit began to put it together. "They knew I didn't have family anymore. Whenever I was asked if I was Jewish, I said yes to my comrades."

He told me, "It didn't matter your faith, or the language you spoke. This was a universal fight for freedom, that's what mattered. I had a job to do. It was war. We were all there to fight for the same cause. All of us were fighting the occupiers. My Resistance comrades felt I was one of them, all of us were fighting a common enemy: evil."

During the second week of fighting Stan was severely wounded in a shootout with Germans at a cemetery in Old Town. He was evacuated and later escaped Warsaw. Decades later he returned to Poland and was given a book on Polish history that included details of his "James Bond–like" battalion. When he began reading the section about himself, he found an egregious error. It said he was killed on the date he was severely wounded in the Uprising. "So," he said to me proudly, "I told the secretary of the reunion group, 'I was just resurrected!' I was glad I was alive and able to make that correction."

My dad laughed, particularly liking that part of the story.

It was after I had talked to Stan Aronson that I pulled out and reread my "Jews Under Nazi Rule" school term paper, from its introduction: "In 1933 Adolf Hitler became chancellor of Germany," to its conclusion: "My paper has proven that the Jews were treated unfairly and severely under Nazi rule. It has proven that people were prejudiced and unfair to Jews because of their religion." What my term paper had really proven was that I could read books by authors like Winston Churchill and with such titles as *Hitler, His Anti-Semitism* and *Judenrat*. It proved that I could research and report statistics, such as there were "approximately six million Jews annihilated during the Holocaust" and "in Poland 2,800,000 Jews were seized by the Nazis." But my school paper had also proven that I really didn't know my own dad.

The real proof—the "eyewitness" we all seek in the news business—was living under my roof, but his firsthand account stayed quietly out of my report. I now understand why my dad let me leave my paper without its dramatic lead, resulting in that minus symbol after the A. Telling me his stories of cruelty and heartache might have helped my grade, but he was protecting me from the nightmarish vision of brutality and heartlessness he had witnessed. He was protecting me from the sadness of his own childhood. Or perhaps he realized that that kind of sorrow remains unspeakable.

7

RIGHT BETWEEN THE EYES

*I*n a few hours and two dozen questions, I had learned more about my father's past than I had garnered in my entire life. As I sat next to him, I was forced to acknowledge that I never knew much about him at all, especially about his formative years. Is this normal in parent-child relationships? Do other children not know much about their own parents' early years, the time "pre-me"? And deeper still, do other children know anything of their parents' triumphs, their tragedies, their fears? I had found the key to a locked chest of my father's secrets, and perhaps to myself. He was talking and I was learning. Had I, for example, made a career of asking questions because my dad never answered mine? Did I become a journalist because my father left me always wanting to know more?

Am I so social because my dad never was, for fear of people asking him about his past, the history of his life?

The one thing that's certain is that I suddenly realized that by the time I was born, the harbored secrets of my dad's life had already transformed him into someone else. Not "Ryszard Kossobudzki from war-ravaged Poland," but "Richard Cosby, American citizen," a man not unlike many in America's "greatest generation": disciplined fathers, who want their children to succeed, their wives to love them unquestioningly, and their employers to respect them. Men who go completely quiet about everything they saw or did during the war. I'm astounded that he never discussed—not with me, not with his wife, not with his employers—that his youth was spent dodging death, fighting to save his country. Why had he built such huge walls around his past? Did he have something to hide? Or was this just the unspoken trauma of war?

I sat in his kitchen becoming conscious that the horrors of war must be like shadows dancing around his mind, never to be touched, but always there.

I suddenly realize I'm conducting the most important interview of my life.

"When did you actually start fighting, Dad?" I ask.

"August 1, 1944," he says, as certain as if it were yesterday. "The first day of the Warsaw Uprising."

"How'd you know to start? And what to do?"

"Well," he answers, "a knock came at the door one day and a messenger told us it would begin at seventeen hundred hours on August 1. Up until right before the Uprising, I had been helping train and keep track of the younger Eagles at the camp we were running about thirty to forty miles outside Warsaw."

"What exactly were you doing at the camp?"

"Teaching boys survival and combat techniques."

"How old were they, Dad?"

"Ten- to thirteen-year-olds," he says. "We had to encourage them at a young age to believe that 'Poland will be free.' "

I would later locate a book about the Young Eagles, which would provide both for my dad and me great historical information, as well as a few surprises. The "Eaglets," formed in 1933, were based on a group called Lvov Eaglets, who fought against the Ukrainians right after World War I. Throughout history, Poles always had to fight to survive. Patriotism was in their blood. The new Eaglets organization was designed to instill patriotism in Poland's young people, and more to the point, to prepare them to fight and die for their country. It is mind-boggling that such young people were being made "combat ready," but if you grew up in Poland, you always had to be ready for war. No wonder my father used to tell us, "You cannot let evil roam unchallenged and that freedom is always worth fighting for." Not a typical life lesson for a young girl in Greenwich, Connecticut.

"I was one of the older guys at the camp at that time," my dad says. "So when Lieutenant Stan was called away to start organizing the fight in central Warsaw I was left in command of all the Young Eagles. He gave me a handful of zlotys, the Polish currency, and instructed me to watch over the kids until he returned. I was frustrated that I was being left behind while Lieutenant Stan, whom I considered a friend and mentor, was about to risk his life for our country. I stayed with the camp for a bit, but then, in a crisis of conscience, I went to the old woman who was our cook to ask what I should do."

"How old was she?" I ask.

"I don't know," he responds, obviously frustrated by my interruption of his storytelling. "She was a grandmother type." He watches as I write "grandmother type" on my legal pad. My father, too, was always good at noticing detail. "I knew the Uprising could begin any day, and I wanted the perspective of someone who had lived a full life and had a family of her own. I needed her to tell me what the best course of action was."

" 'What would you do,' I asked her, 'if you knew that something dramatic was about ready to happen in which you and your family could lose their lives? Would you want your children away at camp, or home with you?' The woman quickly answered that she would want her children as close as possible. I thought hard about her answer while I stayed at the camp a little longer, but about a week later I decided that I had an obligation to return the Eagles to their families and to help Lieutenant Stan fight the fight. I used the money he left me to rent two horse carts, and I took all the boys back into Warsaw to reunite them with their parents. Not long after I got all the boys to their homes, I met back up with Lieutenant Stan and the rest of the adult members of my unit."

"Do you remember the name of your unit, Dad?" I ask.

"Gozdawa Battalion. Named after a famous fighter in Uprising history. He basically came up with the idea to use young underground fighters in the fight for freedom."

"Did your parents know you were doing this yet?"

"They knew I was in the Young Eagles, but I don't think they had any idea I had joined the Resistance. Remember, I had done that three years earlier when I was sixteen, really fifteen. I didn't want them to worry about me. I was always afraid the SS would capture my mother and torture her if the Germans found out her son was in the Resistance."

"Did your parents ever ask you about it?"

"Not specifically," he says. "But they may have suspected, because they did once find a bulletin I had containing all the news on current events and information on German troop movements. They questioned me about it, but I lied and said someone gave it to me.

"My unit was operating in relative secrecy, part of the Polish underground. The different units and cells of the Resistance were kept separate and secret, organizing themselves through messages sent by couriers between anonymous commanders. Our superiors in the underground would issue orders about points of interest and objectives, and the information was disseminated by the women and girls who served as messengers. We had to be ready for just about anything at a moment's notice."

"Did you have uniforms?" I ask.

"We started the Uprising just wearing the clothes on our backs, our civilian clothes, but shortly into the Uprising, we got into a German storage facility and took German uniforms. So, we wore German uniforms, except we added red and white Polish armbands. The armband had a big WP on it, for Wojsko Polskie, translated to mean 'Polish army' or 'Polish military.' It had an eagle between the letters, the symbol of Poland, representing strength and freedom. I think it is originally based on an old Polish legend."

"What did the girls wear?" I ask.

"They wore their civvies and the armband. The armband was important. It was the only way Poles knew not to shoot at each other. Whenever I was worried about being shot by a Pole, I'd wave my arms so they could see the armband. I had it all the way through. I even brought it to America, but I think your mother threw it away." I knew she hadn't.

"What about shoes?" I ask. "Did you wear boots?"

"That's a good one," he says. "Early in the Uprising, I was in the Old Town area, running over ruins and bricks, trying to stay ahead of the Germans, and the old shoes I was wearing were falling apart because the terrain was so tough and full of rubble. One buddy pointed to my shoes and said he knew of a nice shoe store nearby. He took me there, and it was of course abandoned, so I got myself a nice pair of brown suede shoes. Little did I know those shoes would stay with me all the way through the war."

"And what about weapons?" I ask. "What weapons did you have?"

"Ah! Great question!" He laughs. I laugh, too. "I asked Lieutenant Stan the same question: 'What about our weapons?' And with a straight face he told me, 'We don't have any.' He said the weapons were hidden in the woods, and since Warsaw was being squeezed in all directions, we couldn't get access to them. In our whole unit, we only had two measly nine-millimeter handguns. I was stunned. We were supposed to be an elite unit!"

I am stunned, too. It seems like lemmings heading to a cliff, a suicide mission.

"But we had a tactical advantage over the Germans because we knew every street. Though we were woefully underequipped to clash with the Nazis, I was literally fighting to save my own backyard. Most of our units only had a few guns, and ammunition was even scarcer. Because of how difficult it was for us to arm ourselves, fighters in the Resistance jumped at any chance we got to claim a cache of weapons."

"What were the civilians doing during the Uprising?" I ask.

"It was hard to believe that civilians still called the place home, but they did. When the Uprising began, the city went from bad to worse. Already in ruins from the bombings at the beginning of the war, it became what seemed like an endless field of rubble. The streets we were fighting so desperately to claim were lined with what was left of homes, bombed-out, burned-out shells. Many were still occupied by families hiding in their basements."

I later spent time at an exhibit of photos and discussions about the Warsaw Uprising at the Kosciuszko Foundation in New York City. It was fascinating to learn how the covert subculture worked, planning and running a revolution against a well-equipped, well-organized occupying army.

There developed a whole hidden, underground world that operated in Warsaw before and during the Uprising—underground schools, churches, and more than one hundred "first aid stations" and several dozen "hospitals." The scouts created a hidden postal service, delivering thousands of letters daily. There was even an underground justice system, an operating court. If Poles turned against other Poles to help the Germans or were caught collaborating with the Nazis, they'd be given the death sentence. In order not to let a traitor know that they were on to him, trials were often held without the person present. If a person was found guilty, based on the facts, they'd send the Polish execution team to his house and kill him, but not his family.

For the Uprising, General Tadeusz Bor-Komorowski, chief commander of the Home Army, divided Warsaw into operational units. Early on, twenty-five thousand Polish soldiers, only 10 percent of them armed, with an ammunition supply of two to three days, went to war against a perfectly equipped German army having artillery, an air force, armored forces, and all manner of infantry weapons at their disposal. Despite the crushing advantages of the enemy, an atmosphere of hope and enthusiasm prevailed among the soldiers of the Resistance. Poles proudly waved their flags as they gained ground against the Germans. On areas liberated by Polish fighters, the distinctive red and white Polish flags appeared anew.

Caught between fascism and communism, the citizens of Warsaw paid the highest price for their desire for freedom. Warsaw was the first city to raise arms against the Germans, first in 1943 in the Jewish Ghetto, and then, in 1944, by mainly Christian Poles. Hitler wasn't pleased with Warsaw's resolve.

On hearing the news of the Uprising, Hitler said, "Each citizen must be killed, no hostages are to be taken, Warsaw must be razed without a trace. In this way an intimidating lead shall be given for the whole of Europe." Many more Poles stepped up to volunteer for the Resistance. When the Germans dropped propaganda leaflets from planes on Warsaw, mocking and laughing at the Poles, rather than cowering, Poles were further emboldened, their resolve strengthened. Even though anyone caught using a radio was killed for cooperating with rebels, the Poles realized how important the media was in the fight for freedom and operated a secret radio station during the Uprising called "Radio Blyskawica," or "The Lightning," which sent out daily programs to citizens in Warsaw and abroad.

As a journalist, I was fascinated by the ingenuity and tenacity the Poles showed in defying German oppression and recognizing the value in broadcasting, even while they were living in hell. They had few weapons, but realized the airwaves were a way to protect their homeland. I later spoke with Nina Polan, director of the Polish Theatre Institute, who told me the radio station started right before the Uprising and continued until the end. It described battles, made announcements about lost loved ones, and served a key role in strategy. "If they played a certain song," she said, "then the fighters knew there'd be no supply drops that day. Only the top leaders of the Resistance knew the secret code. Citizens at the time thought, 'How can they play this silly song again when Warsaw is burning to the ground?' But the British command had told radio organizers to play it at the right times."

So, despite the Poles' dire circumstances, they were resourceful, even when the Germans cut off electricity, water, medical supplies, and food. When Warsaw's water supply was cut off, the Poles collected rainwater from bomb craters and shared water from wells. While the Nazis were running daily air raids and shelling relentlessly with heavy artillery, the Poles made primitive weapons such as homemade grenades out of unexploded shells or Molotov cocktails using gasoline. They created launchers out of car springs, which could carry the weapons almost two hundred feet.

"In the early days of the Uprising," my dad tells me, "we were lucky—the Nazis underestimated us. They knew how poorly equipped we were, so they sent in units that were basically riffraff— Ukrainian and Cossack troops, soldiers from penal regiments, men who were undisciplined and coarse in their methods. The stories we heard about the Ukrainian soldiers were especially brutal.

"When they took over a Polish house with civilians, they raped the women, and then they butchered everyone in the house. I decided I'd get killed before I fell into enemy hands. I had no intention of becoming their prisoner, having them torture me. It was understood we'd do anything not to be alive when they took us.

"At one point my unit was spending the night in a large supply warehouse. The Nazis had confiscated the expensive items from the Jews when they moved them into the Ghetto—especially fur coats. This warehouse was filled with lots of things, including beautiful fur coats. We were in possession of the warehouse, but we were trapped inside, surrounded on all sides by Nazi soldiers. A few of my buddies were resting in an adjacent building with a few of the girls, and I was on lookout duty. One of the girls, a nurse, approached me.

" 'Listen,' she said, 'would it be all right for me to sit with you for a while? I don't want to stay with the rest of the unit. Those guys are all drinking and making advances. I'd rather stay here with you.'

" 'Of course,' I said, 'but we have to be very, very quiet. I'm on guard duty.' She nodded. There was a big crater in the floor, a hole that had been punched by a mortar. We gathered up a big stack of confiscated fur coats and laid them down in the crater. We sat there together, trying to stay as quiet as we could."

"It sounds like a date, Dad." I smile.

"We were chatting, our voices low, when suddenly we heard the sounds of other voices echoing back and forth all around us. German voices! The girl and I didn't even know each other's names, and there we were, ducked down in that pit in the floor, hiding in nervous silence from the Germans that had now surrounded us.

" 'Shit!' I thought. 'They're going to cut us off from the rest of the squad! I have to tell my boys!' We sat there for a few minutes and I tried to focus on the voices, to pick out exactly where they were coming from. I could see the fear in the young nurse's eyes, and I was plenty scared myself. But the whole time I was thanking providence that it was German voices we were hearing, and not Ukrainian. We knew that if the Germans found us, they would shoot us without any questions. To them we were terrorists, bandits, and we deserved nothing but death. If it had been Ukrainians, and they had found us, they would have raped her to death and tortured me. That I was sure of."

"Really?" I ask.

"Oh, we heard terrible stories about them. They were awful in ways that German soldiers were not. We were told that the Nazis used them as guards in the Jewish camps, that they would murder Jews and then sit down on the bodies to eat sandwiches. We were told they would get drunk and attack houses, raping the women and bayoneting and torturing the men. They'd cut off men's hands and ears, and then castrate them." I lift my hand to my mouth. Tears well up in my eyes. My dad moves on. "The Germans were worthy adversaries, efficient and disciplined fighters. But it was the Ukrainians we were really afraid of.

"Anyway, I'll never forget that the girl asked me how many bullets I had. Every bullet was sacred. There were famous posters plastered around town saying, 'One bullet, one German.' Every Resistance fighter knew his inventory and had thought through exactly how he'd use each piece. I told her I had twenty bullets. She then whispered, 'My name is Henryka. Save the last one for me.' "

Knowing my father, if he had promised to kill her to keep her from being captured, he would have kept that vow. But I believe he'd first have used the other nineteen to kill as many of the enemy as he could.

"As we lay low on that pile of furs, I mentally prepared for the worst, knowing I'd protect her at all costs. Eventually the voices moved off. It was my first close call. I didn't realize until they moved off that I'd been holding my breath the entire time."

It amazed me that even though decades have passed, he was still holding his breath at the thought.

"By my birthday on August 4, it felt like most of the city was in Polish hands. My unit had captured most of our assigned area in Old Town and the City Center. The Nazis didn't count on us being as dedicated as we were. You've got to understand—the troops they sent at first were fighting because they were paid, or because they had been forced to. We were fighting for our home and for our lives. We were determined in a way that no mercenary ever could be."

"With no weapons," I add proudly.

"With *virtually* no weapons," my dad says, correcting me. "I had my Luger."

"When did you eat and sleep?"

"We slept wherever we could, whenever we could, in the nooks and crannies of the bombed-out buildings we operated in. I made a point of returning home to see my mother as often as I could early on. It was the only way I could be sure to get food. She used to feed me beans and pasta, and any rations she had around the house.

"When I was out on operations with my unit, food was hard to come by, and finding food quickly became a struggle. We ate whatever we could find, and sometimes the girls in the unit would bring us rations in the field. Under German occupation everything was immediately rationed, but when the Uprising began, those involved in the fighting were basically cut off from official sources of provisions, meager as they might have been. I was lucky to have a buddy whose sister was a cook—whenever the rations came she would always make sure to give me a little bit extra.

"Sometimes my buddies in the unit and I didn't eat for days. Once, after going without food for a long time, one of the guys in the unit happened upon a case of sugar cubes. I'm not sure exactly where he got them, whether it was hidden somewhere or he bought it on the black market, but for two days I had nothing to eat but sugar. My stomach of course completely revolted on me, and we did what we had to do." He pauses, obviously remembering diarrhea at war. I almost laugh, then catch myself. "After that tense night holding the supply warehouse, surrounded by Germans, my buddies discovered that the Germans had also been using the building to store food. I was on watch one night and a friend of mine in the unit suddenly appeared carrying a can of something.

" 'Rys,' he said, 'have I got a surprise for you.' I looked at the can but the labeling was impossible to read in the dim light; the only part I could make out was the symbol of the Danish crown."

"How do you remember that?" I ask.

"It was reflective," he says, as if it was obvious. "My buddy used his bayonet to pry off the lid and inside was ham, the leanest ham you ever saw. The more time we spent in that warehouse the more food we found. More good Danish ham, and sausages. It was like Christmas in August. Meat had been strictly rationed since the beginning of the occupation, but there we were, in an abandoned warehouse, feasting on more meat than any of us had been able to get in years. It was hard being completely at the mercy of fate during the Uprising, but every once in a while we'd have a stroke of luck.

"Now that I think about it," my father continues, "I had a few pretty incredible strokes of luck. As I said, we were constantly on the lookout for food. Any scraps we could find to keep us going, because we really never knew when we would get another chance to eat. One afternoon I was out looking for something to eat, scrounging on my own at the very edge of our lines. I was picking through the ruins of a building probably five hundred yards away from a railroad embankment. I thought that maybe I'd be able to find a can of meat, or something like that, in the wreckage. It looked to me as if this particular block was completely deserted—my buddies in the unit were camped out a good distance away, and we hadn't heard anything about German activity in the area.

"I was standing in a doorway of this building, leaning against the doorframe, letting myself relax a second, when I noticed some movement far away up the street. I strained my eyes and realized I was looking at men, figures walking down the sidewalk a few blocks away.

My unit was the only one in the area, and I knew where all my guys were. I assumed they were Germans, but since they were so far away I figured it wasn't much of a threat.

"All of a sudden the silence was shattered by this loud noise, a crunch in the brickwork behind me, above my head. I still hadn't seen very much action at that point. But I had been well trained. Without even thinking, my knees collapsed under me, and I dropped to the ground, landing hard in the dust. Lying there in the doorframe, I craned my neck to see what it was that had happened. There on the wall behind where I'd been standing, a bullet had torn a hole through the plaster and brick. It was not more than six inches above where my head had been when I was standing. Somewhere out there, as I'd been carelessly leaning there, a German sniper had noticed me and lined up his shot. He must have been a good ways away, because he'd overcompensated for distance, and his mistake was the only reason that bullet ended up burying itself in the wall and not in my head. I was wearing a helmet, but if his aim had been better it wouldn't have made much difference. If I'd been another few yards away, he would have gotten me right between the eyes.

"It was probably the most foolish thing I ever did, and it was a terrible shock for me. Up until that point I'd felt fear, but that moment made me feel more in danger than I ever had before." My dad stops. Is he coming to grips with his humanity? Recognizing his own vulnerability?

"Eric!" he calls out to the living room. "Time to get ready for work." Then he turns back to me and says, "Today, I need the car, so I have to drive him to work at four-thirty. We have twenty minutes." He picks up his dramatic story, in which he is almost shot between the eyes, without a breath. "From that point on, I never stopped in one place for any longer than I had to, never went anywhere without first thinking about cover. Until then, I had traveled through the seemingly empty streets of Warsaw without any thought. Suddenly, I was no longer a tourist.

"Another near miss happened when my buddy and I were guarding a house on the corner, not far from the theater. It was very quiet, late afternoon. We got a little lax and withdrew a little bit from the front wall of the house, which looked like a demolition site. My buddy said he needed to go relieve himself, so he turned around and walked away. A few moments later, an egg-shaped grenade landed three or four feet in front of me. I have no idea where it came from. There was no sound. We were trained not to ever dare try to grab a live grenade and throw it back. Instead, dive! As soon as I saw it, I made a twist and a backward dive. The grenade exploded in a split second and one of the pieces caught me between the eyes. It embedded in my forehead, and it started bleeding. A lot. Apparently, that area is particularly sensitive to bleeding."

"What did you do?" I ask.

"We were close to my home, so I headed there. By the time I walked in the door, my face was covered in blood. My mother panicked. 'Did you lose your eye?' she asked. There was no water to wash my face."

"What do you mean, 'no water'?" I ask. "What happened to the water?"

"During the Uprising, we ran out of water. The Germans kept it from us, and all the wells went dry. We washed in cologne water taken from an abandoned store we rummaged through. After a few days without water, and standing guard on the hot pavement, I remember recalling photos of Niagara Falls from a book on the United States I had as a child. I started fantasizing about Niagara Falls and hundreds of gallons of water falling into my mouth."

"I'm surprised you knew about America as a child," I say.

"Oh, we knew about America," he says. "Everyone knows about America, but for many it is only a distant dream. Something you see in movies and books, a place to fantasize about."

"So, did the image of an overflowing Niagara Falls help you?"

"It briefly helped me to mentally escape our dire circumstances," he says. "But I was still thirsty and my comrades thought I was cracking up."

"So, what did your mom do about your bloody face?"

"She took me to a nearby first-aid station, which was more like a room in this doctor's house, two or three hundred yards away from German lines. That was a big distance in the ruins. When we got there, the doctor was operating on somebody else. He eventually brought a kerosene lamp over to where we were, picked up the pliers, and said, 'Of course, I'm going to have to yank it out.' I said, 'Go ahead.' What else could I say? In front of my mother, I was supposed to be tough. I didn't blink an eye. It squirted out lots of blood that he wiped off with his hand. He then wiped his hands on his pants, stuck a large bandage on my forehead, and said, 'Be on your way, soldier. Carry on.'

"So, after that, my parents knew for sure I was fighting in the Resistance. I suppose it must have been obvious to them for a while, but it was finally out in the open. I never really talked with my father about it. I was still frustrated with him for what I took to be his passivity. My mother, like a typical mom, just wanted me to be safe. 'Richard,' she would say to me, 'Be careful, keep your head down, and don't get heroic!'"

"Sounds like you had several close calls," I say.

"We all had close calls, but we had some tragedies, too. There are times when even the best training and the most care aren't enough.

A week or so into the Uprising, Lieutenant Stan had gotten wind of a German weapons cache that could be easily invaded and claimed. We had been told that there would be minimal resistance, and since we only had a few weapons among us, it seemed like a golden opportunity to supply ourselves with more. We set out to the position." I imagine my dad in his youth, moving stealthily through the seemingly abandoned streets of a ruined city block.

"It seemed as if the area was completely abandoned. We moved slowly and carefully, keeping alert and doing our best to watch each other's back. It was always strange operating in deserted parts of the city. We found those weapons without much difficulty, and made off with quite a haul—three rifles, an invaluable addition to our skimpy armament. Moments later, however, our happiness at the completion of the important mission was cut terribly short. We were taking cover beneath a small stone wall amidst the rubble of what remained of the Jewish Ghetto.

"Lieutenant Stan gave us the signal he was going to survey the next block and make sure it was clear of enemy troops. He stood up and leaned over the top of the wall, peering through his binoculars at the seemingly deserted street ahead of us. It was a deadly mistake. The gleam of the sunlight on the lenses of the binoculars was all a German sniper needed to sight a target. A shot suddenly rang out, echoing in the empty street. Lieutenant Stan collapsed to the ground. He fell at my feet. I pulled his limp body toward me and immediately checked for breathing, for any kind of movement that might disprove the terrible truth that was stirring in the back of my mind. When I held his limp body close to me, I saw that he had been shot in the head, killed instantly."

"What did you do?" I ask.

"I never cried over the loss of any of my pals. Stan always taught us, 'It's not to reason why; it's our job to do and die.' We all knew our time would come at some point. I gathered my men and the weapons Lieutenant Stan had just given his life for, and I told the girls in my unit to give him a dignified burial. When someone died, you buried him quickly, if at all. You had to worry about the living first."

My father's voice chokes. In the dim early evening light of the kitchen I can see the spirit of the young man he once was in the lines of his face. I've never seen him overcome with emotion the way he is now. I realize that this memory he's dredged up for me is one of the ones he has spent his entire life trying to banish, to wall off and keep out of his mind. There on the streets of Warsaw, holding his friend and leader's lifeless body in his arms, my father's youth officially died.

I think we've had enough for one day.

8

MY HOTEL ROOM

A golden sun was setting over the rooftops of my dad's neighborhood as I left his house and climbed into the backseat of the cab waiting for me in his driveway. I had booked a room at a local hotel. In retrospect, the choice to stay at a hotel alone, rather than at my dad's house, seems like a strange one, not common father-daughter practice. It never occurred to me to ask to stay with him.

As a spirited journalist, always on the move chasing the story, I am used to staying in various hotel rooms in different states and different countries, often for weeks at a time. Staying in a hotel is natural for me, but to be honest, I booked a room because I really didn't know my dad. It would have felt like sleeping in a stranger's house.

My dad and I had grown distant over the years. I had no idea what his life was like, and he didn't know much about mine. Even holidays like Christmas and Thanksgiving had been reduced to a phone call at best. Birthdays were often forgotten, or marked by a card received weeks later, forwarded from an old address after one of my many moves.

As the cab drew closer to the hotel, the glowing windows of houses flashed by. I occasionally caught glimpses of families doing what families do. These simple nights that so many of us take for granted—sharing family conversation over a home-cooked meal or playing board games in the living room—were among the experiences my dad was never able to have after September 1, 1939, when the world changed and his teenage years were stolen from him by the war. Now that I'd gotten a taste of what my dad endured during the conflict in Warsaw all those years ago, I was finally beginning to understand the man that he had become and why my childhood with him was not a montage of PTA meetings and picnics.

I paid the cabdriver and made my way into the Washington, D.C., hotel. As I let myself into my room, my head was swimming with thoughts. I was thinking of all the times my dad had seemed distant, of all the times he had been detached from the reality of our family and emotionally moved on. Resigned to it, my brother and I wanted him to be happy, yet I always wondered why he seemed so reserved, why the events of such a large piece of his life went unmentioned, and why Poland was a topic and a place never to be visited by him again. Although I'd been blessed with success in my professional life, I'd spent my entire personal life confused by what I took to be my father's coldness toward his daughter, by how easy it had seemed for him to leave our family.

Now that I had this amazing opportunity to connect with him, to uncover and sharpen the blurry details of his past, I had the chance to gain a new understanding of how the war left him with a protective shield—a barrier to keep the bad out. Indeed, like so many other young military men and women I've interviewed over the years, Dad learned to shut himself off, to compartmentalize the pain, to push the fear to the back of his mind. It was his one surefire weapon to protect his heart and soul against the terror he witnessed and lived through.

I dropped my suitcase on the floor near the dresser, took off my heels, and sat down on the bed. The first segment of the most personal interview of my life was over, but my work, both on myself and on my dad's story, was just beginning. My job as a daughter was to discover that my dad is a person. My task as a journalist was to find out everything I could about that person.

My career in television has taken me all over the world, many times to dangerous locations. I've always been dogged in my search for the truth, never stepping down from a challenge and never letting anything come between me and a story. I've always had a profound respect for our soldiers and the military—that's something my father instilled in me from a very young age. I remember him as always captivated by military parades, air shows, and any news of our troops. I see now that it all goes back to his early life in Poland—his commitment to fitness, his passionate patriotism, his strictly regimented life, and his deep admiration of those brave souls in the service.

Reporting on our military is a great privilege, I believe one of the most prestigious and important assignments a journalist can receive. I've been lucky to have known and covered these heroic men and women numerous times during the course of my career. From Kosovo to the Middle East to Guantanamo, where I was able to observe firsthand the detainees and their living conditions, I've always been moved and intrigued by the human drama at the heart of such conflicts. Perhaps my interest in covering them comes from a need to know something about my own wartime family history. Perhaps

I was always searching for a part of my father in them. When I was given a chance to travel to Afghanistan to cover our troops serving there, I didn't hesitate.

I knew the trip to Afghanistan would be a perilous one, but I also knew how important it was to tell that story. I wasn't allowed to announce the exact travel details of our journey on the air for fear that our news team would be targeted once we arrived. I took the long military flight, ultimately landing at the U.S. air base in Bagram, and quickly got a feel for the conditions there on the battlefield. I got a chance to tour the base, to meet the men and women who kept it running, and got a taste of what it was like to live as a soldier in this difficult terrain.

I was assigned a wooden bed, the same generic-looking ones the soldiers had. The mattress was rock-hard, and sleeping on the pillow they gave me was like sleeping on a telephone book. I lay miserably on the bed for a moment mulling over my extensive to-do list for the following day, when I remembered that I had packed an extra-high-density pillow in the second tier of my well-traveled garment bag, a trick of mine that I've always thought should be taught in Journalism 101. I learned that if I had my own pillow, I could sleep anywhere. I jumped up to get it, but to my dismay found that the lower zipper on my bag had been crushed in transport. I struggled with it for a few minutes and eventually dragged it outside. I asked the first soldier I saw to help open it, and he immediately slit it open with his large field knife. I pulled the pillow out, went back to my bunk, and lay there in the freezing-cold darkness, trying to find some comfort in a small luxury I'd brought from home.

The next day I awoke early and suited up to go out on patrol. Dressed in a helmet and a thick, heavy bulletproof vest, I climbed into an armored Humvee with machine guns mounted on top. Despite all the precautions, it was still clear how dangerous the unforgiving environment really was. As we drove, a civilian pushing some kind of cart began to cross the road just ahead of us. Our vehicle was moving at a fairly rapid pace.

"Are we going to stop?" I asked the military driver.

He shook his head grimly. "If she doesn't get across in time, we have to keep going," he said. He explained that they had been ambushed before in similar situations—a civilian stops a tank in the middle of the road, only to reveal him or herself to be carrying explosives. They worried constantly about IEDs (improvised explosive devices) planted in and along the roadways as well. Nothing was as it seemed, and nowhere was truly safe. The woman made it across the road before we reached her. There was no ambush, no sudden explosion this time, but I had learned a powerful lesson. I realized how vulnerable these soldiers really were. Despite being part of the most powerful and advanced military in the history of the world, they were still far from home in the middle of a treacherous war zone and had to keep their senses razor sharp. They had already been on the ground in Afghanistan for a while by the time I arrived, and had probably driven that same road in those same tanks a hundred times. But they still couldn't rest, couldn't let their guard down even for a second. "Life is precious," one of the soldiers quietly told me, and that fact is nowhere more apparent or riveting than on the battlefield. They were well equipped and well prepared, but in the end, their survival came down to precision, professionalism, and pure luck.

I imagine my father, a scared teenager in Nazi-occupied Warsaw with nothing but the clothes on his back and his "borrowed" Luger. If today's American soldiers, who have years of training and billions of dollars of technology and firepower to guide and protect them were still vulnerable, what must it have been like for my young dad?

When I left Afghanistan I was in tears. All of the people on my team were deeply moved by the stories we heard from the men and women we spoke with. These troops were all proud to be serving their country, to be fighting for freedom. I also thought back to our visit, before entering Afghanistan, to Landstuhl Regional Medical Center in Germany, where some of the most gravely wounded soldiers were sent to recover. I met a soldier there who looked so young, he could easily have been as young as my father was when he was in the Uprising. He told me the story of how he'd lost almost his entire unit just days before.

"Do you have any regrets about joining the military?" I asked him, thinking that his answer would surely be yes in the wake of such a tragedy. Instead, he shook his head. "I'd go back any day of the week," he said. "I'd do it for freedom and I'd do it for my country." I was so touched by those words, and I think now that if I were to ask him, my father would have very similar things to say. Of course he would be scared to go back after all these years, but now that I've learned more of his story, I recognize the same unwavering loyalty in my dad that I saw in that boy at Landstuhl. I think of that day in the hospital, of that soldier's incredibly young face. Knowing that my father was about that age when he and his small band of brothers answered the call to fight for their country stuns me. To think of him as a teenaged boy, cradling his dying lieutenant in his arms, breaks my heart.

I have seen a man die up close, and it is an image that every now and then recurs in my mind like a vision from a nightmare. My experience with death, however, was much more clinical than my dad's. My MSNBC bosses submitted my name and I was selected to be a witness to the December 2005 execution at San Quentin of former Crips gang leader Stanley "Tookie" Williams.

I had mixed emotions about attending his execution, seeing death up close, even for a man who was accused of multiple murders. I had interviewed and seen this person face to face and listened firsthand to what many viewed as his defiance to admit to any grave wrongdoing. The staff at San Quentin positioned me directly on the other side of the thick glass from a death scene about to occur. There were complications with the lethal injection. The ordeal was disconcerting when it took more than twenty minutes to insert the needles properly, which was much longer than it was supposed to take. Williams became so agitated by the delay that he tried to help them. I can still see Williams's face as he finally died. He was only a few feet from me. Every now and then, this disturbing image and his face flash in my mind, the face of a man I met but once. I cannot imagine how haunted my dad must be when he sees Lieutenant Stan's face at night or those of his comrades whom he fought for and with every minute of every day . . . comrades who never made it past their teens, friends who would have given their lives for him.

As I sat in my hotel room, thinking about the things I'd just learned about my dad, I began to make more and more connections between his experiences during the war and the man I grew up with. He was always prompt and on time. I see now how he learned that time is precious. He also always cleaned his plate, and now I know that too often he had gone without. I remember my dad's cooking was always very simple—stark and plain foods, with few ingredients and minimal preparation time. As a result I never learned to be much of a cook either. Perhaps my dad never learned to cook more elaborate dishes because of the way he had to eat during the Uprising—scrounging for supplies and always ready to move on to the next position.

I've always been happy living out of boxes, and I've always been able to handle whatever life threw at me. I realize now that many of these survival skills came from my father. He used to tell me that it's the difficult experiences that make us who we are. He also has told me many times, "Don't think that life is going to be fair or easy." In school, even an A left room for improvement. When a teacher gave me anything less than a perfect grade, my dad would tell me it was an opportunity to prove her wrong. I think this is the reason I've always pushed myself to excel in my career, why I always jumped to take the riskier assignments, to work hard to catch the big stories. I think of the journalist who my dad said was tortured by the Nazis and sent back as a lesson to others. I shiver at the thought of being physically tortured or killed for reporting the truth, but know there are still countries in this world where reporting is a life-or-death matter. Many times I have put myself in dangerous and difficult spots, from covering the L.A. riots after the Rodney King verdict to facing down the guns of the Montana Freemen. In that instance I pressed for an exclusive interview while holding my hands up in the air, hoping they wouldn't shoot!

Soon after 9/11, I interviewed Palestinian leader Yasser Arafat. At the time, there was intense shelling of the Mokata, his beleaguered compound on the West Bank. Under siege and suspicious, they trusted no one, not even some of their own people. I asked Arafat if he was worried about being assassinated. He responded, "No one will take me but . . ." and then, shaking his hand, he pointed to the heavens. I can see his finger in my face to this day. I spent the following day with Israeli prime minister Ariel Sharon at his beautiful farm in the Negev. I went to grab an orange that was swaying from a tree and found a Mossad sharpshooter perched directly behind it.

When I was getting set to travel to cover the crisis in Kosovo, I learned that two German journalists had just been executed there. My mother pleaded with me not to go, but I knew that it was an important story that needed to be covered. I experienced historic rivalries firsthand when I went from Belgrade to Kosovo. We were stopped at every checkpoint by angry guards, many who hated Americans, and our drive was a frightening adventure in itself.

Our local coordinator, whom we in journalism call "the fixer," said, "Follow my lead." He was Serb, but could not reveal his ethnicity if we passed a rival Albanian checkpoint, as he would quickly have received a bullet to the head, and I could have, too, for hiring him. I'd wait in the vehicle as he hopped out and schmoozed with the diverse guards, trying to talk our way through to the next stop. One time he came back to our van, which we had hastily marked in black duct tape with big letters "TV" on the sides. He said, "I told them you were with Polish TV. They admired the great courage of the Poles in World War II and want to meet you." I got out of our vehicle and took photos with dozens of drunken guards until we could go on our merry way. Even though I really didn't learn any Polish from my father, I knew how to say a few key words for this drunken group, the most important words of all, *"Na Zdrowie!"* Or "Cheers!" At the next checkpoint, he told them I was a Scandinavian TV personality. I could carry that off, too, as my mother was Danish. At the last checkpoint, he said I was a Greek TV star. I told him, "I don't know any Greek," but he told me not to worry, "They don't know any Greek either, and are far from sober!"

Just before we hit Kosovo's war-torn capital of Pristina, we had a harrowing experience. As we drove in pitch darkness, fearful of snipers, worried that our white van was a tempting target, a car pulled out of a side road and suddenly swerved in front of us before coming to a screeching stop. When the mysterious car finally pulled away, we got out of the van to see what had caused the sudden stop. Straight ahead of us, on our side of the roadway, was a huge hole, apparently caused by a recent NATO bomb. We looked into the crater in shock. It was a huge drop, hundreds of feet down a steep ravine. If that car had not swerved in front of us we would've gone straight down to our deaths. That night, I am sure we had angels, as well as luck, looking after us.

It's those experiences—the ones that take you to the edge and that you push through—that better us. It's important to face challenges and see them through. That's what I learned from my dad. I thought I was a fairly courageous journalist, but I realize now that my experience pales in comparison to my father's.

There's a difference between covering and being the story. I'm learning my father's story is one of sheer survival. My dad's life was governed by the precept that anything he believed in, he believed in 110 percent, and would fight to the bitter end to defend. He enjoyed hard work, he enjoyed challenges, and most of all he enjoyed meeting them. That's how I believe he was able to get through those sixty-three days of utter horror in Warsaw. Every day presented a new challenge and an opportunity to overcome it.

When I was younger, I used to resent his drive for perfection. My dad's vision seemed unattainable, and I often felt I could not live up to his high expectations. He put a lot of pressure on my brother and me to wake up early and go running, to get great grades, to basically be the equivalent of West Point grads by third grade. But it was difficult for me to follow his strict regimen and still have time to be a normal kid, to have a normal life. It was hard, I'm sure, for my father to understand all the frivolity and craziness of a first-generation American teenager. For me, it was hard to accept his regimen then, but now

I see that he was pushing me for my own good. Now I realize that he was always urging me to reach the next level, instilling in me the same kind of drive that saved his life in Warsaw. He was teaching me to never accept complacency or second best. And I haven't.

I was seeing my father in a whole new light. I had always known my dad was the kind of man who would never back down from a fight, a man who would die for the things he believed in. I was not surprised to learn that he had turned down a chance to escape to Switzerland and instead decided to stay and fight for his country. He could have taken the easy way out—many people would have—but instead he risked his life in service of his country, because he believed it was what he had to do.

What is it that gives someone that kind of courage? Was it his genes? His upbringing? Or something greater, something less easily defined? At its peak, only forty thousand men and women participated in the Warsaw Uprising. Yet the prewar population of Poland was approximately 35 million. My father was one of an elite few who heard the call to defend his homeland and answered it.

I was sorry I had let so many years pass before asking my dad about his past, but a part of me realizes that he wouldn't have been able to talk about his experiences during the war so candidly if I'd brought the subject up sooner. I know that for a lot of children, their parents' pasts never come up. It made me feel that my connection to my dad was strengthening, that we were both going through a deeply cathartic experience. The walls between us were finally coming down.

I was being given a rare chance to get to know my father not just as a parent, but also as a person. How many children really get to know their parents on such a personal and profound level? As I sat there on my bed, I prayed that this experience would allow me to finally discover who my father really was, to answer the questions I'd carried with me my whole life. My mother's passing had made me realize that my dad was still alive, and that my time to get to know him was limited. Despite all the tribulations, she always reminded me, "Rita, you only have one dad."

9

DEFENDING THE NEIGHBORHOOD

I arrive the next morning at our scheduled time. Dad welcomes me to the house with a hug and an offer. "Want some half grape, half cranberry?" he asks. "I mixed up a new batch." It's only the second day, and we already have a routine.

As he's pouring his juice, I say, "Dad, something occurred to me last night. So far you haven't mentioned if you killed anyone." I realize what a weighty question it is for a daughter to ask and how taking another person's life forever penetrates the soul of a man. He sets his glass down on the well-worn wood of his kitchen table and takes his seat in the chair next to me.

"Well," he says, "after Lieutenant Stan was killed, my unit fell into disarray. But from his death, we had a few more weapons and I learned an important lesson about how to use the sun. Whenever I knew we were going to approach a German position, we would try to do it with the sun at our backs, so that it would shine into the scopes of the snipers. I figured if the sun was glaring into a German's scope he would have a far more difficult time sighting and hitting one of us."

I haven't decided if he has heard my question about killing someone and is building up to the answer or is just completely disregarding it.

"The Uprising was in full gear at that point, and it seemed as if the underground command had better things to do than find us another adequate lieutenant. From then on, we were forced to serve under a succession of poor commanding officers—most were egomaniacs, obsessed with their own advancement and completely uninterested in listening to the suggestions of the men they were responsible for. I know that there were many brave and noble officers in the Polish underground. Somehow it just seemed as if we got stuck with all of the fools.

"It was sometime around here, during the second week of August 1944, that I saw my parents for the last time. Fighting had begun in earnest in Old Town, and I was visiting them at their stark apartment. My father came into the kitchen, took one look at me in my combat gear, and said, 'Well, you stayed in one piece so far. Just keep at it, and stay out of trouble.' I couldn't believe what he was saying. 'Dad,' I argued. 'This is a war! The whole idea is to get in trouble! We're through hiding, we're striking back at the Germans!' " My dad shakes his head and looks down at the table, his expression irritated, but somehow wistful. "My father never understood."

I wonder if my own father is able to see the irony here, if he understands the Kossobudzki cycle that has continued to repeat itself even here in the "Cosby" United States. My father and I never saw eye to eye when I was growing up. Like most teens, I was rebellious in many ways, and I don't think he ever thought I was a particularly respectful daughter. It's interesting, in fact illuminating, now to learn that my dad thought he, too, could never quite measure up in his own father's eyes.

"My father never understood me," he says again, "but my mother did. She prayed for me. It wasn't until I was leaving home for the last time that I realized she'd built a little altar in the apartment. She was always a religious person, but I never knew until that moment that she'd been praying to keep me safe. I was raised as a Catholic, of course, but I was never all that interested in going to church, and as I grew older I sort of had a falling out with religion. Thinking about it now, I'm glad to know that my mother was doing that work for me. Looking out for me!"

I try to picture the grandmother I'd never met, bent over a homemade altar in the corner of her bombed-out apartment in wartime Warsaw. I then picture many hundreds of thousands of other mothers doing the same thing all across the world, at the same time, knowing their sons and daughters were in harm's way, death lurking around every corner. Unfortunately, many of their prayers remained unanswered.

I decide to repeat my question. "Dad?" I say. "This probably goes without saying, but do you think that you killed people during the war?"

"Oh, certainly," he answers without hesitation.

"Do you remember the first?"

"I do," he says. "We were fighting a war, Rita. Killing was a part of duty. But I was always trying for clean kills. Remember the saying, 'One bullet, one German'? I tried to live by that. I always believed it was best to get a guy right between the eyes, so that it was quick, easy, and painless.

"The first time I killed a man was early in the Uprising, only a couple days into the street fighting. We were in a completely bombed-out section of the city, struggling to defend it. The Germans were dug in on one end of the street, and we had taken cover at the other end. We were hiding in an old printing office, determined to force back the Germans. One of them had just thrown a grenade, and we all took cover, ducking beneath the windowsills. When the smoke cleared, I saw across the street that one of the Germans, a man who looked to be about thirty years old, had leaped out of a second-floor window of a burning building. He was trying to reach the street, but hadn't quite cleared the sharp spikes of the wrought-iron fence in front of the building. He'd fallen and was impaled on the spikes. He was still alive, hanging there, moaning. It was a horrible sound, a horrible thing to see."

"What did you do?" I ask.

"Well, that fence that he was stuck on was in a difficult location. He was basically caught in the line of fire. Both sides had an equally good shot at anyone who went out to help him. For a few long seconds both sides just sat in hiding, biding their time, trying to figure out what to do. The only sound for a long time was the horrible moaning. I realized that the right thing to do would be to just end his suffering. I pulled out my Luger, leaned out into an empty doorway just far enough to aim, and fired a single shot. I was probably twenty or thirty feet away, and I got him right between the eyes. He was killed instantly. I considered it a mercy killing. My first kill. I had just turned nineteen." My dad takes a deep breath.

"How did you feel? Were you upset by it?"

"No, I didn't feel any pain at all. I did what I had to do. He fell, he was suffering, and he was my enemy. And the Nazis were vicious opponents. The Geneva and Hague Conventions, resolutions by the

League of Nations, as well as other written and unwritten rules and laws governing how war should and should not be waged between decent men and nations, were completely ignored. They did terrible things to civilians. During the Uprising they forced Polish women and children to march in front of German tanks as they rolled down the street, to deter us from attacking them. They were butchers."

"Did you personally abide by the rules of war?" I ask.

"Not always," he admits. "But after their actions, I suppose all bets were off. When we were guarding the empty theater an incident occurred that, had we had a lieutenant who was a strict Geneva Conventions type, he would have reprimanded me to no end. My buddy and I were lying there in this abandoned theater, minding our own business, and I hear footsteps coming into the square. I'm on one side of the street and there is nobody on the other side. As far as we knew, the Germans were a quarter mile away. My buddy and I were lying side by side, and suddenly down the street walks a German patrol, laughing and joking. I would have thought they were our guys, except they were carrying machine guns, and we rarely had machine guns. Another guy was carrying a pistol. Oh, and they were smoking.

"I said to my buddy, 'Those are Germans and they're lost! I'm going to hit the last guy and you hit the first guy. That will create confusion. They won't know which way to run, and then we just finish them off.' And that's exactly what we did."

"That doesn't necessarily sound opposed to the laws of war," I note.

"But it was," he says, slyly. "I was using a dumdum bullet, which the Hague Conventions don't allow."

"What's a dumdum bullet?" I ask.

"We used to saw off the tip, which reduced the distance it could fly, but when it went into the flesh it mushroomed. Today, I think they call them 'soft-tipped.' When I hit the last guy, I ripped almost half his head off. That was not very nice. My buddies congratulated me, and so on. But even though I know that any German would have felt satisfied to end my life, I didn't feel very happy about it. We took all their weapons, and the bodies stayed there for days.

"Now, this brings up something that I probably shouldn't tell you about, but I took a lot of kidding about it, so I remember it vividly. One day one of those lieutenants whom I totally disliked came to me and he said, 'Corporal'—he didn't even know my name, or my code name—he said, 'Corporal, I want you to go to the building on such-and-such street, there's a temporary cage for German prisoners, and I want you to bring five prisoners to our position.' I had no idea where that cage was. I had no idea we'd even taken prisoners. I walk where he tells me, and I meet this Polish guard, I don't know what his rank was, I just remember he was physically big, and I said to him, 'My lieutenant told me I have to get five prisoners and march them to our position. The guy says, 'Sure, who do you want?' And I said, 'Well, this isn't going to be a fashion parade, so give me the biggest bullies you can find. There's going to be something very unpleasant happening to those guys.' So, he gives me two very nasty-looking Ukrainians."

"How'd you know they were Ukrainian?" I ask.

"Because they were stripped to their waists and they had big U's painted on their backs, in black or red. I said to myself, 'Oh, that's wonderful,' because we knew they had been butchering and raping our civilians whenever they could get their hands on them, and probably thousands of Jews in the Ghetto, too. So, he gave me two Ukrainians, one mailman, and two German army guys. The mailman is there—and I felt like asking him, 'What the hell are you doing here? You're not a military guy.' But at the beginning people didn't know what the different uniforms were, and the moment they saw a German in uniform, they figured he's a German soldier! So, I had a mailman, two army guys, and two Ukrainians. I had my five guys.

"So, I marched them along to bring them back to our position as the lieutenant requested."

"You were alone with these guys?" I ask.

"I was alone but they had their hands tied behind their backs, and I had my Luger, so I knew they were not going to run. I turn them over, and the lieutenant says, 'Okay, thank you.' But one of those German guys asks, 'Can I go and piss?' So I said, 'Lieutenant, he has to relieve himself.' And the lieutenant said, 'Okay, take him.'

"We get to the bathroom, and I said to myself, 'This is funny, either I open his fly and hold it for him, or I release his hands.' I decided I was not going to take any chances. The German uniforms had buttons at the crotch. At that time, Polish uniforms also had buttons, no zippers. Only Americans had zippers at their flies. Anyhow, I unbuttoned his fly, and with a little help . . . well, you know, Rita . . ." My dad blushes. "I had to do it that way. If I released his hands, he's going to swing, and I'd be the laughingstock of everyone if I could not even take care of one pissing German!

"So, he takes care of business and I walk him back and give him to the lieutenant, and the lieutenant and a few guys left with the five men. My job was finished."

"That sounds like you were being nice, Dad," I say. "You were letting him keep his dignity, and he was your enemy."

"Yes," Dad agrees, "but while I was marching those five guys, they kept asking, 'Are we going to be shot?' They thought they were going to be lined up against a wall and shot. And I kept saying, 'Oh, no, we're not going to shoot you.' What I said turned out to be true, but I didn't know exactly what was in store for them. However, the day before a German tank was attacking our barricades, and it had Polish civilians, women and children, tied up in front of it. Their hands were bound together. They had nowhere to go, and were being pushed by the tank. The Germans figured if they got close enough using our people as a shield, they could penetrate our barricades. They knew we wouldn't shoot our own people. They could have just as easily dispensed with these human shields, because we didn't have antitank guns."

"What happened to these helpless women and children?" I ask.

"The Nazis ran them over."

We sit in stillness. The suffering is incomprehensible to me—those poor people, and my dad powerless to do anything about it. "So my lieutenant took our five prisoners, tied them together, and put them on our side of the barricade. The German guys didn't care. They shot them one after the other. So, in a way I lied to them. I told them we weren't going to shoot them, but I didn't mention their own guys."

"The Nazis were ruthless, with no regard for human life. Once, when I was patrolling an area in Old Town, I witnessed a Nazi sniper who was really enjoying himself using a civilian for target practice."

"Target practice?" I ask.

"I was behind this short wall and could see this civilian, wearing a dark suit, on the ground. The sniper, who was on an upper floor of a building across the open square, was having fun just shooting this helpless civilian who was clearly not armed and couldn't shoot back. Every time he got shot, he twitched, which made me think he was still alive. I was counting the bullets because typically most German snipers had five shots between their magazine and the bullet in the chamber. After the fifth shot, I knew I would have five to ten seconds when the sniper went to reload if I was going to save this man. Immediately after the fifth shot, I scrambled to the man, grabbed his legs, and pulled him behind the wall. He was bleeding profusely, but when I checked for his pulse, I realized there was none. It was too late. Even though he was just a stranger, that moment remains vivid to me. I felt so much rage that a human being could be used for target practice."

I realize my dad wasn't frozen in rage, his rage resulted in brave action. He threw himself into the line of fire, risking his life in hopes of saving another.

"That's hard, Dad," I say, trying to bring some relief to the heavy moment. "Do you remember any good moments?"

"Even moments of levity generally turned to trouble," my dad says. "I remember one day a private picking up an abandoned guitar in one house we were guarding. He began plucking away on that guitar, entertaining us with a song for a few minutes. Suddenly, there was an explosion, a crushing, wailing sound. And then silence, no more guitar music. I looked up. The guitar was on the ground and the private's chest was gushing blood, a horrible wound. I tore a piece of my shirt and plugged his wound with it. I called for the first-aid girls. They arrived in minutes and took him off."

"Do you know what happened to him?" I ask. "Did he die?"

"I lost track during the Uprising, but years later, when I was in London, I stayed at a student hostel. One day a young man entered the hostel, and I recognized him as the guitar-playing private from Old Town. I said, "You made it!" and he said to me, "You made it!" He showed me the huge scar on his chest, and a few days later he left, and I never heard from him again."

"When you were in Old Town, did you and your unit think it was winnable?"

"We had to," he said. "Who wants to think he is in a losing battle?

But, as the fighting intensified, it became clear we were up against a machine that couldn't be stopped. In addition to tanks, it became common for the Germans to use Stuka dive-bombers against our positions. The planes would circle over the city, waiting for signals from infantry on the ground. When German soldiers needed to call in a bomber, they would fire flares into the sky, and then the planes would just follow the flares.

"I thought that I was a safe distance away from the German lines. We were at least a hundred yards away from them, a distance that kept us relatively protected from ground attacks. It was still dangerous though, because the Germans could have easily used mortars to attack us from that distance. We wanted to get in closer, because that's where the Uprising fighters had the best chances. The Nazis had better technology, so they were much better suited to long-distance fighting. Because we had so few weapons we had to try to get as close as we could and then use our shots carefully to pick them off one by one."

"So there were three of us out on patrol that day, moving slowly and carefully toward the German lines. We were sure that we were still pretty far away from where the Germans were camped, but suddenly a bright red flare rose into the sky, hissing its way up over us. In just seconds the droning sound of a Stuka's engines filled the air, and the three of us scattered. The other two guys I was with took to the other side of the street, and we all ran as the plane dove toward us. For a few seconds all I could hear was the roar of the propellers. I ran for cover as hard as I could, not knowing if the German pilot in that plane was going to drop a bomb or just machine-gun me outright.

"I dove into a partially demolished house and did my best to take cover. When the plane got close, the pilot dropped a bomb.

And, boy, did he have good aim. The bomb slammed through the roadway and the sidewalk and must have exploded somewhere in the basement of the house. Everything began to crumble around me. The floor immediately collapsed, and I started sliding down into the basement, pieces of the house raining down on me as I went. Bricks were falling on me from above, and my ears, still ringing from the force of the explosion, were filled with the sounds of falling rock and splintering wood. When I came to my senses, I threw my rifle and immediately began clawing at the rubble that was burying me, trying to keep my head above it. I was screaming out for my two buddies, but they couldn't hear me over the sound of the collapsing house.

"The plane flew off; the pilot must have been patting himself on the back for getting rid of one more bandit Pole. I somehow managed to drag myself out of the house, which was now nothing more than a pile of smoking rubble on the side of the street. I must have looked horrible—blood was pouring out of my ears, and my chest looked like someone had just taken a swing at me with a sledgehammer. My buddies saw me emerge from the wreckage and started running toward me. I was relieved to be alive, but suddenly the expressions on my friends' faces turned from joy to horror, and they started backing away from me again.

" 'Guys!' I shouted, 'Come here! Help me.' One of them turned and shook his head, pointing at my waist. I had been carrying a stolen German grenade clipped to my belt. At the time the Germans were using grenades that we used to call potato mashers. We called them that because that's exactly what they looked like—a cylindrical explosive canister with a long wooden handle and a string fuse. The handle provided leverage and allowed the Germans to throw the grenades farther. Anyway, when the building collapsed, a falling brick had crushed the explosive canister. The cap was hanging off and the fuse string was dangling. And the whole thing was still attached to my belt.

"I panicked. I didn't know what to do. I couldn't believe that I had survived basically having a bomb dropped on me and now I was going to be killed by my own grenade! I don't know how long I stood there, but when it didn't explode immediately, I realized that if the grenade was still live I was wasting precious seconds. I very gingerly removed my belt, carried it carefully back to the wreckage of the house, put it down against a still-standing piece of wall, and quickly walked away. The underground later called in experts to dispose of it.

"I had survived, but I was still hurt pretty badly. I was covered in dust and grime. But the real problem was that the force of the explosion had severely damaged my ears. For at least a week, my hearing was basically shot, and my ears were running the whole time. Every morning, wherever I had slept was stained with pus and blood from where my head had lain. None of the guys in the unit wanted to bunk with me."

"But," I say, "you survived."

"Again," he says, "I only survived because I was lucky."

I always thought my dad's intermittent hearing was either him purposely trying to give me a hard time or the result of his not understanding English too well. I remember a few years back that my dad's ear doctor asked me for an autographed headshot, the large photo that on-air journalists and celebrities often give out and sign. After he received mine, he sent me a thank-you letter and took the opportunity to convey that, in addition to a successful career, "There is no greater gift you can give yourself than to have children and a family." That ear doctor, whom I've never met, told me more about my dad's personal feelings about my life than my dad has ever said to me in four decades.

Back in the kitchen, I asked about the dive-bomber. "Was that the worst moment?" I ask.

"Oh, there were a lot of 'worst' moments," he says. One of the worst things that comes to mind has to do with a tank. Remember, during the war the young Resistance girls often served as messengers, moving through the battlefields to relay information between the different units. By this time, when we occupied a building, we made sure we could vacate the building without going into the street. Every house had a cellar, a basement, where people kept food and coal. We punched holes in the basement walls from one house into the next. After a couple of weeks of fighting, you could walk underground for what seemed like miles. We also set up barricades so the girls who delivered messages wouldn't be shot in the street."

I think of my dad as a young man walking through the basements of bombed-out houses in Warsaw, seeing families cowering together, frightened the Nazis were going to find them and execute them. I look at my dad now and realize I'm finally punching through his walls, getting him to reveal his truth, discovering the man behind the curtain. I now am seeing a man who was in many ways a stranger to me. I'm getting to know him personally. "Dad," I ask. "Did you have a girlfriend?"

"For a long time, I really liked that girl Henryka, the one I met at the fur warehouse who was also a member of our unit. I even took her by to meet my mother, so we could get some food. It was a dangerous job, being a messenger, and Henryka was very good. Maybe the best. German snipers were everywhere, and they would jump at any chance they got to pick off a girl carrying a message. Henryka was lucky, but she was also smart. She knew the ropes.

"One day she came to me with news that the Germans had left an abandoned tank not far from our location. Because we had all been issued forged documents and were supposed to be part of a motorized bodyguard unit for the commandant of the Warsaw Uprising, a few of the guys in my unit had gotten the chance to learn how to drive tanks, so they decided to go and try to steal it. At the time we were scrounging for handguns and bullets, waiting on the Allies to send in help or airdrops or something. Some of our unit was fighting with sharp sticks and pitchforks—can you imagine what a victory it would have been for us to have a tank? But something about it didn't seem right to me. The Germans were unbelievably disciplined. Why would they just leave a tank for us to take? I told Henryka about my misgivings and begged her not to go with the men who were planning to commandeer the tank.

" 'Rys,' she told me, 'this will be a huge advantage! Fate has brought us this chance, and we would be fools not to take it.'

" 'Please,' I said to her, 'it has to be a trap.' I also was weary from fighting and needed some brief rest. So, I gave her my prized Luger, and she went anyway, despite my pleading. She and men from several units went to oversee the operation. The drivers were able to sneak into the tank, and they got it running. They drove it back to a kind of town square that was under the control of the Resistance. They met with no German opposition whatsoever—no soldiers defending it, no snipers making it difficult for them to get to it. No one stopped to worry about why it had been so easy to steal. Everyone was celebrating what seemed like a huge victory for the underground. There were hundreds of people gathered around it, young men and women, admiring their spoils. Suddenly, there was a huge explosion. I was several blocks away when it happened, but the ground shook with the force. The Germans had packed that tank full of timed explosives. Everyone in the area was killed instantly.

"I rushed to the square, but obviously I was too late. It was worse than you could ever imagine or I could ever speak aloud. The square was stained with blood, great bright sprays of it up the walls. There were rivers of blood. The smell of burned flesh and blood hung in the air. Other Resistance fighters were already around, sifting through the wreckage and trying their best to identify their friends. There were no remains that were even remotely identifiable. I tried to find a piece of Henryka and my other friends, but there was simply nothing left. I spent a long time in that square looking for the remains of my friends, for the remains of little Henryka. She was only seventeen years old, and suddenly there was nothing left of her life. Nothing to even say she existed."

"Except you telling me now," I remind him, as he wipes away the tears filling his eyes. I suddenly realize that my job, telling people's stories, in a way keeps them alive. "Obviously, she existed very much." He looks at me and smiles, perhaps agreeing that his memory of Henryka keeps her alive. "How did you go on fighting after something like that?"

"The tragedy with the tank was the beginning of the end for Old Town and our motorized unit. At least a dozen of my buddies from the unit were killed when that tank exploded, and I no longer had a weapon. We had a couple of days of total chaos afterward. I went to the local first-aid station to look for survivors and ran into one of my schoolmates who was there. He was badly wounded and told me his fighting days were over. He gave me his last grenade as a present. He asked if I could bring him some food the next day in return. When I came back the next afternoon, I was horrified to discover that the first-aid station was destroyed. All that was left was a pile of bricks.

The Germans, we learned, often intentionally hit buildings that had a roof marked with a large red cross, knowing there would be many more victims inside, victims who could not quickly escape."

"What did you do next?" I ask.

"We did what we could do," he says with notable sorrow. "After the tank explosion my unit disintegrated. The lucky few of us left standing were shuffled around and absorbed by other units, but the Resistance was being squeezed out. Less than a month into the Uprising, the SS came in and took over the main old city of Warsaw. And when we had no other choice, we tried to escape any way we could."

"How?" I ask. "Weren't all of the routes in and out of the city controlled by the Nazis?"

"Most of them were," he says. "We had to take the one route they wouldn't follow. We had to take the sewers."

10

Into the Sewers

*W*e were fighting a losing battle in Old Town. By late August, it became obvious that, despite the many successes we had enjoyed, the Resistance fighters had little chance of victory. The SS arrived and kept us completely blocked in. Warsaw was consumed in flames. Cut off from the rest of the city and the remainder of the Resistance forces, we had to find a way to escape to City Center. Our superiors told us that escape was the only way to survive, and that the only way to escape slaughter was to travel through Warsaw's sewer system."

Resistance forces had been operating in the sewers for some time. The endless, twisting tunnels ran back and forth beneath the city and provided excellent cover for Resistance agents.

"Could you even stand up down there?" I ask.

"The passages were only a few feet wide, and some were tall enough to walk upright. But in places it was just three feet high or so. Many people had to be physically whipped at the top of the manhole to make them abandon their backpacks so they wouldn't get stuck in a tunnel. There was a great system set up down there because all traffic had to be 'one way.' We were so careful; it wasn't until late August that the Nazis finally caught on that we were using the sewers so effectively to communicate and travel through the city. The Germans were reluctant to enter the sewers, and instead, in an attempt to end the traffic of Resistance fighters and refugees, had resorted to dropping grenades down manhole openings, raising the water level to flood us out, and pouring in poisonous chemicals. They also had posted guards at strategic exits. Fortunately for us, their efforts had been mostly in vain because we had a pretty good communication system down there."

"What was it like realizing you were losing the battle, that you had to resort to going into the sewers?" I ask.

"It was a difficult thing to take in, for sure, but in the weeks leading up to our escape it had become a sort of unspoken truth. It was a sad fact that everyone in the unit had come to know, but no one wanted to admit. My buddies were furious when the order to retreat came through. Many among us saw the decision as an insult to the thousands of men and women who had already been killed in defense of Old Town. We had all suffered losses, and to just give up and concede the loss of a district that many of us had grown up in was devastating. And to be forced to sneak out through the sewers like rats added insult to injury. But we knew we had no choice. We wanted to survive.

"We stuck it out as long as we could, but the situation became hopeless. Warsaw had become a city of graves. We had run out of space to bury the dead. It was bad enough when Lieutenant Stan was killed, but soon I found my friends falling around me, more and more every day. It was especially difficult because these young men weren't just my comrades in arms; many of them had been in my unit as a Young Eagle. I'd basically grown up with them.

"Toward the end, a friend of mine was killed, and it was a terrible shock for me. He was a beloved member of our unit—no matter what the situation, he was always positive. I don't know how he was able to keep such a sunny disposition when everything around us seemed to be falling apart, but everyone else was glad for it. We'd be under fire, mortar shells exploding all around us, and he would be cracking jokes. And the best part of it all, his sister was the cook who often gave us extra food.

"We were in a position in Old Town that we thought was relatively safe. The sounds of far-off gunfire echoed all around us, but by that point the noise of war had become just a part of the atmosphere. It would have been strange if there were no sounds of battle. I was relaxing in a safe place, inside a building that was still relatively undamaged, letting my guard down for a moment. I was jarred from my daydreaming by the muffled sound of a nearby explosion, and after a few minutes an officer appeared at the door.

" 'A sergeant has been hit,' he told me. 'He's been killed by a mortar shell.' I had nothing to say in return. I was strangely unaffected by the news. I suppose you'd say numb. I knew that I should be feeling a terrible sense of loss, but the only thing I really felt was a kind of deepening of the emptiness that had already become a constant for me. 'I need you to check his pockets,' the officer told me. 'He's carrying important documents that we need to recover.' I nodded and made my way out the door to the camp.

"A body was lying on a door propped up on pieces of rubble. Despite what I'd been told about a guy being killed by a mortar shell, he looked strangely peaceful and whole. Apart from a light spray of blood on his face, he looked as if he could have just been sleeping. But as I got closer, I realized that I knew this soul. It was the brother of our unit's cook, a jovial man who no longer had the smile on his face. I had to remind myself to stay focused, I was sent there on a mission.

"I approached him and went to check the chest pockets of his uniform. When I reached into his jacket, I got the shock of my life. My hands slipped right into his chest cavity—his whole torso had been ripped apart, from his chest up to his neck. I had touched his insides with my bare hands."

"Did you almost throw up?" I ask.

"I flinched for sure," my dad says. "I was certainly horrified. It wasn't so much the fact that I was disgusted about touching his insides, but rather the fact that this human being could be butchered this way, like an animal. I thought again of all the friends who had been killed by the tank explosion, all the lives that had been erased by the fighting. Until that point, I had been resistant to the idea of escape. I thought we would never be taken alive. It was then I realized that if any of us wanted to live to see the war end and Poland be freed, we had no choice but to abandon Old Town.

"The evacuation began at night. It was believed that if we made our escape under cover of darkness the Nazis would not be prepared for a fight. We were wrong." He clears his throat and takes a sip of his drink. "The initial plan was to send the remaining fighters over the rubble into City Center, a dangerous dash over open ground for a distance of a half mile or so. Unfortunately, the Nazis had positioned themselves less than a hundred yards away from our intended route by the old theater building. They didn't want us to get out of Old Town alive. The Germans must have known that we were going to push in that direction, because when the first squad moved forward in front of the old Bank of Poland, the Nazis opened up with machine guns. I've never seen anything like it. There were so many bullets, and every fifth round or so was a tracer."

"What's a tracer?" I ask.

"Bullets with hollow bases," he explains, "filled with phosphorus to glow in the dark. They enabled the soldiers firing the guns to keep track of where their shots were going. When the Nazis opened fire there were so many bullets that the street turned from dark night into what looked like daylight. The noise was so loud that you couldn't even hear the screams of the men who were being hit, just this all-consuming roar of gunfire. The shadows of falling soldiers were thrown starkly against the walls of the bank, dark shapes flailing against the building's pale stone façade. There were mortar shells falling, too, but they were reduced to bursts of dust and debris—the din of the machine guns swallowed up any sound the shells made. The first few squads were eliminated in a matter of seconds. It became clear that we were going to have to dig in and wait it out while groups of Resistance fighters escaped in the sewers behind our position a short distance away."

"What did you do next?" I ask.

"We had to fight with everything we had to keep them from overtaking the bank. Before too long we began to run out of bullets, what today's army would call 'going black on ammo.' But luckily we'd sent a message to the Nazis. They seemed to pull back. The SS soldiers were disciplined warriors, smart enough not to make an attempt to push forward once we'd shown that we were ready to fight them man-to-man to the death.

"We were ultimately told that aboveground was an impossible escape route, that we, too, would have to go through the sewers.

"In an odd twist of fate, it turned out that the best entrance into the sewers was no more than a hundred yards away from the house I'd lived in with my family before the Uprising. It was strange seeing my own street so completely transformed by war."

"Where were your parents at this point?" I ask.

"I had no idea," he says. "I hadn't seen my parents in a couple weeks at that point, but I didn't have any time to wonder where they were or if they were safe. It was get out now or die. At that point the evacuation was in full swing; we were one of the last units to leave Old Town. It was decided that the first people to go into the sewers would be the high-ranking officers, followed by the nurses and medical personnel and their patients if they were well enough to travel."

"And if they weren't?" I ask.

"They were left behind," my dad says, his voice steady, but quiet. "Our job was to hold the position long enough for everyone to get into the sewer, and then to follow ourselves.

"We had to retreat and set the perimeter again, and then several hours later, in the middle of the night, before the Germans had time to reset their guns in the new location, we made our break for the sewers. We climbed down, one by one, keeping our heads low, into the hidden manhole entrance of the sewers. The moment we entered, everything was swallowed by darkness, and the sounds of battle above us were instantly muffled and replaced by the eerie sound of running, dripping water. As soon as I dropped through the entrance I landed deep in filth. The smell was overwhelming. My brown suede shoes were covered in waste. For a few seconds I couldn't move. It was chilling, to say the least. When I was finally able to trudge forward, all I could feel was the grime squishing under the soles of my shoes.

"We had a guide with us, a man who had worked in the sewers before the war and knew the way. My spot was at the end of the procession, as a sweeper. It was my job to keep track of the other people in line, and to pick up any stragglers, anyone who might have gotten separated from the rest of the group. By the time we went in, there were only close to twenty of us in my unit left alive."

I try to imagine my dad falling into the darkness of the tunnels beneath the city, escaping from one hell aboveground only to find another below. "Did you feel claustrophobic?" I ask.

"I probably would have, if it hadn't been so dark," he answers. "It was so pitch black in there that you couldn't really tell how much room you had. Where we entered, the ceilings were surprisingly high. I was right around six feet tall in those days, and I was able to stand almost upright without hitting my head on the ceiling. But the heights varied and so did the sludge. It seemed in the spots we were standing upright that the current was stronger. The floor was very slippery and covered with excrement and debris. I'm just glad I only found out later about all the corpses."

"Corpses?"

"If you made a wrong turn in the sewers, you weren't likely to ever get out alive."

"How did you remain calm?" I ask.

"It was life or death, Rita," he says. "During the entire time we spent down there we were forbidden to talk or make any unnecessary noise, because the Nazi soldiers above us might hear, especially as we went by manholes, and drop grenades down on top of us. So we had to line up and hold on to each other and trudge single file through the maze, as quietly as possible. As we continued moving the ceilings got lower, and we had to keep our heads down.

All the Resistance fighters were wearing helmets, so our passage was punctuated with loud clanks every time one of us would accidentally raise his head and knock his metal helmet against the ceiling.

"After we had traveled for a few minutes I noticed the sounds of something sloshing through the muck behind me like an elephant. Someone had caught up to us. I was no longer the last person in the line. I could just barely make out the shape of a woman behind me, huddled close to the wall. I stopped for a moment and whispered back to her, as low as I could, 'Who are you?'

" 'I'm So and So,' she replied, her voice low and fearful. 'I'm an officer's wife.' I cursed inwardly. This operation was already danger-ous enough when we were a squad of trained Resistance fighters. Suddenly a civilian had been added to the mix, and not just any ci-vilian but an officer's wife. 'If she collapses,' I thought to myself, 'I'll have to carry her. If I have to carry her I'll have to slow down, and if I slow down we'll lose the rest of the group. We could be lost forever in this hellhole!' As I said, we'd all heard stories about people getting separated and turned around in the sewers."

I imagine my dad and the officer's wife creeping through the muck in darkness. I thought of the sewers running for miles under the city, endless twisting passageways, like tunnels in an anthill. The nauseating smell, the fear of flooding, and the booby traps planted by the Nazis. I can't imagine the terror. "What if you got separated from the guide?" I ask.

"I tried to push the thought from my mind and reassure myself. At first I had complete confidence in the guide. What choice did I have? He was responsible for all of us, and certainly seemed like he knew what he was doing. I didn't find out until much later that he was drunk the entire time. I suppose any human being who's reduced to trudging through darkness and filth on a daily basis for months would have to be."

I think of those guides operating for hours, sometimes days, under the surface, like moles, taking groups back and forth between entrances and exits. They were basically working in a toilet.

"The job would have been impossible if they hadn't spent most of their time drinking copious amounts of vodka.

"As we continued to move through the sewers we all began to get more tense. It seemed as if the tunnel was stretching on forever, and there was no light or sound except for the occasional beams that filtered down through manhole covers and the sloshing, sucking sounds of our feet dragging through the filthy water. We walked and walked, the air becoming thicker, the stench more oppressive."

"Did you have any idea how far you had to go?" I ask.

"None of us had any idea how long it would take to reach our destination. We just put our trust in the guide and hoped for the best. We had no other choice."

"That would have made me crazy," I tell him.

"Well, after several hours of this tense, silent movement I began to hear the woman behind me whimpering, panicking. After a few minutes I turned and whispered to her, 'Are you wounded?'

" 'No,' she replied. 'But I can't stand this darkness!'

" 'I'm sorry,' I hissed at her. 'But you're going to have to take it. We all do.'

"She was quiet for a few minutes and then began muttering to herself, her voice creeping higher and higher. 'We'll never get out. We'll never get out,' she was saying over and over again in the dark. Before too long I'd had all I could take. It wasn't just that she was endangering all of us by making sound. Every terrified noise she made also caused me to become more and more tense.

"I turned to her. Frustrated and stressed, I momentarily thought of slapping her. Instead, I said, 'Shut up!' 'I'm afraid,' she replied. 'We're all afraid,' I told her. 'But you're not just endangering yourself; you're putting the twenty people ahead of you at risk, too! These are my buddies. I won't let you put them in danger.' After that she got hold of herself.

"I really have no idea exactly how long we were traveling down there. The guy ahead of me was carrying a very heavy machine gun, and the cone of the gun had been banging against my forehead the entire time we were walking. We were pressed so close together in the tunnels that I couldn't move away from him, and I knew that if I complained to him he would just suggest that I take a turn carrying the weapon. He was a big man, and the machine gun was huge, so I just gritted my teeth and tried to ignore it knocking against my face. After all, I was terrified to let go of his back for fear of taking a wrong turn and being left alone with a crying officer's wife and no one behind us or in front of us.

"The smell of the sewers had been overpowering from the moment we'd entered the tunnels, and as we continued walking my suede shoes stirred up the sewage flowing on the floor; all of the noxious gases trapped within it began to rise up. It became difficult to breathe. At first I had tried to breathe just through my mouth, but eventually even that proved to be little defense against the overwhelming stench. It was so thick that I began to feel light-headed, and wondered if I would be able to stay conscious through the slog to the exit.

"After what seemed like days, the tense, endless night finally turned to daylight. Ahead of me there was the sound of splashing footsteps and then the soles of boots clinking and dripping on metal rungs of a ladder. A shaft of white light pierced the darkness, and I caught a glimpse of someone's legs disappearing through the man-hole opening up above us. He called for us to follow. One by one we ascended the ladder, taking big, gulping breaths of air when we made it to the surface, thankful to have escaped the hellish tunnels. More than five thousand members of the Resistance escaped during that frantic 24-hour period.

"As I was helped to the surface they cautioned me to keep my eyes closed. 'Your eyes are adjusted to the dark. It will be painful to open them all the way after such a long time in the tunnels.' I nodded, squinting. After I climbed out of the hole, I heard immediate gasps from the men who had already come to the surface when they saw my face.

" 'Rys!' a buddy said. 'Were you wounded?' I shook my head, confused by what he was asking.

" 'Not that I know of,' I replied, looking to check out my body.

" 'You're bleeding!'

"I lifted my hand to my forehead and found blood on my fingers. That damn machine gun! The cone had knocked against my forehead so hard and for so long that it had cut deeply into my skin. Blood was streaming down my face from a gash above my eyes. I had been too dazed and frightened to say anything to my buddy in front of me."

My dad smiles and points to the small, pale scar that is still evident today on his forehead. I've finally gotten the story behind the two scars on his forehead—one between his eyes from a piece of an egg grenade's shell, and the other from a machine gun. Now, what about the much larger scars covering the rest of his body? What horrors lay ahead in my father's untold story?

11

COLLAPSE

*A*fter we left Old Town through the sewers, it became clear that things were not going to end well. We were lucky to have gotten out when we did. Many Resistance fighters still trapped under siege in Old Town never got the chance to escape. The fighting there and elsewhere in the city became incredibly brutal, with nearly constant air bombardment. Some Resistance soldiers had taken to only hand-to-hand combat, as supplies and ammunition continued to dwindle. The situation became more and more hopeless. We had been fighting so hard for so long, and without any real aid, that we simply had nothing left."

"What did you do when you got out of the sewers?" I ask. "Where were you?"

"We settled in to guard City Center," he says. "Several of my relatives lived there, including my favorite uncle, Teddy, who lived on Jerusalem Avenue. Before the Uprising, I used to go to his house once a week to learn English. I decided to go visit him and make sure he was okay. When I got there, I found his street had been destroyed. I walked down the street praying that his house would still be standing. I ran into a man cooking some food on an improvised stove. He looked shell-shocked. I asked him about my uncle's house. He pointed at a sea of bricks and said, 'There were no survivors.' I stood there for a minute, said my good-byes, and went on my way."

"Did you think it was hopeless, Dad?" I ask.

"As we fought on, many of us at City Center were still hoping for some kind of aid from the Soviet army. There were some drops from the United States and the British, but most of them ended up in German hands. Some Russian shipments did come, but they were dropped without parachutes, so the weapons were smashed on impact and the bullets that did make it were often the wrong caliber for the weapons we did have."

"Did you keep hoping the Soviets were going to help?"

"Some of my friends in the Resistance fantasized that the Russians would still come and be our saviors. I had my doubts about the Russians helping us. I didn't believe that they wanted to liberate us. We knew the Russians were nearby, we could see them in our binoculars. They were right across the Vistula River. But day after day they never came across the river. Their plan was to stay across the river and watch Warsaw burn." This is, I realize, a suspicion that he had learned from his own father's prejudices—but he was right. The Russians did watch from the other side of the river as Warsaw went up in flames and the Resistance fought desperately on.

"For a short time it seemed that the fighting would be forever locked in a brutal stalemate. Many in the Resistance were determined to fight until the last bullet."

"Were you, Dad?" I ask. "Were you going to fight until the last bullet?" He pauses. I think of him, having made it through so much fighting, taken so many risks, crawling out of the rubble on his belly and slogging through the darkness and the filth of the sewers, and he hadn't yet sustained any truly life-threatening injuries. When does one finally say, "Enough?"

"Yes," he says, "I suppose I was prepared to fight to the death. But I was growing tired and was always hungry."

"How hard was it to get food in these conditions?" I ask.

"Well," he says, "I do remember eating meat once after we made it to City Center."

"How'd you get meat?"

"Well, our headquarters were nearby, and that's where we would go to meet the delegate."

"What do you mean, delegate?"

"I suppose he was like our secretary of defense. He was a government representative with the underground. He thought he was running the whole show, but he really had no place with us. No one liked him at all. He was probably the one person we were all secretly hoping that the Germans would get. He had this big dog, a mongrel the size of a Great Dane. That dog was well fed, while the rest of us were starving.

"There were two pretty Resistance girls—these girls who tried to take care of us. They came to me one day and said that they had prepared something special for me. 'Taste it! Taste it! See if you like it!' they said proudly. They gave me two slices. I hadn't eaten any meat in more than a month. I was wolfing it down. The girls asked me if

I liked it, and I said, 'Fine, fine!' The girls were giggling at me like crazy. I thought it was because I was eating with my fingers, sloppily shoving the meat into my mouth, as I hadn't had any substantial food in many weeks. I polished it off quickly. After I finished, one of them asked, 'Did you like it?' I nodded. Then, the other one said, 'You just had a slice of that beautiful dog of the delegate we all hate!"

"You *ate* dog?" I ask, my eyes wide. "The delegate's dog?"

"Yep, when that dog broke free from his leash, those girls grabbed it, killed it, and stewed it."

"Oh, my God, Dad, a dog?" I'm horrified.

"A dog. It tasted like a very lean wild rabbit, or hare. Definitely much better than horse." I guess he'd eaten a horse at some point, to know the difference.

It saddened me greatly to hear this story, for my dad had always loved animals, especially dogs. More than anything else, this really showed me just how starving he was, and what men in his position had to do simply to survive. "Did you see other dogs during the war?"

"You know," he says, "come to think of it, there were no dogs in Warsaw during the war. The delegate's dog was one of the very few pets I can remember seeing."

"What did the delegate do?"

"Oh," my dad says, "when he found out that dog was missing, he sent officers all over. Even into German lines! Can you imagine risking men's lives to look for that dog? I wish the delegate were alive to hear me tell this story. He'd probably be 120 years old by now, but I'm sure he always wondered what happened to that dog."

"What about the girls?" I ask. "How could they do that?"

"It was their duty to help us. They knew if we didn't eat, we didn't fight."

I would learn later that World War II was the first time in the history of wars that so many women had contributed in such immediate and significant ways. In the Resistance, they made weapons, carried out medical duties, served as messengers, and even fought on the line right beside the men. An estimated five thousand women participated in the Warsaw Uprising, including at least one elite unit commanded by women whose role was to execute high-ranking SS and Gestapo officers. The women died at an extraordinary rate. To my dad's knowledge, none of the women in his unit survived.

"I had great admiration for all those women. Women risked a lot to save the injured and keep others alive. By the way, my cousin Rita joined the Resistance."

"Rita was a Resistance fighter?" I ask, both surprised and honored.

"Yes, I found out right before the Uprising. She came and asked if I could get her a role in a certain unit."

"Tell me about her, Dad."

"Oh, she was a smart girl! She was attractive, athletic, and could always take care of herself. She never panicked. She was a real gutsy lady, but she was also very fun and had a great sense of humor. She could charm a lot of people. Rita had big ambitions. Since I had no brothers or sisters, she was like my sister. But to this day, because we were all so secretive, I still don't know exactly what she did.

"She ended up in a women's prison camp in Germany. After the war, she joined a Polish unit helping in the officers' mess in Germany, and then traveled with the unit to England. There she met an older man, a captain, in London and they moved to Canada, where she took up ballroom dancing."

I remember her coming to visit us in Greenwich once when I was around five years old. She had brown hair in a fancy hairstyle, wore an elegant outfit, and had a beautiful, warm smile. I remember how delighted she was to meet me, knowing I was named after her, but until now I had no idea she had fought in the war at all. I just remember a kind, older woman giving me lots of toys and candy. "I'm glad and really honored," I tell my dad, "that you named me after a Resistance fighter, someone gutsy." Turns out she was a courageous young woman who had nerves of steel. But as I sit at the table with my dad, I understand it's more than that. I'm astonished by the sudden realization that I'm named for my dad's past.

"All the women in the Resistance were as determined as we were," my dad says. "They were all so brave. Women were always reported MIA, and I feared what really happened to them. The women who carried the stretchers were known as the 'soldiers of mercy,' and it was as risky as fighting. They were often captured or killed, as were the female messengers. The two girls who cooked that dog eventually fought with us side by side the last few weeks on the lines. But that was near the end. Shortly after that, I was gravely injured."

"Is that when you got all the large scars on your body?" I boldly ask.

"Rita," he says, "do you remember asking me about my scars as a little girl?"

"I didn't ask you," I tell him. "I asked Mom at Somes Campground once while you were out fishing."

"You may have," he says. "But you also asked me."

"I did? I don't remember."

"How could you?" he says. "You were very little, little more than a baby. You touched my arm one day and asked, 'Does everybody have a hole in their arm, Daddy?' And I said, 'No, not everybody. I was just unlucky. I was in the wrong time, and the wrong place.'" Tears well up in my eyes, and I choke them back. "That's exactly what it was, Rita," my dad says, "when I got hit by shrapnel, it was a fluke. If I had just smoked one more cigarette, I wouldn't have been at the location yet. Or if I had not smoked the last, I would have been gone before it hit."

I realize my dad has thought about his fate, especially at this moment, more than once. "When did it happen?" I ask.

"It's the worst ones that you never see coming. Things were bad, but we had some hope. After we got to City Center, in between fighting, I was also picking up supplies like ammo and running it back to my unit. A few Russian planes were finally coming, and I was going to try to get the supplies that were being airdropped from them."

"How'd you know they were coming?" I ask.

"They had an observation plane that would fly over a certain part of City Center, and when they'd chosen a spot they would airdrop supplies. I remember one time they dropped flour and the bag exploded. Little kids came with spoons and tried to scrape up and salvage as much flour as they could in buckets."

"Little kids?" I ask.

"There were a lot of young guys hanging around. I think these were the Boy Scouts, and everything that could be eaten was precious. After the drop, we knew the area was active. My lieutenant assigned me and another guy, code named Private "Hart," to go and pick up the ammunition that was supposed to be dropped that night. When we got to the location, we saw some flour and busted-up bullets."

"What time of day was it?" I ask.

"It was twilight," my dad says. "Right near dark. So, I say to Hart, 'Let's go find somewhere we can sit and wait. When we hear the plane, we'll go and get it.' He thought that sounded fine. I remember laughingly saying, 'So that way they won't drop it on us. If a crate of ammunition lands on our heads, we'd have a headache for a while.' We found a middle-aged Polish woman and her teenage daughter living in a basement right next to the drop area.

"I called out, 'Excuse me, anybody there?' The woman said, 'This is my house.' I said, 'We hope we're going to be getting some supplies from the Russians. We have to wait for it.' She said, 'Why don't you sit with us, and I'll make some fake tea for you.' "

"Fake tea?" I ask.

"Yes," he says, "Fake tea. We had long ago lost real tea; this was basically just hot water with some sort of leaves steamed in it. The woman was also loaded with cigarettes. Maybe she was selling them on the black market. We started smoking like crazy. We got to talking with her and her daughter, and a few hours later as we were puffing away, we thought we heard a noise. I said to Hart, 'Let's go out and scout the area.' The whole area was abandoned, except for the woman and her daughter.

"Being shot or stabbed or executed never scared me all that much. The only death that really terrified me was death by explosion, death by shrapnel. It wasn't the pain—if anything, being blown apart by a grenade or a mortar shell was the quickest, easiest way to go. The thing that frightened me the most was the fact that if your body was torn apart by shrapnel, you were completely annihilated. Erased. When that tank exploded and all my friends were killed, the worst part wasn't that they had died. Death is sad, but it's a part of life. What I couldn't believe, what really haunted me, was the fact that so many people had died there, and they were unrecognizable forever. No one ever knew exactly how many were killed because they were completely blown apart.

"I worried about what my parents would think if such a thing happened to me. If I were shot defending my country, at least they would have a body to bury. My friends would have a place to come and pay their respects. If an explosion blew me away, and my body was completely destroyed, no one, not even my closest buddies, would be able to recover me. And that filled my heart with fear.

"I never did feel much fear during the Uprising. I was stressed, and I was tired and hungry and frantic to keep my city and my buddies safe, but I only ever felt real fear once. Maybe it was a premonition for what was to happen to me now at City Center. Early in the Uprising, I had been stationed in a building with a private and ordered to keep watch for advancing German troops and report back if we saw any movement. We'd received intelligence that the Germans would be moving into our area soon, but we hadn't seen any of them.

"The house they'd stationed us in was on a completely demolished block, yet somehow it had remained undamaged. It was a strange image, this one untouched house surrounded by piles of rubble where its neighbors had stood not that long ago. As I said, the Germans never appeared, but they must have known that we were there waiting for them, because after an hour or so they began to fire mortars at us. This was not out of the ordinary—there was a constant risk of mortar fire, and the Germans would often shoot them randomly in the hopes that they would get lucky and hit a Polish squad.

"This particular attack seemed different, though. The mortar shells were falling fast and dangerously close—one every twenty or thirty seconds. This wasn't random fire. The Nazis must have known we were there and were trying to flush us out. Soon the shells were falling so close to us that the shrapnel was hitting the house, flying in through the broken windows and peppering the empty white wall behind us. We took cover beneath the windowsills and I watched that wall as the shrapnel tore into it.

"As I stared I was suddenly seized with an uncontrollable fear. I watched as those shards of hot metal flew over our heads, shredding the paint on the wall and falling like burning hail over our heads. I knew that if I stood up I would be torn apart, instantly disintegrated. I thought about my parents, I thought about how I was an only child and how they would never know what happened. I thought about Henryka and the dark sprays of blood in the square after that tank exploded. Total erasure. So many mortar shells were falling around us; it seemed inevitable that one would come whistling through the empty windowpanes and explode inside the room, and then where would we be? We'd be gone, snuffed out, erased. I realized that I was trembling, shaking uncontrollably.

"After a few moments of this, I managed to cast my gaze across the room to the private who was with me. I had a strange moment of clarity, a split second in which the sounds of the exploding bombs seemed to fade into the background and my senses took hold of me. 'Rys,' I said to myself, 'you're a corporal. You've been placed in command here. This boy is looking to you to lead him. If he sees you balled up here under the window, shaking like a leaf, he's going to try to run, and if he tries to run, he's going to be torn to shreds before you can blink.' That was all it took for me to pull myself together. I snapped out of it. I shook my head and tried to get the kid's attention, but he was more scared than I had been, already a zombie. His eyes were wide and fearful, blankly staring at the dusty hardwood floor and the pieces of metal and plaster that were raining down on it. I breathed a little easier when I saw how frightened he was and realized that even if he had seen me, there was nothing that could have made him move from the position short of my grabbing him by the hand and making a run for it.

"After what seemed like an eternity of the deadly mortar shells raining down, the Nazis must have decided that they were wasting ammunition and stopped firing. We were supposed to remain in position for another hour or so, but as soon as the coast was clear I gave the order to move out. Both the private and I were still a bit shell-shocked, but his head was clear enough for him to follow orders."

I've heard that one of the most frightening things about artillery shells is that you rarely hear them coming. They are designed to explode in the air right over their objective, but where the shrapnel goes is haphazard. Sometimes men are inches apart, and one is seriously injured while the other is fine. There's no warning: The only sound you ever really hear is the explosion, and by that time it's already too late.

"So, Dad, are you saying the worst scars on your body came from shrapnel?"

"Yes," my dad says.

Finally, the mystery has been solved. "Were you scared?" I ask.

"There was no time to be scared," he says. "We weren't even moving through a field of battle. One second Hart and I were enjoying our time smoking cigarettes with that lady and her daughter, and the next, boom! I was walking with him, side by side in an abandoned courtyard full of rubble. We were walking along, looking for the airdrop of ammo, feeling secure in the knowledge that no Nazi activity had been recorded in the area. The area was so far from Germans that you could dance and yell, 'Hitler is an asshole!' and nobody would hear you. Suddenly there was a flash, and the world exploded. I was thrown into the air, and I landed hard on the pavement, Hart about twenty feet away. I could see that he had been cut to pieces, that he was bleeding from a hundred different wounds, but I couldn't move to help him."

"Were you in pain?" I ask.

"There was no pain—I knew that I must have been really badly wounded, that I was in serious trouble, but I don't remember it hurting. I've never felt anything like it since—it was simply like my strength was leaving my body, like a balloon losing its air. I could feel my life draining away. So, there you have it, I got wounded by a mortar shell! You see, back in that house earlier in the Uprising where I was shaking, it just seemed like I knew that was how it was going to happen to me. It was the only shell that landed all night."

"Who helped you?" I ask.

"The woman and her daughter ran out of their house. I didn't yell 'help' or anything like that. They obviously heard the explosion, it was basically in their backyard, and I remember they were trying to stop the blood, but I had so many holes in me that I felt like Swiss cheese. All I knew was that I was getting weaker and weaker; my life was draining out of me. See here, see this." My dad points to the holes he has still in his right arm. "This was bleeding, this one and this one, my arm was completely paralyzed, I couldn't move. One here, one here—I've still got small fragments." He shows me a little node on his wrist. "Remember when you were a little girl, and I would make that move up and down my arm?"

"No!"

"Oh, you used to love that. I could make it crawl beneath my skin."

Perhaps I do remember after all, but I was so young and it is only a faint recollection now.

"So, this woman asked me, 'Are you badly hurt?' And I said, 'No, but I'm getting very weak.' It was night. I was bleeding from everywhere, but we couldn't see. She asked, 'How about your buddy? I can't carry him; neither can you. But there's a first-aid station close by.' She took me there, while her daughter waited with my buddy. A doctor wrapped makeshift bandages around my wounds, putting pressure to try to stop the bleeding. The numbness began to fade away because the nerves began to act, and I was in great pain. They didn't even have any vodka to give me."

"Vodka?"

"Normally, they'd give you alcohol if they didn't have any anesthetics. We had no morphine because the war had depleted all resources. So, that woman ran to her house and brought back a carton of cigarettes. She stayed with me all night long holding cigarettes to my mouth, and we smoked those cigarettes together as I clung to life. You know, to this day I don't even know her name. I never asked."

"What happened to your buddy?"

"They sent some guys out, and they brought him back. The surgeons rushed him onto an 'operating table,' but the people were saying in the first-aid station that it was too late, that he was gone. If we'd just had one more cigarette."

"Do you think about that often?" I ask.

"What?"

"Fate," I say.

"You know, there is a destiny. Everybody has a destiny. Why would I get hit right then, when I didn't expect it? Even the Germans didn't know they got me. They always shot from a distance away. They probably never even suspected somebody was there. Some soldier just picked up the shell, dropped it in a tube, and BOOM. It was a shit chance. As I said, wrong time, wrong place. If I was either faster or slower it might not have happened."

"If that hadn't happened, then what?" I suggest.

"Right. People got shot. It was the last weeks of the Warsaw Uprising. I really believe that this was destiny. I wouldn't say I got what I deserved, but I got what was waiting for me."

My dad, Ryszard "Rys" Kossobudzki.
Handsome, young, and determined.

Happy times with his family in Poland, before the war stole his youth and destroyed his country.

right: Playing with one of his favorite toys, a sword. Only a few years later, he'd be holding a gun.

below: The Eaglets became an important part of the underground fight against the Germans. Dad (second row, second from right) with his family of brave, young compatriots.

above left: Lieutenant Stanislaw "Stan" Srzednicki, my dad's Eaglet leader, role model and a courageous fighter, in full uniform.

above right: Dad's cousin, Rita, for whom I'm named, was a Freedom Fighter.

left: Hanna and Konstanty Kossobudzki, the grandparents I never knew, survived the war by selling black-market goods from a secret, hidden compartment in their store.

Jews were marched at gunpoint from the Ghetto, not knowing what Nazi cruelty awaited them.

The Jewish Ghetto being torched by the Nazis. They left virtually no building standing.

More than a year after the Ghetto Uprising, Resistance fighters launched their own uprising. Citizens of Warsaw fought in the streets and defended their neighborhoods from behind crude barricades.

The Nazis left behind a city of rubble. After the war, less than 15 percent of the buildings in Warsaw remained standing.

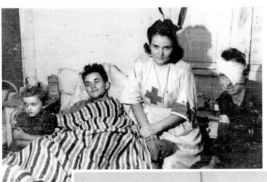

In the makeshift insurgent hospitals, conditions were grim and there was no anesthesia. During my dad's operations, Resistance fighters sat on his arms and legs to hold him down.

From the hospital he staggered to a boxcar, which carted many Resistance soldiers to POW camps. Many Jews were taken by railcar to extermination camps, where millions were killed.

left: "Welcome to Stalag IVB," one of Germany's largest POW camps of World War II.

below: Food was scarce, and even though the "soup" was only water with a few slices of turnip floating in it, men lined up for it, getting just enough to stay alive.

below: This is my dad's POW tag, perforated across the center. When a prisoner died, half was buried in his mouth, the other half placed in his records.

Supplies were meager at the camp; the Red Cross was the only reprieve and is credited with saving many lives, but soon these valued parcels became few and far between.

Alex Chelmicki, scarred by a flamethrower, became my dad's best friend. His idea for how to use cigarettes would save my dad's life, and in turn, my dad would save his.

During our tour of Auschwitz we looked at the guard towers, which loomed ominously over every camp, as well as the treacherous double barbed wire.

At Auschwitz, it was emotional for my dad to see the eerie similarities within the German war machine. He and his friend Alex slept in bunk beds like these, with Alex on the top bunk, Dad in the middle.

Baraque: 34a

Tente:

Date 15.I 1945

Nom et prénom
du pris. de guerre: Kossobudzki Ryszard

Nr. d'immatr.'on 305147 Né le: 4.8.25 à

Diagnose: Splitenwun no Obexun

Le L.A.L №. 15.2.45

Valide / invalide / repos   jours.   Signature du méd.

Abtr. Stalag IV B
Lagerarzt

Cachet (pas valable sans cachet)

1./0624

The form my dad received soon after he arrived at Stalag IV B. In German it says "shrapnel in upper right arm." Note the barracks number in the upper-left-hand corner—34A.

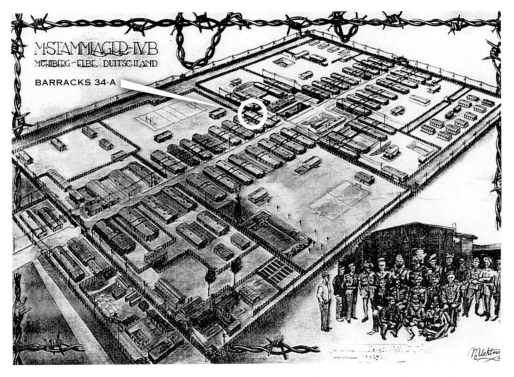

My dad's barracks, 34-A, not too far from the fence where he'd make his escape to freedom and U.S. forces.

Overcrowding and undernourishment were significant problems at Stalag IV B for the tens of thousands of prisoners from dozens of countries.

Mom and Dad on their wedding day in England. Never one for extravagance, Dad still looked dapper . . . in a borrowed suit.

My dad (second from right) in Venice with American soldiers. After having been saved by U.S. troops, my father has always greatly admired the American military.

My parents sailed to America on the famous *Queen Mary.* My dad was listed as Kossobudzki and "stateless."

Christmas at our house during a rare holiday together. From left to right: me; my brother, Alan; and Nicky, Dad's favorite dog.

Though I knew nothing about his role in Warsaw's Eaglets, my dad encouraged me to join the Brownies and Girl Scouts. I was consumed with earning badges.

My dad ran 33 marathons, even winning the Marine Corps Marathon in his age group in the 70-and-older category. He once figured out he's run the distance around the equator two and a half times.

Dad was in great shape, but always wore a shirt even when he taught swimming. I realize now it was an effort to cover up his physical scars.

Nicky guarding our patchwork tent. Even our family vacations were about survival.

Wearing a bulletproof vest and helmet in the middle of nowhere, while covering American and Afghan troops fighting terrorists in Afghanistan.

I was the first journalist to witness an interrogation at Guantanamo Bay. At the time I didn't realize the irony; I was covering detainees, and my father had been one himself.

It was an honor for me to meet Pope John Paul II, who was a pivotal force in bringing an end to communism in his native Poland. He had tremendous respect for Resistance members.

left: My dad finally receives his long-lost remnants of war, which helped set the stage for his return to Poland after sixty-five long years.

below: A hero's welcome! Last time he left Poland at gun-point; now he is a free man being honored by President Lech Kaczynski of Poland. It was an amazing moment for me to witness.

Laying a rose at the spot where his girlfriend Henryka and hundreds of others were tragically killed by the tank explosion. He says this event in his youth left him forever numbed.

Outside 23 Bracka Street, the makeshift hospital that saved my dad's life, there is a Virgin Mary statue with an eternal light marking a mass grave of other Resistance fighters who weren't so lucky.

My dad and thousands of others escaped the Nazis by trudging through dark sewer canals. Besides the nauseating stench, the underground passageways were littered with decomposing bodies and vermin.

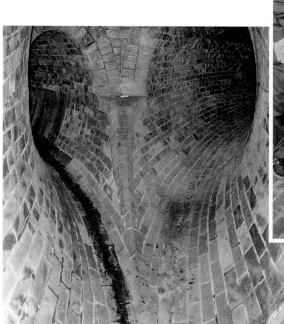

Dad admiring the statue commemorating the brave Resistance fighters and those who escaped the horror of the Nazis through the terrifying sewers.

It was easy to take a wrong turn within the pitch-black narrow tubes. Doing so meant being forever lost in a deadly labyrinth.

My dad wept when he was reunited with comrades he fought alongside six decades ago. Code names (left to right): Felek, Grom, Rys, and Beniaminek. "Felek" told my dad, "It's okay to cry."

Dad's incredible meeting with Tadeusz Goralski. The two men discovered they entered the same POW camp only minutes apart. There is now an eternal bond between them.

In Warsaw, at our first Thanksgiving together in more than thirty years, my dad said, "I'm a changed man."

12

Operations Over

*T*he days that followed remain a painful blur. I drifted in and out of consciousness, unsure what was a dream and what was really happening around me. I felt weaker than I ever have before, as if my life was being dragged out of my body bit by bit.

"I remember being carried by people I'd never seen through what seemed like an endless maze of gray streets. The city seemed strange to me. The Warsaw that I had grown up in, the city I knew every inch of, had become a place I no longer recognized. I was carried through blocks of houses, endless ranks of homes reduced to ash and rubble. I didn't realize it at the time, but the Uprising was breathing its last breath. Poland's chance at freedom was dying around me as I also questioned my own mortality.

"I'm not sure how long it took us to get to the hospital from the first-aid station, but I do remember being dropped several times on the stretcher as my buddies who were carrying me had to duck quickly from German sniper fire. At one point, I flipped out of the stretcher, falling several feet, and my face slammed into the rubble. When we finally arrived, it was not what I had been expecting. The nurses and soldiers around me had been chattering the whole way back about the 'hospital,' and I had been expecting something official. The building we stopped at was nothing more than an apartment block, on a main route called Bracka Street, that had somehow avoided the grievous damage its neighbors had received.

"There was no security check at the door; we were simply crammed inside. There was chaos all around us. No one had the time to check our credentials. The building was populated by about a dozen men and women, Resistance fighters tended by two volunteer nurses and doctors. The hospital was very low on equipment, and I was immediately set down on a bed."

"Can you remember how your room looked?" I ask.

"The room had six beds in it, I know because I counted them later. Patients always occupied them. I lay there on the bed, staring up at the unfamiliar and unusually high ceiling, trying to get my bearings and failing to do so. When I began to focus, I realized that everyone in the hospital was totally silent—everyone around me appeared to be sleeping. At least I hoped they were sleeping. The only noises were the sounds of battle that could still be heard booming from all corners of the city. Somewhere out there in the streets of Warsaw the Uprising was still raging, my friends were still risking their lives. Were my parents still alive? Would I ever see them again? How close were we to the end? I closed my eyes and fell into a deep, dreamless sleep."

My dad sits quietly for a moment, catching his breath from the weight of telling his story.

"I'm not sure how long it was that I slept, but I was thankful to wake up when I finally did. I didn't know that in a few minutes I would wish I hadn't. Pale morning light was filtering through the windows at the other side of the room, and as I lay there I heard the sound of an opening door and a doctor entered the room.

" 'A new patient!' he said. 'The nurses tell me you were caught in a mortar explosion. You're lucky to be alive!' I nodded weakly. 'The problem with mortars,' he said, 'is that you're never out of the woods right after the explosion. Shrapnel has a nasty habit of sticking around and causing terrible problems. Infections. Gangrene.' I had no idea if the explosion had left any shrapnel in my body. All I knew was that I had been wounded in several different places. I hadn't even been able to check the wounds myself.

" 'The problem with field hospitals like this,' the doctor continued, 'is that we're really not very well equipped. But you're a Resistance fighter. You're used to that sort of thing.' He chuckled. I think he must have been trying to be funny, but his attempts at humor were not doing much to lift my spirits. Around me, the other patients stayed quiet.

"The doctor kept talking. 'We barely have enough food to go around, so as you can imagine we don't have X-rays or anything like that. Or,' he said, his face taking on an expression of grim resolve, 'any anesthesia.' I closed my eyes. I didn't want to think about what might be coming next.

" 'That shrapnel,' the doctor said, 'if there is shrapnel, it has got to come out, or it's going to cause you all kinds of problems. You were lucky enough to survive that explosion, but the real threat is infection and we can't have that. Boys!' he called, and two young men appeared from the same door the doctor had entered through. They walked over to my bed and stood on either side of me. The doctor approached and produced a large pair of medical forceps from a pocket of his coat. 'Hold him down,' he said to the two boys.

"The guys held my legs, and the two young nurses came in to hold my arms down on the bed. I wanted to shout, to protest, but I knew that it had to be done if I was to survive. 'We'll have to start with that right arm,' he said to me, 'it looks like that's where you got the worst of it.' He reached down to pull the tattered, blood-soaked remains of my sleeve off my arm. The soiled fabric stuck to the dried blood on my skin. It was unbelievably painful as he lifted it off."

"Did you look at it?" I ask my dad. "Did you see what it looked like?"

"Yes, I turned my head and looked over at my arm. The explosion had torn a huge chunk out of my flesh. I had been bleeding profusely up to that point, which I took as a good sign. In my head I somehow thought it meant that the wound was not going to become infected."

"Is that what you learned in the Young Eagles?" I ask.

"No," he says. "I mean more like a hunch. The doctor reached down with the forceps and, without any hesitation, plunged them into the open wound on my arm. The pain was immediately white-hot, the worst thing I've ever felt. I'd never experienced pain like that before and I haven't since."

"Can you describe the pain?" I asked.

"Rita, there are no words for that kind of pain." He seemed relieved that I didn't need further explanation. "The doctor began digging around inside the wound, moving the forceps deeper and deeper, using his sense of touch to search for the shards of metal that he was convinced were still lodged somewhere beneath my flesh. I wanted more than anything to scream, but I tried to avoid it at all costs." My dad stops. He looks at me with realization. "You know what?"

"What?" I say.

"Even in the blinding pain that the doctor was causing, I was concerned with how I must look to everyone else in the room, my fellow Resistance fighters. I was still self-conscious. Can you believe that? I didn't think it would be too manly or brave to scream in front of all of my comrades, so I bit down on my tongue. I really wish that the doctor had given me something else to bite down on before he began the procedure, a book or a piece of wood or anything. Instead, I bit down on my tongue until blood filled my mouth.

"Out of the corner of my eye I could see the doctor pulling things from my flesh and I could hear the clink of metal as he dropped them on a tray. Black, bloodied shards of shrapnel, little things that I couldn't believe were causing me so much pain. One by one he extricated them and dropped them onto his tray. I'm not sure how long he was at this job—it was probably only fifteen minutes or so, but it seemed like an eternity of teeth-grinding agony. When I had just begun to feel I couldn't possibly take any more, the doctor stopped and wiped off his forceps. Looking more to the nurses and young men than to me, he said, 'That's enough for today,' and then he turned and left through the same door he'd come in through. The nurses stayed to dress my bleeding wound."

"You made it," I say, relieved my dad had gotten through the event and the story of it. I notice my palms are sweaty.

"No, Rita," he says, "This process repeated itself every day for three or four days. Every morning at about the same time the doctor would appear with his forceps and dig around inside the various wounds I'd received all over my body.

"The final day the doctor went deeper than he ever had before, deeper than seemed possible to me at the time, and the pain was so intense that I nearly lost consciousness." I picture the doctor there hunched over this teenager, seeking out the metal bits of hatred the enemy had left within my dad's flesh. "He finally seemed satisfied that he had removed every bit he could and gave up. 'I hope I've found all the fragments,' he said. 'Now we just have to pray that the wounds heal well.' He left and I never saw him again after that day, but I will never forget his face."

"What did he look like?" I asked, curious about the demeanor of the guy who could do this thing to my dad.

"Round, affable, the kind of man who looked like he would be a good drinking partner. Had I met him under different circumstances I never would have believed he'd be capable of doing the work that he did so nonchalantly. That look of resolve that he wore as he dug around in my arm is forever burned into my memory.

"Once the torture of my treatment had ended I fell into something of a routine at the hospital. Little by little my strength returned to me, but I remained confined to my bed for most of my time there. The beds on either side of me were occupied. To the left was a young woman in her twenties, a Resistance messenger. She never spoke, but her face wore a constant mask of pain. I learned from one of the nurses that she had three or four bullet holes in one of her legs. She'd been shot accidentally by her commander in the Resistance when he'd gotten careless with a submachine gun."

I can't believe the detail with which my dad can remember these sixty-three days and the tumultuous period before and after. It's as if there's a frame-by-frame shot list of the nightmare that has played over and over again in his mind. Rather than letting it go little by little, it seems he's remembered more and more vivid details as the years have passed. His long pauses, the pain on his face, the trembling and almost prayerful rubbing of his hands at points, speak of the heartfelt truth of his recollections. His recitation is an unabashed, hurtful diary of raw emotion unfolding before me in a way I never imagined. I pressed him for more particulars. "Who else was in the hospital room?" I ask.

"On my right was an older guy, in his late thirties, another former Resistance fighter. He was in the same division as me, but not in the same unit. The last time he saw me was that day I'd been tasked with guarding the mailman and other German prisoners, the day I'd agreed to take one of them to the latrine. When he saw me in the hospital, he pointed and said, 'There's the Resistance fighter that takes Germans to the toilet.' "

"What did you say back to him?" I ask, angry that this man would humiliate my dad, especially in his near-death condition.

"There was nothing for me to do but try to ignore him—he was older than I was, and it was true I took an embarrassing job that was almost always delegated to younger soldiers."

"What was he doing there?" I ask, notably incredulous.

"He'd been shot in battle and had a bullet lodged in his buttocks. Despite this injury he was still cocky in the hospital, mocking me from his bed, making sarcastic comments about me as well as the wounds I'd sustained. I had little choice but to disregard his taunts.

"Before too long he received a heavy dose of poetic justice. Another doctor came to do to him what he had watched happen to me for several days. They rolled him over to get the bullet out. The wound was clean, but the bullet had buried itself deep—there was only one way to get it out again. The doctor had to use a scalpel to cut into his flesh, deep enough to find the slug. Of course, there was no anesthesia. The man screamed like a pig as the doctor worked, waking up all of the other patients in the room. It was terrible to see someone in such pain, but I couldn't help but feel a certain sense of satisfaction that I'd endured similar pain with far fewer theatrics. After the doctor performed this operation, the man was considerably quieter. . . . He never insulted me again."

"What was going on in the outside world at this point?" I ask.

"It was difficult for us to know. I couldn't leave the hospital, and I was stuck in my bed to take in the sounds around us and try to piece together what might be happening. It was clear that the fighting was growing more and more intense, and moving closer and closer to our position." Outside that hospital on Bracka Street, Warsaw was being lost street by street, house by house. "Several houses neighboring the hospital were destroyed by German rockets. We all began to grow very nervous, both patients and staff."

"What did the doctors tell you about the situation?" I ask.

"The doctors weren't a permanent part of the staff. There were only those two nurses who stayed at the hospital, keeping it running. I suppose the doctors were treating people wherever they could in the city where they could get to safely. There was certainly not a normal routine."

"What did you do to occupy your mind?" I ask. "To keep yourself from going crazy?"

"You know, it's funny. As I lay on my bed, listening to the sounds of mortar shells exploding not far from us, I knew that in the event of an emergency, those two nurses would be unable to carry everyone out of the building in time. So, with little else to do, I spent a lot of time making dour calculations about what I would do in the event of a direct attack. I was still very weak from blood loss, and my wounds made it difficult to walk, but I decided that if the hospital was bombed I would roll down the stairs and crawl out." I am struck that even in his near-death condition his instinct was to plan how to survive.

"In the days and nights that led up to the end of the Uprising and the surrender of the Resistance forces, I was constantly afraid for my life. Every night the shells burst closer and closer, the sounds of explosions and gunfire becoming louder and louder. It was scary as hell, being trapped in there, unable to run or hide."

I imagine my dad lying on that bed by himself, not knowing what was going on in the world, not knowing where anyone he loved was or even if they were alive. "You must have felt completely helpless," I say.

"I did." He nods. "Lying there on my bed, listening to the labored breathing of the wounded soldiers surrounding me and the seemingly endless concussions of the bombs outside, I prayed."

As hard and as courageously as they fought, in the end the Polish Resistance was no match for the Nazi war machine. After sixty-three days of relentless fighting, the Uprising collapsed. "We threw in the towel," my dad says. "We had to. We were at the mercy of the Germans." Unbeknownst to those fighting, talks had begun in mid-September between the Resistance leadership and the Nazis. But false hope that the Soviets were finally moving to Poland's aid and a last-minute infusion of reinforcements had brought an end to the negotiations, and the fighting had continued, long enough to grimly wound my father. The Polish commander-in-chief reached out to the Soviets for aid, but nothing of real substance was given. The Germans quickly reasserted their military dominance and the last vestiges of the Resistance were crushed.

On October 2, the Resistance forces capitulated, and almost immediately the fighting was over. The Germans agreed to treat Polish insurgents as prisoners of war instead of as civilians, but this request was not wholly honored. The Polish fighters who were still alive were quickly disarmed. Many Resistance soldiers were shipped off to concentration camps, many of them going to their deaths.

"When the Uprising was defeated and the fighting finally ended," my dad says, "there was a free-for-all for supplies. The city was filled with abandoned houses, many of which had been left full of the personal belongings of the people who no longer lived in them. Everyone combed through homes and cellars, searching for anything of value and taking it. Some of my buddies from my unit came to visit me at the hospital, and brought me valuable supplies they'd liberated."

"What?" I say. "What did they give you?"

"A blue suit, a pair of socks and underwear, a brown suitcase to keep my things in, and a huge lot of cigarettes—close to two thousand of them. I don't smoke anymore, but at the time it was the most precious gift anyone could have given me. Soon after I got them, those cigarettes would save my life.

"Besides the presents, it was wonderful to see my comrades. These were young guys I'd fought with, guys I'd risked my life with for months. We thought that now that the fighting was over, things would go back to the way they were during the beginning of the German occupation. We were wrong. I didn't know it at the time, but this was to be the last time that I ever saw any of them again."

"What did you think when they told you about the surrender?" I ask.

"I know I should have felt disappointed, that I should have lamented the fact that so many of us had fought and died for what ultimately proved to be a hopeless cause, but really I just felt a sense of vague relief. After those helpless nights on my bed, it was nice to know that I was going to live, at least for a little while longer.

"Before too long the Polish war chest, whatever resources they had left from the failed Uprising, were distributed among the soldiers who had served. A man came to the hospital one afternoon to give everyone their money for fighting in the Resistance, and my share amounted to seven U.S. dollars."

"You mean Polish dollars, right, Dad?" I say.

"No, it was American dollars, Rita!" he answers. "It was the first time I'd ever seen dollars before. I asked the guy, 'What is this?' He told me, 'It's your share. It's American money.' And, almost as soon as I got it, someone stole it."

The Americans and other Allies had used pressure to make sure the Germans would classify Polish Resistance fighters as POWs, and give them full "combatant's rights" in accordance with the international convention. Only then did the leader of the Polish Home Army agree to a surrender of the Resistance fighters who were still alive. Most were taken into mass captivity by the Germans in October 1944 and shipped to various camps throughout Europe. Of course, this didn't mean the next phase of life for these new POWs would be easy.

"It was lucky that my friends were thoughtful enough to bring me clothes, because up until that point I'd worn nothing but the bloody underwear I had on when I'd been brought to the hospital. The rest of my clothes had been torn apart by the mortar shell. The only useful things I'd arrived there with were my pair of brown suede shoes, the ones I'd found in that shoe store during my tour of duty in Old Town. They were a good pair of shoes, probably the most expensive in that store, and they were getting ready to go with me on a wild ride. One afternoon a doctor arrived. 'Pack your bag,' he said, nodding at my suitcase, which stood on the floor beside my bed. 'You're going to Germany. Good luck.' "

13

THE TRAIN TO GERMANY

*N*one of us in the hospital was ready to move—I had gained some strength since my injury, but I was still in no condition to walk on my own, much less board a train and travel somewhere into a foreign country.

" 'You're being evacuated,' the doctor told me, 'All wounded Resistance fighters are being evacuated immediately and sent to Germany. We're all going to the train station. A Red Cross train is waiting there to take everyone across the border.'

" 'But where are they taking us?' I asked.

" 'Who knows?' the doctor said, shrugging. 'But I'm sure it will be all right.' He seemed strangely cheerful given the circumstances, but he was a member of the Resistance, so he would be going wherever we went. 'As far as I know we're safe,' he continued, 'the

German army will take care of us. They'll respect the international convention.' He gave me a smile that seemed overconfident. I'd witnessed the brutality of the Germans and the soldiers they employed. They hadn't respected the terms of the laws of war up to that point. Why would they begin now that the fighting was over, now that they had absolute power over us?"

"Did you think about somehow escaping?" I ask. "To get away before the train took off?"

"We had little choice but to obey. Where was I going to go, especially in my condition? Warsaw lay in ruins around us. Most of us didn't have homes left to return to. One by one the injured soldiers I had spent the past few days with in the hospital were pushed, carried, and wheeled outside into the street.

"I had actually seen the street the day my friends had come to visit and told me that the Uprising was over. There seemed to be a short break in the shelling, so I was determined to get out of my bed and see for myself. It took all the strength I could gather, and the pain was intense, but I lifted myself to sit up on the bed and slowly put on the blue suit they'd brought me." I picture my dad laboriously putting on his blue suit in his condition. "It was a surprisingly good fit—if you didn't look too closely, you might think it had been tailored for me to wear. I stood and headed for the door, leaning shakily against the wall.

" 'Wait!' one of the nurses called after me. 'You're not strong enough! It might not be safe!'

" 'Don't worry,' I told her. 'I'm not going far. I'll be careful, I just need to see what's happening out there.' I hobbled down the stairs and pushed the door open. I looked out at my city for the first time in days. I couldn't believe what I saw. The street in front of me, as far as I could see, was in flames, homes and buildings all leveled or burning. I stepped onto the stoop and leaned against the wall, staring in shock at what was going on around me. There was the crackle of flames, punctuated by the occasional shifting of debris or the whoosh and crash of burning rafters falling in. At first I thought what I was looking at was the remains of the shelling that had been going on for the past few days, but then I realized this was impossible. 'Houses don't burn for a week,' I said to myself. 'Something is going on.'

"Before long I noticed movement up the block from my location, and as I squinted I could see people, I suppose German engineers, armed with flamethrowers. They were moving methodically down the street and setting fire to each building. I stood there in disbelief, watching their progress. It was at that moment that I understood how complete the Nazi victory had been. The smell of smoke was thick in the air. I feared that not even the hospital would eventually be left standing.

"I made my way back inside as quickly as I could and dragged myself up the stairs. I was so winded that I could barely get words out.

" 'Half the street is in flames!' I told the nurse. 'Did you know that the Germans are out there burning houses?'

" 'I did,' she replied, her face pale and expressionless. 'But I didn't want to worry you, so I thought it would be best not to tell you.' I collapsed back onto my bed, my mind racing a hundred times faster than my body could move. Would the Germans come here? Had we lived through the Uprising only to be burned alive in this makeshift hospital?

"The nurse seemed to understand the thoughts that were going through my head and she put a hand on my shoulder. 'Don't worry,' she said. 'We've hung a Red Cross flag out front. The army will respect that.' I didn't trust the Germans to respect that flag—as I said, I'd seen what they were capable of. Remember how they leveled my classmate's first-aid station right after the tank explosion? But by the time we were forced to evacuate, our hospital was the only building on the entire block that was still in one piece. The windows were blown out, but other than that everything was in place. So it appeared that the Germans would be true to their word this time.

"It took a lot of energy for me just to get to the street that day, and I was bedridden afterward. My wounds caused me an incredible amount of pain, and there was no escaping it. I was still terribly weak from all the blood I had lost, and unable to support my own weight for more than a few steps. We had no plasma in those days, so I was taking a very long time to regain my strength.

"When we finally did leave the hospital to be sent to Germany, the nurses recognized my weak condition, and at first they offered to carry me on a stretcher, but I declined, saying they should give it to someone more seriously wounded. We joined a sad procession of the injured and their attendants. The walk to the train station was not a long one, but our path was strewn with obstacles. Debris lay everywhere—rubble from ruined houses, broken furniture, smashed horse carts. The two nurses helping me did their best to make my passage as smooth as possible, but this was a tall order, given the circumstances and the amount of rubble we had to cross.

"I was starting to get dizzy. I leaned heavily on the two nurses and we continued our journey as I staggered toward the train station. After a few hundred more feet I began to feel as if I might pass out. This was the farthest I had traveled since my injury, and I had still not recovered from the massive blood loss. My arms became completely useless, and my wounded legs were so weak that I was incapable of anything more than a halting shuffle. I lost consciousness more than once before we reached the station, but the nurses carried me on.

"For whatever reason the train had bypassed the big stations and pulled up at a little depot. There weren't any big buildings around, and the Red Cross train was the only one at the platform. I decided that it must have been some kind of freight drop-off point—a loading station. The train was huge, about thirty cars, each with a large red cross painted on the side. Even in my state it was obvious to me that I was not looking at a passenger train—these were cattle cars. The nurses walked me up to the train and one of them held me up while her colleague asked where I should be put. I couldn't make out what was being said, but after a few moments a door into one of the train cars was slid open and someone set up stairs. With some difficulty I was helped up the steps, and another nurse helped push me inside. She motioned to a wooden 'bed' on the floor, laden with straw.

" 'This is your bed,' she said. They were tiny, smaller even than those in the hospital, but I was so exhausted and grateful to be off my feet that I immediately fell into it. 'Rest,' the nurse said to me in a tender voice, 'we're loading from all the different hospitals. There's going to be a lot of time before the train leaves.' "

"What else do you remember about the train, Dad?" I ask.

"The steel and wood interior of the boxcar was much more pleasant than the exterior. It was surprisingly clean inside, with spotless floors and a noticeable absence of smells. There were some containers of disinfectant in the corner of the car. I mentioned to the nurse that they must have a problem with lice or cockroaches.

" 'No,' she said, 'the Germans make sure that this train is kept spotless.' As I turned my head, taking in the featureless walls, I noticed a small bucket in the corner, which we all had to share as the bathroom. The other beds gradually filled with other wounded soldiers. After a while an old guard appeared, almost fatherly look-ing. All of the soldiers assigned to guard detail on the train were old. They were the leftovers, but they were armed.

"I closed my eyes and let the sounds of shouting nurses and groaning wounded soldiers become a swirling hum of white noise around me. I drifted off for a bit, and was jolted awake when the train lurched forward. It seemed to be moving incredibly slowly. At first I thought that we must just be picking up speed, but the longer we traveled the more clear it became that we would just be making our journey to wherever it was that we were going at a snail's pace."

"What was the ride like?" I ask him.

"The train had obviously not had much maintenance attention. It was rattling all over the place, creaking and grinding its way along the tracks. The wheels were not oiled, the axles were worn out, and the couplings were on their last legs. It was an unbelievable racket, especially when we hit switches in the tracks. Whenever that hap-pened the sound was like a sudden explosion, like we were passing over mines. And the shaking was uncomfortable on my injuries, to say the least.

"As we continued on our long, slow journey I gradually began to regain the strength I'd lost on the walk to the train. When I felt up to it, I heaved myself off the straw bed and staggered over to the open door to see what I could see. The guard hadn't bothered to close the big sliding door we'd used to enter the car, and he was sitting on a little stool by the edge, staring listlessly at the tracks sliding by below. The guard knew that in our condition no one in the train car was in any position to threaten him, so he sat there, bored, holding his weapon and staring at the passing countryside.

"All through the day the train continued its slow, creaking jour-ney across Poland toward the German border. Before long the sun had sunk low in the sky and long shadows were stretching across the land. It was early evening when the train began to slow down and eventually screeched to a halt. I picked myself up out of my bed again and made my way to the open door to see where we were.

"Instantly, I was overcome with a strange feeling of déjà vu. 'I know this place,' I thought to myself. The guard picked up his rifle, hopped out of the train, and vanished. I stood there at the open door, staring out into the night and marveling at the coincidence that had befallen me. 'My God,' I thought. 'This is Grodzisk! This is where my parents bought their summer house!' I looked out at the station and moved my gaze away from it, down the road a bit. There, not more than a couple hundred yards from where the train had stopped, I saw what looked like small, shining lights in the windows of a house that I swore could have been my parents' country home. My heart leaped. I hadn't seen or heard from my mother and father since early in the Uprising. I had no idea if they had lived or died, if they were still in Warsaw or if they'd fled to the safety of another town, another country. To this day I don't know if I was truly looking out at the summer house, but just seeing those small lights made me feel that they had made it, that they were out there somewhere. It strengthened my resolve to get out of this alive, to find them.

"For a moment, I considered making a run for it, right then and there, off the train, but then logic kicked in and I decided against it. I was still grievously wounded—I knew that I wasn't up for running from German guards, even if they were all as old as the man who'd been watching us on the train. And I remembered what we'd been hearing about the Soviet army's movements, and I imagined what it would be like if and when they were here. It was not going to be a happy land. If I were to be arrested by the Russians, as a former

Resistance fighter, I would be sent to Siberia at best. I believed that I would have my chance to find my parents again, but this wouldn't be that chance.

"I sat back down on the straw bed, and before too long the old guard returned and the train creaked and groaned back into motion. I watched as the Grodzisk station disappeared into the darkness behind us, and the lights from the building I believed was my parents' house faded from view."

"Did you get any sleep?" I ask him.

"That night, I fell asleep and slept better than I had in days. I was shaken awake the next day when the train screeched to a stop once again. Bright daylight was shining onto my face through the door, and voices were shouting in German outside. The vicious German police, just as nasty as the SS, suddenly surrounded the train with huge, barking German shepherds, cars, and officers. We couldn't understand what they were saying, but it was clear enough what they wanted. We were all ordered out of the train at gunpoint. Those who were unable to walk on their own were loaded into cars. A soldier saw me stagger and screamed at me, gesturing to the open door of one of the vehicles with the barrel of his gun, but I shook my head. I didn't want to show any weakness. If I could muster the strength to walk on my own two feet I was damn well going to. We were marched through a good-sized town."

"Were there people there?" I ask.

"It seemed completely empty," he says. "It was haunting. If there were people there, they didn't even look out their windows as we passed. The German dogs were snarling and snapping at our heels as we walked. We were marched all the way through town to a dilapidated district, a deserted place that seemed to be slowly crumbling away into nothingness. The Germans left us suddenly in what looked like an abandoned prison. As we all sat there, wondering what was going to happen next, a few of us began to entertain ideas of escape and also serious concern.

" 'Where are we?' we began to ask each other. 'What the hell are we doing here?' No one wanted to give voice to the dreadful thought that was festering in all of our heads, that this was going to be the end of our journey. That we'd traveled all this way only to be shot and forgotten. I remember as clearly as if it were yesterday, one guy said, 'Well, they can only kill our bodies. They can't take our souls.' I nodded in assent, but it did little to assuage my fears.

"We sat there waiting for many hours with no food or water, and then, seemingly out of nowhere, the German police reappeared and marched us back to the train."

"Did they say anything about why you had been there, or what had gone on? Did anyone tell you?"

"No one told us why. There was no logical reason to suddenly get us to leave the train, other than that someone had planned to kill us, or take us elsewhere. My belief is there was some 'conflict of interest' between different German units, and they were fighting over what to do with us, whether to kill us or carry us on.

"We were roughly loaded back onto the cars and sent on our way. It wasn't until later on that I found out where we had been, and how close to death we must have come. The town we stopped at was Lodz, a major industrial city and the site of a massive Jewish ghetto. In August 1944 the ghetto was liquidated. For those long hours, we were held in a district that had once been home to more than 220,000 people. Only five to seven thousand of them survived.

"We were lucky to escape with our lives. I think the German police stopped us because people of significant power wanted us killed. Again, somehow, we had luck on our side. When we were loaded back onto the train and sent on our way we didn't know where we would end up, but we all felt that we had been spared. As long as we were alive, there was still hope."

14

THE CIGARETTE KING

*A*fter we left Lodz, it wasn't much farther until we reached our first stop in Germany. Our final destination was still a mystery. After what had seemed like an eternity of jarring rail travel, the boxcar finally heaved to a stop in Zeithain, Germany, about an hour north of Dresden and south of Berlin. We were ordered out of the train cars, rounded up, and marched a short distance from the station to the massive German war prisoner hospital."

"Do you remember when this was?" I ask him.

"It was mid-October."

"What did the POW hospital look like?"

"It was quite large. It was stark and orderly. It was by no means a luxurious place—it had been constructed to house hundreds of mainly Russian POWs, and now thousands of wounded Polish soldiers."

"What did you have with you?"

"Well, let's see, the suitcase filled with cigarettes. And I was wearing my blue suit, new socks, and my brown suede shoes. It was all I had to my name."

"Did they say anything to you?" I ask. "Tell you to do something?"

"We were marched inside and quickly assigned barracks. I was completely exhausted by the time the nurse gave me my bed. I was still incredibly weak and had not yet recovered from the massive blood loss I'd suffered."

"What about your wounds? Were they bleeding?" I ask.

"My wounds were still open and I was constantly worried about infection. The trip from Warsaw to Germany had done some damage, but mostly it had taken the wind out of me. I was so tired that I collapsed onto the bed and wondered if I'd ever be able to get up again."

"When you did wake up, what happened?" I ask.

"When I woke up, I noticed they had brought in another soldier and put him in a bed next to me on my right with only a small aisle separating us. He looked in sad shape. He had been wounded as critically as I had, but in a different way. His hands were gnarled and twisted, and the lower part of his face—his nose, mouth, and chin—were covered in what looked like horrible burns, which he got from a German flamethrower."

"How so?" I ask.

"It looked like his skin had bubbled. For several hours the two of us lay there in silence. I couldn't tell if he was awake or not, but after an hour or so he sat up a bit and spoke to me."

" 'What happened to you?' he asked, nodding in the direction of my bandages. My head was swimming, but I managed to get out a word in answer.

" 'Mortar,' I said.

" 'You're lucky to be alive.'

"I nodded grimly, then I confessed what had played out numerous times in my mind, but I had never said out loud: 'My friend wasn't.'

" 'Don't think about that now,' he said. 'You're here. You're alive. We might still get out of this.' He introduced himself. 'I'm Alex. Alex Chelmicki.' "

"You know his last name!" I say.

"Of course I know his last name. He would become my closest friend and confidant in the long months to come. Over the next few days, we got to know and lean on each other. I even helped feed him because his hands were still raw and blistered. I was amazed that he was able to stay as positive as he seemed despite his wounds. Alex had fought in the Polish Resistance, too.

"Alex and I bonded over the difficulties we'd both endured. It was nice to have someone to talk to, but camaraderie only went so far in that hospital. The place was not built to provide care for serious injuries—the doctors and nurses that were employed there were only able to perform the most rudimentary procedures, and the hospital was terribly underequipped. As the days passed my injuries became worse and worse. My shrapnel wounds were still bleeding and oozing pus, and because of how poorly we'd been eating I was developing a bad case of anemia."

"Did they give you anything for your wounds?" I ask.

"All they could do was apply bandages. But my wounds were eventually cleaned in another way. One day, when one of the nurses was redressing my biggest wound, I saw lots of green pus and felt a strange, writhing movement in it. 'What is that?' I asked her. She smiled and said, 'The maggots have found you.' The sight nearly made me sick, but the nurse seemed strangely pleased. 'They'll help to clean it,' she said. 'We don't have much in the way of antiseptic.' "

I couldn't help but make a face in disgust and feel a little nauseated.

"Rita, this was still wartime," Dad reminds me. "There was no plasma to replace the blood that I'd lost, and no penicillin to stave off infection. The best the doctors at the hospital could do was give shots of glucose to combat malnutrition and anemia, but they were terribly stingy with their doses and didn't give me any. There was, I suppose, so little of it. I felt weaker then than I ever have in my life— even the smallest movement was a terrible strain, and it was nearly impossible for me to get out of my bed. If Alex hadn't come up with a plan to keep me alive, I believe I would have died, slowly wasting away from blood loss and anemia.

"One day he sat up in his bed, and said, 'You know, I've noticed that a lot of the doctors here are pretty heavy smokers.'

" 'So?' I said.

" 'So,' he continued, 'cigarettes are rationed pretty strictly here. People want to get them. Even doctors have to find them wherever they can.'

"I felt light-headed. I was having a hard time following him. 'Right . . . ' I said, closing my eyes and trying to fight back the pain.

" 'So,' he said, 'you're sitting on a gold mine of cigarettes! You've got that suitcase underneath your bed packed full of what—two thousand of them? Those doctors will be a hell of a lot more likely to give you some glucose if you send some of the cigarettes their way.'

"I nodded. 'There's just one problem with that plan,' I said, through gritted teeth. 'The doctors don't have cigarettes on duty. How will we know which ones we can bribe?'

" 'I thought about that already,' Alex said, grinning. 'Anybody who smokes here, smokes a lot. We just have to look at their hands. Any doctor with a real addiction will have nicotine-stained hands.' He held up his own terribly damaged hands and wiggled his fingers. I smiled. He had a real idea. I took his advice and the next time a yellow-fingered doctor made the rounds I reached out and grabbed the hem of his coat as he walked by.

" 'Listen,' I whispered, 'I need a shot of glucose.'

" 'I'm sorry,' the guy said, 'but those shots have already been given out today.' I pulled out a twenty-pack of cigarettes, and without a word held it out to him."

"What did he do?" I ask.

"He took the cigarettes from me and quickly slipped them into his coat pocket. Immediately, his bedside manner changed. Then, he said, 'I'll see what I can do for you.' "

"Did he?" I ask.

"That doctor returned ten minutes later with a shot of glucose, and from that day on I received another one every other day for a few weeks. It was incredible how quickly I began to recover once I started trading my cigarettes for those lifesaving shots." I think of a neglected houseplant that looks dead, but springs instantly back to life when watered. "I became the cigarette king. I could have traded cigarettes for extra food for myself, too, but I didn't want to take it out of a starving man's mouth. The glucose shots were the best trade I made in my life. In a week or so my wounds finally began to heal and I could comfortably get up and walk around the hospital with Alex. I never really thanked him for his smart thinking, but he had probably saved my life. I would have never thought about bribing a doctor."

"How long were you at the hospital?" I ask him.

"We arrived there in October and stayed for several months."

"How did you spend the time?"

"I was confined to my bed in terrible pain for most of the time we spent there, but Alex and I entertained each other with stories and company."

"Besides Alex, anything else good you remember?" I ask.

"There were a few bright moments. Eventually December rolled around, and before long it was Christmas Eve. Of course there was no official celebration—we were prisoners of war, after all. But the Polish medical staff at the hospital was able to make it something of a festive occasion. We were lying quietly in our beds on Christmas Eve, some of us praying, all of us thinking about our families. I didn't expect this night in the hospital to be any different from the others that had come before it. Suddenly, I heard some kind of commotion from outside the door, and a pair of Polish nurses burst into our room shouting, 'Merry Christmas! Merry Christmas!' They made their way through the barracks, pouring something out of a few big jugs they were carrying. When they reached me, one of the nurses handed me a little tin cup and filled it with about three-quarters of an inch of clear liquid. 'Merry Christmas!' she said cheerfully, and continued on her way.

"I raised the cup to my face and watched Alex as he did the same in the bed across from me. We both looked up at each other with surprise as we realized what it was we'd been given.

" 'Vodka!' Alex said, his eyes lighting up. Someone on the medical staff had been good enough to save a few rationed potatoes and had been making moonshine. The jolly nurses had all clearly sampled the stuff already. Alex and I toasted each other and drank from the little tin cups. Our bodies were weaker than usual, and it was particularly strong stuff. So, before we knew it we were in a rare happy mood. We spent that night singing Polish songs with the other men in their beds, and it was a rare and wonderful bright spot in my long ordeal."

I'll never look at Christmas the same way again. Such a small gesture in troubled times can be the greatest of gifts. While my childhood Christmases have not always been picture-perfect, this story reminds me of what's at the heart of the season.

"I stayed in the POW hospital in Zeithain until January 1945. As wounded prisoners began to regain their strength, the Germans began sending them away from the hospital to a destination we still hadn't been told about. We knew that we were being moved to a POW camp, but we didn't know the details, or where it was exactly. When I was finally well enough to move, I was selected to be shipped out. Alex's wounds had still not completely healed, but we had become close friends by that point and neither of us wanted to abandon the other. He volunteered to leave the hospital with me so that we wouldn't be separated.

"It was January 12. The moment we stepped outside the hospital we were met with a blast of freezing cold winter air. We were with a small group of maybe ten other prisoners, and not a single one of us was dressed for the weather."

"What were you wearing?" I ask him.

"The same thing I'd been wearing for three months! I was still in the blue suit that my friends had given to me in Warsaw."

"What about Alex?"

"Alex was wearing a white sweater, a torn shirt, and some beat-up old slacks."

"Where'd they take you?" I ask.

"We were marched for probably ten miles through the freezing cold snow, spurred on by Germans armed with rifles with long bayonets. We moved at a painfully slow pace. We couldn't have gone more than a mile or so each hour, so the walk was very long."

"No one told you where you were going?" I ask.

"No."

"No one asked?"

"Rita, we weren't asking questions. We'd know when we got there. That was the rule. After several hours of walking we saw a town in the distance. At first we wondered if this place might be our destination, but it quickly became obvious that we would not be staying. As we marched through the streets of a small village the sidewalks filled with young boys, Hitler Youth who screamed at us in German and pelted us with snowballs as we passed. It was disturbing to hear how much anger and hatred there was in their young voices."

I thought of my dad's experience in the Young Eagles, thought about the fear and rage he'd felt as conflict descended on his own city. It made me sad to know that the war had stolen his youth, and probably the innocence of these boys, too.

"Before long we left the town behind. When we reached our destination we were all exhausted from the difficult trek. I was finally feeling as if I might not be on death's door, but I was still not prepared to walk for miles in the freezing January weather. Many of the men that were with us had been in worse shape than I when we left. Our journey ended at Stalag IV B, a massive German prisoner of war camp near the town of Muhlberg and east of the Elbe River. The camp's gate loomed ahead of us, a gigantic wooden entrance with a glass-windowed guard tower perched at its top."

"How'd you know its name right away?"

"It was spelled out on the gate. 'M. Stammlager IV B.' Shortened, it means 'Stalag IV B.' Prison camp number 4 B."

"What happened when you arrived?" I ask.

"We were immediately led through the gates and taken to a huge building where German soldiers lined us up, stripped us all naked, sheared off our hair, and recorded our registration numbers."

"Do you remember your POW number?" I ask, testing him.

"No," he says. "I'm lucky that I remember my Social Security number. I vividly remember those tags, though. There was a long, sturdy chain and a metal plate, perforated down the center. On each half I think it said, 'Stalag IV B' and our number. If we died, one half was supposed to be put in our mouth and the other half placed in their records."

Not wanting to envision half of that tarnished tag I found in his suitcase of memorabilia, broken and jammed into his mouth, I asked, "What happened after you got your numbers?"

"From there, we were all pushed into a room that was like a gigantic shower. We were still naked and the room was freezing cold. The tiles were like slabs of ice underneath my bare feet. German orderlies approached us with guns that blasted us with some kind of disinfectant powder. They hosed all of us down, paying special attention to crotches and armpits."

"Was Alex still with you?"

"Yes. We were inseparable."

"What about the powder on his wounds?" I suggest. "It must have really hurt."

"He never mentioned it, but I'm sure it hurt like hell. There was no use complaining. What good would it have done? From there we dressed and were sent to the Polish POW commandant to be assigned to our barracks."

"Did you and Alex get assigned the same barracks?" I ask.

"Yes. We made sure of that."

"What did it look like?"

"The building was really big."

"How big, Dad?"

"It was home to around 150 prisoners. All the beds were set up in bunks, three stacked on top of each other."

"Were you assigned a bunk?" I ask. "Or did you pick it?"

"Bunks were negotiated among the prisoners. My legs and arms were still in bad shape from the shrapnel wounds I'd sustained, and climbing was difficult. A guy already had the bottom bunk, so I asked for the middle bunk and Alex took the top. The bunks had mattresses, but they were filled with wood shavings and were pretty uncomfortable."

"What did you do after you got your bunk?" I ask.

"The two of us sat there on our beds, a bit shocked at our circumstances, I suppose, taking it all in. More and more men were arriving every minute. Alex and I joked, trying to make each other feel better, but talking did little to quell the fear that was growing in the back of my mind. We had no idea what was going to happen to us at Stalag IV B. All we could do was hope for the best."

15

WELCOME TO STALAG IV B

*R*aus! Raus!' Every morning at five o'clock a guard would enter the barracks with our wake-up call, and say, 'Out.'

"They'd march us outside, line us up, and count us. After a few weeks some of the guys who had extra sets of clothes didn't even bother getting dressed for the morning head count—they would roll out of bed, put on their coats, and walk outside in their pajamas. The count always went pretty quickly because it was pretty rare for people to escape. This is not to say that it never happened."

"They didn't give you anything to wear?" I ask.

"No." He laughs. "We had whatever we had on our backs when we came in. We were never issued uniforms or anything like that. I wore my blue suit every day, and when we went to bed, I slept in it. It was the only outfit I had, so I had to make the most of it. The barracks were cavernous and often got very cold, but every barracks had one coal stove for heat. The only problem with it was that coal itself was strictly rationed, so we could only use the stove for a few hours a day."

"How many barracks were there?"

"I'm not sure. I don't remember counting. The camp was huge, a massive hodgepodge of soldiers and dissidents from many nations. The Germans didn't bother with individual POW camps for different countries. Instead they shipped prisoners from all over the world to any one of many places like Stalag IV B. I've heard that there were something like twenty thousand men there, thirty or forty different nationalities. Essentially it was a city, an artificial city whose citizens were all prisoners. And we were divided into barracks based on where we were from. I was with the Poles. Next door, our neighbors were Russians, nearby the Dutch."

"Was the camp dirty, Dad?"

"The Germans were very particular about the cleanliness of the barracks. But that's not to say that the accommodations were a hotel, either. The sawdust beds were uncomfortable, to say the least, and as you can imagine, with a couple hundred guys in close quarters, most with only one outfit to their name, there was a lot of body odor and fear of disease. The Nazis were completely intolerant of lice, or anything like that. If the guards so much as heard a rumor that someone in the barracks had lice, we would all immediately be marched to the showers we'd been sent through upon our arrival, and once again stripped and blasted with disinfectant powder. Your clothes would be disinfected, too—I don't think there was a single louse in the Polish barracks."

I try to picture my father being treated that way, naked and hosed down with disinfectant like an animal. He is such a proud man, the experience must have been humiliating for him. "Did that happen to you often?" I ask.

"Oh, many times," he answers. "But only as a precaution. It happened probably every two or three weeks, just to keep everyone clean. The bad part was that the powder itched and burned. The minute they sprayed it at you it filled your nose and mouth and made you sneeze and cough."

"So, what happened after they took a head count each day?" I ask.

"After we were counted, some of us had outside work detail, which enabled me to sneak some items back to the camp, like extra coal, which Alex and I found when we worked at the rail yard."

"Would you talk to other people?" I ask.

"Well," he says, "it was difficult to communicate with a lot of the men interned there because of the language barrier, but Alex and I bonded with some of the other Poles. A lot of the Polish guys in our barracks had also fought the Nazis during the Warsaw Uprising, and we spent a lot of time trading stories. We'd all been through so much horror; we'd all lost so many friends. We bonded over these experiences. Telling our own tales brought us all closer together. We also made friends with a few of the Dutchmen as well. They had a hidden radio and were giving us updates on how the war was really going, not just what the Germans wanted us to hear."

"In addition to work, what else did you do to pass the time?" I ask.

"Oh, lots of things. Somebody made a chessboard. In our barracks we had the chess champion of Warsaw. Other guys would bet rations or a cigarette just to play him in chess. No one ever beat him. Guys all over camp would come to play him inside the barracks. One day ten guys played him at the same time. They still lost. I've heard there was live theater at the camp, but I think that ended before I got there. I don't ever remember seeing a theater, so it must have been abandoned. I do remember a group of American cowboys, five Texans, would come around with guitars and sing western cowboy songs. We loved that. We called them The Troubadours. Everyone who wanted to listen to them had to pay half a cigarette for about a half-hour performance. They brought happiness once a week to the Polish barracks.

"Remember, I was there near the end, so people were mostly lethargic because there was so little food and a lot of us had been injured. All I was thinking about was tomorrow, hoping it would come. What happened yesterday, to hell with it! I was very single-minded. I was looking toward the future. I had decided I was going to move to Niagara Falls."

"Niagara Falls?" I ask, thinking back to what he'd told me about his daydream during the Uprising, when, delirious with thirst, he'd remembered the book on the United States he'd read as a child. "Because you were thirsty?"

"Interestingly, I don't remember ever wanting for water at the camp. We almost died of thirst in Warsaw, but at IV B I seem to remember that water was the one thing that wasn't rationed. That was lucky. There was one small faucet in the camp for hundreds of men, so obviously it wasn't clean, but it was sanitary enough that none of us got dysentery or anything like that."

"So, thinking of Niagara Falls at that point wasn't because you needed water," I press.

"No," he says. "Not this time. I was thinking about a better life. America represented opportunity for a better life. Along those lines, I tried to study a lot."

"Study?"

"Yeah, I'd try to practice my English. There was a Polish guy from Detroit who had moved there from Warsaw before the war. He would come by to practice his Polish on Alex and me, and I encouraged him to teach us English. He was a funny guy. We suspected he was a little bit Jewish, but we'd never ask him. It was lucky that no one knew about it. If the Germans found out, he could have ended up shot or in a concentration camp, instead of with the POWs.

"That brings up something important. There were certain unspoken rules of prison camp."

"Unspoken rules?" I ask.

"Things that were just understood," he says. "Number one: Never ask a guy about his background, where he came from. Talk only about what he wants to do in the future. Never touch on the past unless he brings it up. Number two: Never come up with questions to embarrass a guy. You could draw him out a little if you became a friend, but you'd never ask a question directly that might make him uncomfortable."

"Like what, Dad?"

"Like 'How were you hurt?' Or, 'Where are your injuries?' Those kinds of topics were off-limits." It does not go unnoticed by me that this rule was carried with him to America, and right into the house I grew up in. As a child, I learned never to ask a question that might make my dad uncomfortable. Nothing overtly personal. Perhaps it's one of the reasons I became an inquisitive journalist, overcompensating for the lack of opportunity to satiate the curiosity of my childhood. "Instead of those kinds of questions," he continues, "you could ask, 'Hey, what are we going to do when we leave the camp?' and 'Who do you look forward to seeing?' and things like that.

"And number three: Don't steal from your own, especially food. There was a very unfortunate incident that happened with this guy in our own barracks. There were two older prisoners, and they traded something with the guards for margarine. This guy stole some of the margarine and got caught. The punishment was 'down with the pants.' A guy who was our barracks leader, a huge man, picked up the heaviest belt and gave the thief twenty lashes on the naked ass. It was harsh punishment, but he deserved it. No one would ever steal from another again in our barracks."

My mind suddenly flashes to my childhood birthday party at the local ice-skating rink when I was eleven or twelve years old. Before the affair, I threw a tantrum, upset that my mother hadn't gotten me the expensive birthday outfit I wanted. I was furious with her, frantically screaming and flailing my arms.

"My father stepped into the scene, and I mouthed off at him, selectively employing a few sharp curse words. Yet as the words left my mouth, it was immediately obvious that I had gone too far. I had challenged his authority. He promptly bent me over his knee and whacked me with the palm of his hand. One forceful blow from my father was enough to settle any and all disputes. I can still remember my expression when I saw his strong hand targeting my rear end. Today, there's a fine line between "stern but lovable disciplinarian" and "abuser," but as I write this I must admit, I well deserved it. I certainly knew not to do it again. Much like touching a hot stove, the cause and effect are easily remembered. I realize now how petty I must have sounded complaining about the wrong outfit to a man that wore the same suit night and day for almost seven months.

I also feel as if I now have a better understanding of my dad's strict sense of discipline. Whether he learned it in the Young Eagles, fighting in the Resistance, or as a prisoner of war, he lived by a rigid moral code. I move on by asking, "Where did you get your food at Stalag IV B?"

"Our diet in the camp was terrible. Every morning, once we'd been lined up and counted, we were given breakfast. Our first meal of the day consisted of nothing more than a slice of brown bread, about this thick." He holds up his hand and sticks out his thumb.

"About as thick as my thumb. There were all kinds of rumors at the time that the Germans were putting sawdust in the bread to cheapen the baking process—I don't know if that's true, but I wouldn't be surprised. It sure tasted bad enough. To go along with the bread we all received one slice of cheese and one tiny slice of margarine. The cheese was like nothing I'd seen before, or since. I'm convinced it was not a dairy product." I imagine my dad and Alex, sitting around their barracks, joking about what it really was. "It was this terrible, sickly yellow color, and the slices were round—like slices of banana.

"When the bread arrived, the greatest crime you could commit was trying to sneak the biggest piece, the biggest cut. You could get into a lot of trouble if you were trying to be smart about it. The bread was rectangular, not round. Like bread we have now from the store." I imagine a crude-looking loaf of Wonder Bread. My dad jumps up from the table excitedly. "This is a classic!" He enthusiastically brings out a plastic-wrapped loaf of bread. I notice it's potato bread. He sets it on the table.

"The bread was narrower," my dad says. "There was a special knife, and a loaf this size was for seven or eight guys. One guy was the designated cutter, and every one of us gathered around and watched as he took the special knife and dissected that bread like a surgeon." My dad uses his finger as the knife to demonstrate the meticulous slices the "barracks bread-surgeon" would make. "Click, click, click. If he cut a piece that was too small, it was going to be his because he was the last one to pick up. He was going to be left with the last piece. We were really hungry; so nobody wanted the smallest piece. Every crumb counted."

"Did you ever cut the bread?" I ask.

"Once, only once, did I try cutting. My hands were trembling badly. If you cut too many small pieces, you could really get in trouble with the other guys."

"So, that was breakfast." I say. "What about lunch?"

"We had no lunch, but dinner consisted of soup, the same terrible soup every day. It's actually wrong to even call the stuff they served us soup—it was just hot water with a few pale slices of turnip. Sometimes the turnips weren't even cooked all the way through, so they were like little frozen poker chips floating in the soup. We never got any bread with dinner, just that one bowl of soup. To this day the smell of turnips, whether they're fresh or frozen, turns my stomach. I haven't eaten them since.

"On Sundays they gave us a special treat—tomato soup with noodles! Of course, the tomato soup was not made from real tomatoes, and the one or two pathetic noodles that were floating in it were probably not even really made from dough, but it was a welcome change of pace.

"Everyone wanted to be the one who carried the soup because it came with certain advantages. The guys who were served first sometimes got nothing but water. The further you got down in the pot, the higher the chance there'd be a turnip in your serving. The very last guys served were the ones who brought it over. They also got to clean the pot. Sometimes there'd be leftovers stuck to the bottom, an extra noodle or turnip. Unfortunately, I couldn't carry the soup. It was a big, heavy cauldron. I don't know how many gallons it carried, but probably a hundred pounds of liquid. Only the biggest, strongest guys could carry it. I didn't have enough strength in my arms at the time.

"Every now and then, we'd get parcels from the Red Cross. We'd get excited when we'd see the white Red Cross truck pull into camp. Hundreds, sometimes thousands of us would line up against the wires, sometimes waiting for hours as they unloaded the trucks. We would cheer after each package came off the trucks. Those were definitely some of our happiest moments in the camp. We received four or five shipments from the Red Cross when we were at Zeithain, but I only remember receiving one or two at IV B. They contained crackers, chocolate bars, cigarettes, and coffee, and we shared one parcel among several prisoners."

My dad pauses for a moment. "The charity of the Red Cross saved my life more than once," he tells me. "From the trains that got us out of the burning rubble of Warsaw to the rations they sent while we were in the camp, my experience during the war would have been a very different one if it wasn't for the aid we received from them. A big part of the reason I became so involved with teaching swimming for the Red Cross, the reason I did it for three decades after I moved to the United States, was that I wanted to find some way to repay them for giving me so much hope, and for keeping me alive. It's a small thing, but I felt I had to do it." I never realized until this moment why my dad was so dedicated to the Red Cross all those years.

I'm suddenly struck by the vision of my dad in the pool teaching little kids how to swim. He always wore a T-shirt. My whole life I had never given it any thought, but the pieces fall into place and I realize that he was self-conscious about his scars. He didn't want to be asked about them. He tried to keep them covered, his past covered, even when he was in the pool.

"Once the Red Cross parcels arrived," my dad continues, "cigarettes became the unofficial currency among the prisoners of the camp."

"You must have been rich," I say, "with all those cigarettes your friends gave you."

"By the time I arrived at Stalag IV B, Alex and I had already traded all of them for necessities at Zeithain."

"Alex?"

"Yeah," Dad says, "but it was okay, I wasn't much of a smoker at the time, so I was able to save up more cigarettes when I got to Stalag IV B, and ended up using them for a lot of different goods and services during my stay.

"I found out that one of the guys in my barracks had been a student in the Warsaw Underground Polytechnic School during the war. He was brilliant, and very generous with his time. I used to pay him a half cigarette per lesson, and he would teach me and a few of the other guys algebra and calculus. At first we had paper, but when we ran out he would scratch the numbers and formulas into the sand with a stick. Stalag IV B was built on sand. The Germans wanted that so that it would be hard to tunnel out. I used my last ten cigarettes to buy those math classes, and in twenty lessons I had learned quite a bit. Those lessons were of great importance to me, not just because of the valuable math skills I learned. At the camp, with nothing else to do but stand around all day or do work detail, it was very easy for your mind to become dull. Taking those math lessons helped to keep my brain agile even while my body was weakening. In a way, they helped to keep me from wasting away."

I feel a pang of guilt as I think of the disagreements that I had with my father about academics when I was in school. He had always pleaded with me to stay committed to math, especially algebra and calculus. But I was always more interested in liberal arts. Now, thinking about how important math was for him during those long months of internment, I wish I had listened more closely and understood what it had meant to him decades ago.

But there were even more creative ways to keep the mind active in camp by fantasizing about what to eat. "The guys who were most popular were the people who worked in culinary arts. We'd give them a couple of cigarettes to design menus for us. I was friendly with a guy who was assistant cook at a top restaurant before the war. He'd say, 'I remember in 1938 we had a banquet for Italian and French diplomats.' And I'd say, 'What did you serve?' He'd describe every dish. 'We started with homemade pâté as the hors d'oeuvre, and then we had fancy soup. And for the meat—oh, prime beef. We shopped in the best slaughterhouses. We cut our steaks this thick.' " My dad uses his fingers to show the thickness of a college textbook. "That culinary guy was our hero. Every few days he would design a new menu for us.

"A lot of our talk revolved around what we were going to eat when we were free. I decided I was going to go into a restaurant and order every dish they had on the menu."

"Was there something in particular that you always craved or dreamed about, Dad?"

"A steak. A two-inch-thick prime steak, with a pound of fried onions on top. Followed by a couple of glasses of vodka. Thinking about good food always cheered us up.

"Oh, there was another thing that always cheered Alex and me up. Right in the middle of camp there was this super compound, a hut with barbed wire around it. Inside was a very well-dressed Russian woman officer. To this day, I don't know if they were baiting us or what, because some of those guys were without women for five years. Alex and I used to go once a day and stand outside her compound to watch her, just for the fun of it. I'd say to Alex, 'Let's go see the girl.' There was always a crowd of men around her. The comments were unthinkable. If they could have broken through that wire, I don't know what would have happened to that woman. They would have probably kissed her to death. I told Alex if we escaped, we'd take her with us!"

"Were you always thinking about escape?" I ask.

"Yes," he says. "There were many plans being concocted about how we could get out. The worry was also what we would find on the other side of the barbed wire, especially since we'd have to escape at dark."

"Did you have lights in the barracks?" I ask. "Was there electricity?"

"We had one sixty-watt bulb for the whole barracks. You couldn't read unless you were standing directly under the light. And the electricity was notoriously unreliable, especially in our final month there. The power would disappear without warning, sometimes for days at a time. The first time it happened we thought it must have been because the Allies had bombed a power plant and we all took it as a good sign, but eventually it came back on. As time passed it became clear that cutting the electricity was actually a tactical move on the part of the Germans running the camp—whenever American or British planes flew nearby, the Nazis would immediately shut off the power so the pilots wouldn't notice the camp's lights. They were concealing us, keeping us hidden away from the eyes of the Allies."

"Did any of the pilots notice the camp regardless of the electricity?"

"One funny thing I remember is when a German bomber flew over once and dropped a large empty gas tank from the sky and it fell on the side of the outhouse. Boy, did it make a noise. We all looked, and one of our guys was in the outhouse at the time, and was so freaked out that he ran out with his pants down!"

"There was another close call I remember. One evening, as we all lay in our bunks trying to fall asleep, a loud droning sound began to grow over the snoring and coughing that usually dominated the inside of the hut. I sat up in my bunk, straining my ears to make out what it was that I was hearing. The sound slowly grew louder and louder, and guys were all waking up around me.

" 'Planes!' someone said. 'There are planes!'

"The moment those words were uttered, the chatter of a machine gun tore through the air, and a stream of bullets came slicing through the roof of the barracks! Bits of wood from the splintered ceiling were spraying everywhere, and immediately our combat instincts took over—everyone rolled from their bunks and dropped to the floor, even Alex, who was on the top bed and was probably seven feet off the ground. He landed hard next to me and I could see the fear in his eyes. The gunfire stopped and we lay on the floor listening as the droning slowly moved away from the camp. When it was obvious that the planes were moving away, we ran outside to see what had happened. In the pale twilight, we could just make out the shapes of two planes flying away from the camp; a German fighter was being chased by an American, coming out of what must have been a very low dive. We stood there watching until the guards ordered us back inside the barracks.

"I think that what must have happened was the German pilot and the American had been in a dogfight, and the German ran out of either ammunition or courage and tried to make a run for it. He must have known about the POW camp and headed our way, thinking that the American wouldn't dare risk firing on a bunch of prisoners of war. He came toward the camp as quickly as he could and went into an extreme dive, the American in hot pursuit. That American pilot apparently didn't know we were there, because he had no qualms about opening fire over Stalag IV B."

"Did the German plane get shot down?" I ask.

"I don't know. As far as I know, he escaped. That was the only time that planes ever came near the camp, and the only time that the war ever really touched us there.

"We knew the Allies were coming closer, though. We believed the guys in the Dutch barracks near ours were listening to the radio they'd snuck into camp, and we'd hope for any hints about what was happening in the outside world. The Dutch also had a big map of Germany that they updated with military positions every two or three days. The Dutch guys in that barracks were good men. I became close with quite a few of them in my time at Stalag IV B. I would wander over to their barracks often to practice my English and watch as they used the radio to map out the movements of the military fronts on either side of us.

"Directly west of us the Allies were moving forward at a painfully slow pace—and on the east, the Russians were making good time. We couldn't figure out why it was that the Russians seemed to be moving so much more quickly than the Americans and the British. At the time it seemed as if the Americans were having a really bad time of it, like they were losing the war. The German guards liked to make us believe that.

"At one point, a bunch of new American POWs was brought to Stalag IV B. They were in terrible shape, the worst-looking prisoners we'd seen brought in since we'd been there. They had all fought in the Battle of the Bulge, and they were terribly emaciated and run down. Word got around pretty quickly that these guys were in bad condition, so we did the best we could to take care of them. We sent them some cigarettes and a few cans of food from our most recent Red Cross parcel. Everybody gave up what they could."

"Charity?" I ask.

"Gifts," he says. "We delivered cigarettes and meat to them to help them feel better physically and mentally. We hoped it would cheer them up a little bit."

My eyes well with tears at the thought of my dad giving up what very little he had to help the American POWs. I pull a book from my bag and hand it across the table to him. After finding the Stalag IV B prisoner tag among my dad's things, I had found a book, *Stalag IV-B: An Ex-POW Tells His Story*, and gotten in touch with the writer, Reverend A. W. Ishee. The book is a harrowing story of terror, heartbreak, and physical and mental abuse as he managed to survive the camp after being one of twenty-five thousand U.S. soldiers captured during the Battle of the Bulge, the single bloodiest battle that American forces experienced in World War II. "I've spoken to him," I tell my dad.

"You have?" he asks. "What did he say about the camp?"

"It was a very emotional conversation," I say. "One of the most moving conversations I've ever had. As soon as I mentioned Stalag IV B, he choked up."

"Where is he now?" my dad asks.

"He's eighty-five years old and a pastor in Laurel, Mississippi. He believes his faith got him through the experience and said that in his darkest hour he made a vow to God that if he got out alive, he'd devote his life to the church and his faith." My voice breaks a bit, remembering Reverend Ishee's voice quavering. "Dad, he said that when he arrived at the camp he was filthy, covered in blood, and had lice all over him."

"When we saw the condition of those American soldiers entering Stalag IV B," my dad says, "we were a little worried that we were going to lose the war." I think now of my dad, emaciated and hungry, donating his food to help the battered arrivals. You have to look pretty awful for starving POWs to say you look bad. I didn't tell my dad, but I said a prayer that the food he gave up had helped Reverend Ishee.

"He described the camp as much more brutal than you have," I tell my dad.

"He did?" my dad asks.

"He said the Nazi guards used to beat them with rifle butts and that he was punched and hit often. He also said that it wasn't just hunger, that they were actually starving to death. He told me they were stripping bark off the trees and eating sap, leaves, anything, just to survive."

My dad nods his head. "All of the Polish prisoners were thin and weak at that point. I was down to skin and bones. Our diet and work schedule didn't keep us very healthy."

"Reverend Ishee also said he wasn't able to wash for so long that his underwear rotted off him," I say. I then pull out my notes from Reverend Ishee and read to my dad. "He said, 'We were just a bunch of kids who went over and learned how to fight when we got there. We felt like we were fighting for our own country, but also we felt like we were fighting for the whole world. Some said they weren't going to make it, but I said I'm not going to give up. I'm going home. I had my mother . . . ' " It was at that moment in the conversation that Reverend Ishee trailed off and stopped speaking for a while. His silence spoke volumes. I look up at my father. He, too, is silent. His chin quivers. I continue. "Reverend Ishee said, 'We didn't know if we were going to win the war or not. We just prayed to God to have mercy.' "

"We were all confused about why it seemed to be taking the Allies so long to reach us," my dad says. "With only the sporadic communiqués from the Dutch radio to go on, we had no idea that the Americans had made a deal to stop their advance at the Elbe River, and to leave the liberation of the area to the Russians. As time passed and the Russians moved closer and closer, the Germans became more and more noticeably concerned about the war's end. We didn't know what would happen when the Russians arrived, but we were all scared of that horrifying thought. All I knew was that I had to get out of that camp, and that I wanted to find a way to get to the American front. I knew that if I was going to do it, I would have to do it soon."

16

THE GREATEST ESCAPE

$\mathcal{M}$y dad's resilience amazes me. Here he was starving to death, with healing shrapnel wounds, wearing the same suit he'd had on for six months, and yet he's not complaining. He was managing to study English and calculus, and to keep his will alive in a German prisoner of war camp. "Dad," I tell him, "the way you're talking so matter-of-factly about this, you act like it was a vacation for you. Most humans could never endure that."

"Life in Stalag IV B was certainly difficult," he says, "but through-out our time there, I had hope. I knew the Americans would come through. I believed that we were only passing through; that we were temporary tenants of the camp. We were all just occupying space, killing time in a sort of stopover, waiting for our chance to escape."

When I covered the war over Kosovo for Fox News, I reported on three American soldiers who were taken prisoner near Belgrade. It was the first time I experienced bombing as a journalist, hearing the thunderous blasts, the air-raid sirens. I witnessed the condition of the POWs and saw how disoriented they were after just a few weeks. My dad was being held for months by the cruelest army on earth. "But, Dad," I say, "you sound so positive about something that was so bad."

"Rita," he says, "in times of trouble you have to remain positive. If you don't keep your spirits up, your mind occupied, and do what you can to make sure your body remains strong, you become weak. And remember, the weak die first. Alex and I tried to keep each other going, thinking about the future." I momentarily see my smiling high school senior picture with an optimistic verse above from Fleetwood Mac's well-known hit song "Don't Stop." In my family, we were taught to never look back.

"Dad, what do you think was the hardest thing about being a captive?"

"I suppose the most difficult part of the episode, besides lack of food, was the isolation. Not knowing what was going on in the rest of the world. Not knowing what my parents were doing. Not being fully aware of anything besides what was happening within the barbed wire of Stalag IV B. One of the biggest problems for us was the sheer boredom. It was easy for life in the camp to boil down to seemingly endless cycles of routines—go to sleep, wake up, line up, go to work, go to sleep. Rinse, repeat. Finding a way to break up the monotony was crucial. We had to find something to do, like the games we'd play, and my studies. Also, I always jumped at the chance to volunteer for the work crews."

"But why would you volunteer to work for the Nazis?" I ask him.

"It was a good way to get exercise—a lot of the guys who spent their days standing and sitting in the barracks and yard became not just thin but very weak. I wanted to build my strength, not lose it. I often even accepted bribes to take other prisoners' shifts."

"The guards would let you do that?" I ask.

"The guys who ran the work crews weren't interested in anything besides head count. They weren't going to go to the extra effort of checking POW numbers. As long as they ended up with the number of prisoners they'd been told to round up, they were satisfied. It was easy for a lazy prisoner to slip a friend a cigarette or two in exchange for shift coverage. So, I'd get cigarettes that I could trade for food and useful exercise—sometimes even outside the camp gates."

"Did you see other people when you left?"

"No," he says, "Stalag IV B was isolated, this little bubble removed from the rest of the world. The only time we'd see new people would be when a fresh crop of prisoners arrived. They'd bring with them bits of information about what was going on in the rest of Europe, and in the rest of the world, but for the most part we were a society unto ourselves, until one fateful day in February when the war nearly came to our doorstep."

"What happened?" I ask.

"The bombing of Dresden."

On February 13, 14, and 15, 1945, the British Royal Air Force and the United States Army Air Forces conducted an all-out aerial bombing of the German city of Dresden. The Allies' firebombs utterly destroyed the city. The event is one of the most controversial attacks in the modern history of war—the bombing may have been a smart strategic choice, but it also resulted in the deaths of up to 135,000 civilians, both Germans and others.

"How close were you to Dresden?" I ask.

"Dresden was not very far at all from Muhlberg, where Stalag

IV B was located. The night the bombing began the British planes were the first to arrive, followed by those of the U.S. Army Air Forces. We were close enough to know they hit the city four different times, and it was obvious how much damage they did."

"How?" I ask.

"It was like a manmade hurricane, sucking the oxygen out of the air. The glow from the fire was so bright you could have read by the light of it."

"Did you know what was happening?" I ask.

"We were pretty sure."

"How did the prisoners react?" I ask. "What did they say?"

"Oh, at first we were overjoyed, it was a celebration. The flames were shooting so high it was like looking at the Northern Lights. The entire sky was lit. The first night we were all dancing in our barracks, cheering. 'Burn, baby, burn!' everyone was shouting. 'Look at those Krauts getting it!'

"At first all we could think about was how much of a victory it was for the Allies. But our happiness was short-lived. There were a lot of prisoners of war in the hospitals there when the bombing began. A few days after the bombing we found out that a lot of really badly wounded and sick soldiers from Stalag IV B had been brought to Dresden just a few days before. That took the wind out of our sails a bit. We all felt guilty about cheering on the bombing when so many of our buddies, our comrades in arms, had been killed also."

I find out later that the acclaimed author Kurt Vonnegut, a young army private from Indianapolis, was in Dresden for the bombing, having just been sent there from Stalag IV B. He had been captured in the early days of the Battle of the Bulge and brought to Stalag IV B, but on January 12, the same day my dad was stripped, deloused, and checked in, Vonnegut was checked out along with about 150 others and sent to Dresden for work detail. Vonnegut's famous novel *Slaughterhouse-Five* was based on his experiences as a shell-shocked POW in Germany during the firebombing of Dresden. I spoke to Mark Vonnegut, the sixty-two-year-old son of Kurt Vonnegut, about his dad's reflections on Stalag IV B. "The irony of it all is that he was glad to be sent to Dresden because he thought the Allies wouldn't bomb it, because there was no major industry or factories there at the time. Dad thought he was lucky when he got to leave Stalag IV B." He survived the bombing only because they were housed in an underground meat locker, slaughterhouse number five.

"Dresden was, however, a signal to all the guards that the tide was turning, that the war was not going well for the Germans," my father explains.

"Did any of them get violent?"

"No guard ever laid a hand on me in the camp," he says. "But I do remember seeing guards lose their cool. For instance, there was this smart aleck, a Polish guy in our barracks. He must have been the youngest guy, about seventeen years old. One day he started teasing this one-armed guard. Really making fun of him. The guard walked over and slapped that kid hard on the face, so hard it knocked the young guy to the ground. When the guard left, our senior sergeant turned to the guy and said, 'Serves you right.'

"In fact, as the days dragged on and the Russians and Allies closed in on Germany from either side, I think the guards must have known that their time was running out."

"Around the end of March, there was one guard whom I remember actually having some unusual conversations with. I met him taking my usual morning walk inside the grounds. He said, 'Hey soldier, where are you from?' So, I told him. And he said, 'Oh, Warsaw Uprising! You were very brave. You really gave us a hard time.' I think he was trying to butter me up. And I congratulated him, too. I said, 'We fought like you were fighting. You did great, too, until the Russians turned around and started chasing you west.' He asked me, 'What do you think is going to happen now?' I said, 'The Russians will take half of Germany. The Americans and the British will take the other half. And you guys are all going to be in prison. You're going to be in their hands. You'll be sent to Siberia to dig in the coal mines.' Everyone knew how rough the Russians were on German prisoners. Over one hundred thousand German prisoners were taken at Stalingrad, and eventually only five thousand came back. The mortality rate under the Russians was high. I said to him, 'I only hope you end up west, especially in American hands.'

"I knew it was near the end when one afternoon a guard showed up at our barracks to select workers for a new project. 'All right,' the guy said, 'I need a team to build trenches outside the camp today.' He began pointing to the prisoners who were loafing around the bar-racks, assigning us one by one to the work group. When he finished I hadn't been chosen, so I tapped another prisoner on the shoulder.

" 'Hey,' I told the guy, 'I'll take your shift for five cigarettes.' That was the going rate for a day's work.

" 'Done,' the guy said, slipping me the smokes. I thanked him and went to find Alex. He hadn't been picked either, but liked working less than I did. 'Listen,' I told him, 'there's a work crew leaving in a few minutes to go outside the camp and dig trenches. And you and I both know the only reason they'd need trenches outside this camp.'

" 'Antitank trenches,' he said.

"I nodded. 'The Russians must be getting really close,' I said. Of course I didn't like the idea of being 'liberated' by the Russian army, but the fact that the Germans were nervous enough to have us dig-ging trenches around Stalag IV B seemed like a good sign. I wanted to do everything I could to make things difficult for the Nazis, to get us as close to escape as possible. 'We don't want to prevent the Russians from finishing the war more quickly,' I said to Alex. 'Let's go.' "

"So, what did the two of you do?" I ask my dad.

"Well," he says, "Alex and I went with that work crew. They marched us out of the camp a few hundred yards and handed everyone shovels. When we arrived we saw that the trench-digging project had become a twenty-four-hour operation. There was another shift of prisoners leaving the work site just as we were arriving. They all looked exhausted."

"Working around the clock?"

"Well, you have to remember that it was March. It was still very cold in Muhlberg, and the topsoil was frozen solid. The earth below wasn't frozen, so they had teams of prisoners digging constantly to keep it from freezing. When we arrived we were divided into two work crews, one to go down into the hole and dig, the other to stay up top and move all the dirt away from the trench. When we were divided up, Alex was left on the surface, and I was sent into the trench.

"Before I climbed down, I took him aside. 'Listen,' I said. 'Here's what we're going to do: stand above me while I shovel, and for every load of dirt that I throw out to you, pick it up and throw it back in. That way we'll get the exercise, we'll keep warm, and we can throw a wrench into the works for the Germans.' He nodded, and we set to work. We were there for five or six hours—and the guards in charge of supervising us were not paying particularly close attention to what was going on. So we kept up the illusion of working hard, when really we were just treading water, so to speak.

"One day two or three German officers in uniform even came by our barracks and tried to recruit some of us to be parachuted for the

German army into Poland to fight the Russians who were there. The Germans said, 'This is a chance for freedom.' But not one of us volunteered. There was no way I'd fight for the Germans. Or survive in Russian-occupied territory. That was no road to freedom."

"So, how did you get out of Stalag IV B?" I ask.

My father smiles. "Well," he says, "we escaped."

"How? When?" I ask.

"We just waited until it seemed like the time was right, and we took a risk and went for it. We knew that the Russians had reached a point that was very, very close to Stalag IV B. The German guards knew it, too—they were noticeably nervous. They were more concerned about themselves and their own futures. But they still made it clear we had to respect their rifles!"

"So, did you know that the time to escape was approaching?"

"Well, remember we got those sporadic reports from the Dutch guys with the radio. There wasn't any organized escape plan until the very end, but I knew something was going to happen soon. We would need all of our strength to escape, because we were going to have to leave the camp on foot and walk through the countryside to the Allied front. We knew it was many miles. By that point the only thing of value that I really had was my blue suit—so I sold it for a big loaf of dark brown bread. I shared the bread with Alex and two other guys from our barracks, and it was like a feast. We were heroes for the day with that blue suit. Remember, the only bread we ever got in the camp was that terrible sawdust bread the Germans gave us. So we cut that dark loaf up and devoured it, and it made all of us feel energized. We were ready for whatever was coming."

"Wait," I say. "What did you have to wear? Wasn't the blue suit all you had?"

"The Germans had a pile of leftover uniforms from World War I," he says. "They had holes and patches all over them. I looked like a clown, but I didn't care. For a few days we were full."

"Who made the decision to escape when you finally did?" I ask my father.

"Well," he says, "it wasn't really something that everyone agreed on. It was a progression of events. As we moved into April things continued to deteriorate at the camp. The Red Cross deliveries had stopped coming because of the nonstop bombing, and that meant many of us were really beginning to starve. Sometime around the middle of April the power had gone out again. We weren't sure this time if it was a strategic move by the Germans to avoid detection or if it was the Russians—we'd heard that they had started hitting power stations, and it could have been that they cut out the electricity. Either way, the camp was in darkness, no lights, and no generators. Pitch black.

"A senior sergeant from our barracks came in and spoke to all of us. He said, 'Several of us have come to the conclusion that the Russians are approaching us pretty fast. Tonight I think we're going to make a break for it—whoever wants to go should be ready.'

"And it was clear that it was not something that the entire camp was going to be taking part in. Our sergeant knew about it, and maybe the leader of the Polish prisoners was in on it, as well. We figured there were several points in the fencing that had rusted through—it would be easy to cut through and escape that way."

"Were there still guards in the towers? Wouldn't they have seen you trying to escape?"

"There were still guards in the towers. It was still risky—the possibility existed that we would have the bad luck to be caught by one of the guards, but it was a risk that we were willing to take. It was obvious to me that our time had come, that if we were going to get out of Stalag IV B we were going to have to do it now."

"When did it happen?"

"It was around ten o'clock at night. Nothing moved, and there was very little sound except the murmur of voices from inside the barracks. The sergeant who had come to tell us about the escape plan said, 'All right. Who wants to go? If you want to be a part of this plan, raise your hand.' I immediately raised mine. Alex was sitting next to me on my bunk, and he kept his hands folded in his lap.

" 'What are you doing?' I asked him. 'This is our chance!'

" 'I'm not going,' he said.

" 'Why not?' I asked him.

" 'Richard,' he said, 'I have risked too much in my life to take the chance. First of all, we have no idea if the guards are going to shoot or not. We don't even know where they're all posted! What are we going to do if we get to the fence and the guards open fire?'

" 'It's a risk we're going to have to take if we want to get out of here,' I said.

" 'That's the least of our worries,' Alex continued. 'Even if we manage to get out of the camp without being shot, how are we going to get to the American front? We have no idea what's between us and them. We would have to walk at least twenty or thirty miles, and we could run into some German defense! They'd just shoot us on sight! No questions asked. And even if we don't run into the army, we're going to be moving on foot through the German countryside. The locals aren't going to exactly be friendly, either. We'll have farmers sniping at us from every barn!'

"I had told Alex a story of my visit to a Polish fortuneteller in Warsaw during the occupation. A friend and I had gone to this small apartment with lots of curtains and a crystal ball. The guy was very unusual looking, with a long beard. He read my palm and gave me a piercing look. 'You're going to be exposed to a great danger,' he told me. 'But it will not destroy you. You'll be running ahead of it. You'll always be traveling west. Go ever west.' At the time I remember laughing at how bad that idea was, since west at that point was Germany. But as I sat there in our barracks, trying to convince Alex to escape with me, the old fortuneteller's prediction came rushing back to me. I told Alex, 'Don't despair. Our fortune is to go west. Always west. That's where our destiny is. We are not cut out to be slaves under Germans or Soviets. If the Soviets come, we'll have to go east to Russia. And we don't want to go there.

" 'We've got to go now, Alex,' I told him, 'this is our only chance. If we go west, toward American troops, we'll be free men. Once we're in American hands, we definitely will never be abused. We'll be taken care of. We've got to go west, and tonight is as good a night as any.' That persuaded him. He slapped me on the shoulder and said, 'Yes, we're going.' I think he knew just as well as I did what would happen to Polish prisoners when the Soviets arrived."

"What?" I ask.

"Like the Germans, the Russians were not bothering to honor the terms of the international laws of war, and they certainly weren't very fond of us Poles. We figured that if we were 'liberated' by the Russians we would probably end up being sent to Siberia to the coal mines, or worse, shot on sight."

"How many people decided to go?" I ask him.

"I'm not sure, exactly. I was told by a Polish officer later on that approximately a thousand of us escaped Stalag IV B around that time. There were maybe a hundred of us in our immediate group—mostly Poles, but also a few Russian POWs who didn't want to end up back under the Soviets."

"The Russians didn't want to be liberated by their own people?" I ask.

"The Soviets did not admire their own men who were taken captive. The Russian POWs would have been 'liberated' right back to Siberia," he replies.

"A thousand of you?" I ask.

"Yes," he replies. "After I saw the movie *The Great Escape*, in which seventy-six men escaping from one camp was considered a phenomenal number, I said, 'Well, ours has to be the greatest escape ever.'"

The Great Escape was one of my dad's favorite movies while I was growing up. It's the story of an escape that took place east of my dad's camp, near Zagan, at Stalag Luft III, in March 1944, about a year before my dad's successful attempt. Seventy-six men, including some Poles, crawled through a tunnel they made and escaped, but only three managed to achieve freedom. The remaining seventy-three were all recaptured by German units, and fifty of them were lined up and executed by the Gestapo on the orders of Hitler himself. Even though my dad had seen the film many times before and knew the tragic end, he'd still cheer them on, talking to the TV and practically jumping out of the sofa as they dug their ingenious tunnel and Steve McQueen jumped on a stolen Nazi motorcycle.

"So, how did you actually escape, Dad?" I ask.

"We all packed up fast—after all, we had very little to take. The guys who weren't going kept telling us, 'Don't be stupid! Don't leave the camp! You're safe here, don't go outside. You'll get a bullet in the head for sure.' But once we had decided to go, we were determined, and we moved as quickly and quietly as we could from the barracks to the edge of the camp. I believe somebody cut a hole in the wire fence with a homemade pair of cutters, and we all slipped through as stealthily as possible."

"What about the guards?" I ask. "Where were the guards?"

"They were there, but remember, the electricity was out. It was pitch black. We just had to be cautious."

"They could have shot you from the guard towers!" I say.

"They would have been shooting blindly in the dark," he replies. "It was a chance I had to take. In the end there was no alarm sounded, there was no shooting, just us running into the darkness."

"How'd you know which way to go?"

"We followed the sergeant. We sure weren't going to head off in our own direction into unknown enemy territory, and the sergeant seemed like he knew what he was doing and which direction to head. We knew that we were supposed to head west. The map that the Dutchmen had kept told us that the Americans were camped on the other side of the Elbe River. Freedom was waiting for us somewhere on the other side of that river—all we had to do was get there."

17

GOD BLESS AMERICA

*I*t was April 20, Hitler's birthday, and a ragtag bunch of skinny Poles were giving him a present. They were on the outside, gunning for American lines, praying they were headed in the right direction, and worrying what every turn might bring. Being on the outside was now more dangerous than being inside.

"Emotions were very high," my dad says. "As we escaped, people kept telling us, 'Don't leave!' That didn't make it any easier, but suddenly, after months behind barbed wire, we had cut loose and stepped out into the world to make our own future."

"What happened when you got outside the fence?" I ask.

"We split into small groups. Again, I think my group was no more than a hundred to start. And we just walked into the unknown to try to get as far away from Stalag IV B as quickly as we could. That first night we kept moving through the forest, heading southwest, following the sergeant. It was nerve-wracking, moving through those woods at night. It was a dense forest. Even though we had the light of the moon to navigate by, it was still difficult. But just knowing that we were free was an incredible feeling."

I imagine them jumping at moving shadows, freezing at every snap of a twig. "What happened next?" I ask. "How'd you make your way through the German countryside without getting shot?"

"For the first day or so we spent our time hiding in the woods. There were a few guys with us who spoke fluent German, and they snuck into a village we'd passed in the night to try to gather information on what was going on around us. The sergeant wanted to know as much as possible about the military positions in the area, so we wouldn't be caught off guard or accidentally run into a detachment of German troops. That would have put our escape to an end pretty quickly."

"Wasn't it dangerous for Polish prisoners to talk to anyone, even German civilians?" I ask my dad. "I thought you were all concerned about Germans taking up arms against you."

"Well, Rita," he answers, "it was a risk we had to take. We were willing to risk a fight against some farmers if it meant that we could avoid running into actual soldiers later on.

"The German-speaking scouts left early in the morning of the first day, just as the sun was rising. They weren't gone long, and when they returned they were in incredibly good spirits."

"What did they find?" I ask.

"Two things. First off, they dumped on the ground a lot of potatoes that we cooked on a fire in the woods. And they also found out some good news. When the scouts got to the village, they were of course worried about the reaction they'd get. They approached slowly and carefully, doing their best not to arouse any suspicion. But when they arrived they found the entire town draped in white flags of surrender! The villagers had hung all of their white bedsheets out of their windows—they were capitulating without question! Even the mailman had taken off his uniform!" My dad laughs, and I wonder, for a moment, if he's serious. "So there was no fortification whatsoever in the area—no troops, no tanks, no resistance at all."

"That's lucky," I say. "So it was smooth sailing all the way to the American front?"

"Not quite," he answers. "That particular village was safe for us, but there were still pockets of German soldiers in the area that posed a real threat. The scouts also had news that there was still supposedly a large SS presence not too far north of us. The townspeople knew the Nazis were there and were determined to fight until the last man. The townspeople said that if we had the misfortune of stumbling into them, they wouldn't think twice about turning machine guns on us, mowing us down, no questions asked. So north was definitely out.

"There was one other thing that made our trip difficult. We were on the opposite side of the Elbe River from the Americans. The sergeant knew of a bridge that spanned the river that would be easy for us to cross, but the people in the village told the scouts that the bridge we'd planned on taking was under Nazi control. There was, however, a temporary pontoon bridge farther south that was more or less unguarded. That was the one we planned to take."

"Where did you stay at night while you were making your way to the river?" I ask. "Did you all just sleep in the woods?"

"No," he says. "We all slept in barns, and I finally talked to some of the other Poles that had escaped with us. I met a lot of guys that I hadn't gotten to know in the camp. I would say that 90 percent or more of us were former Resistance fighters who had fought in the Warsaw Uprising. Most of the guys were young, around my age, but there were quite a few old-timers as well. Some of the guys had been caught by the Nazis in 1939. That means that they spent *five years* in the prison camp. Five years! I was in Zeithain and Stalag IV B for six months and it felt like an eternity to me. I couldn't believe that these men had survived for that long."

"What about the Russians that had escaped the camp with you? Did you talk with them at all?" I ask.

"Actually, the Russians had all peeled off and left us by that point. I think they must have felt that it was unsafe for them to stick with Poles, so as soon as they could they just slipped away. Who knows what their plan was or where they went.

"When we got to the pontoon bridge there was one problem," he says, with a mischievous grin.

"What was that, Dad?"

"It was guarded by one lone Gestapo guy," he says. "With a rifle. But of course there were about a hundred of us, so we just ignored him completely." He starts laughing. I laugh with him. "We ignored him! And we just marched across this bridge, and we whispered to one another, 'If that guy makes a move, it will be the last move he ever makes.'" He laughs again, heartily. "I mean, can you imagine, one hundred against one? All he could do would be to shoot four or five of us."

"Then where did you go?" I ask.

"After we crossed the river, we stayed in some little village somewhere until it got a little darker."

"So, how long did it take you to actually reach the American front?" I ask.

"The entire trip took about two and a half days. We only had a vague idea of what direction we should be heading in, so we just had to follow the sergeant, depend on the kindness of villagers and what they were telling us, and hope for the best. We were told that the American troops were near a town called Grimma, and we figured that if the Americans were anywhere nearby, that's probably where we should be. So we did our best to get our bearings and set off in the direction of Grimma.

"On the last day, we walked all morning through the countryside. It was nerve-wracking, knowing that we were traveling through what was essentially enemy territory. I couldn't stop thinking about what we would do if the intelligence that the villagers had given us was wrong, if we were to round a corner and suddenly be faced with a detachment of SS troops. I tried to keep these thoughts out of my mind and just focus on the goal ahead of us.

"After a few hours of walking my fears were suddenly realized. We came upon a small town there in the countryside, a village that was little more than a few shops clustered around a square. We decided to go into the town, hoping we'd be able to find out how close the American front was. As we approached the square, my blood froze in my veins. Passing through the square, just yards away from us, was a squad of SS officers, marching a group of prisoners at gunpoint. Without even thinking we all took cover, hiding in doorways and behind trashcans, wherever we could to stay out of sight. I was so frightened, and so angry. I couldn't believe that we had come this far, gotten so close to freedom, only to have our escape cut short this close to our goal. A part of me wanted to jump those Nazis right there, but I couldn't risk their opening fire on our group. All we could do was sit there and wait for them to make their way across the square, prodding those poor prisoners along. I don't think any of us breathed the entire time."

"So, what happened?" I ask, transfixed by the suspense.

"We were lucky," he says. "Or those Germans weren't paying attention. Either way, they eventually passed us by, and when we were sure they had gone we left that town as quickly as we could and headed back into the countryside toward our goal. I felt like I'd really dodged a bullet.

"After a few more hours of walking, the air was suddenly filled with the whine of plane engines. We all glanced skyward, trying to spot the source of the sound. Remember, up until that point the sound of planes always meant dive-bombers. If you heard those propellers approaching, you knew to find cover quickly. I'd already had my own near-death experience with German planes when that building collapsed on me, so I didn't even think before I acted. The moment I saw the plane approaching from the west, Alex and I made a beautiful, synchronized dive into the ditch at the edge of the road. Without a word, everyone scattered.

"We all lay there in the ditches beside the road, some of us praying, all of us holding our breath to see what would happen next. I watched the plane as it approached. It didn't look like a bomber, but that was no guarantee of safety. The German pilots had a nasty habit of circling around enemy infantry and when they spotted them, broadcasting their coordinates back to base. If your location was reported you knew that it wouldn't be too long before bombers arrived. We had no idea what to expect."

"Did the pilot see you?" I ask.

"He did," my dad answers. "As the plane approached again I saw the sun glint off a window opening in the canopy, and the pilot dropped something out. It landed in the road ahead of us. 'Grenade!' somebody shouted, and we all dove again into the ditches and braced ourselves for the explosion. The plane buzzed over our heads and as it passed one of the guys noticed a star painted on the underside of its wing. 'Nazi planes don't have stars,' I thought to myself. After a few seconds there was no explosion, and the sergeant said, 'That's not a grenade!' We all stood up and dusted ourselves off, trying to make out what it was that had been tossed out of the plane."

"What was it?" I ask.

He smiles. "It was a chocolate bar," he says. "A chocolate bar with a note tied to it with red ribbon. The sergeant untied the ribbon and opened the note, but the whole thing was written in English. It had been an American plane! 'Quickly,' the sergeant shouted to us as we gathered around him, 'I need someone who can read English.' Stalag IV B had its fair share of American and British prisoners of war, and a few of us had picked up some English. One of the Poles came forward and read the note."

"What did it say?"

It said 'Welcome. You are safe to walk now during daytime. There are no troops between you and our lines. You have fifteen miles to walk and you're free.' He gets visibly choked up. He struggles to hold back his tears. "There's no way to describe the happiness I felt. Everyone was overjoyed. Right there in the dusty road we all started shouting and dancing. We were fifteen miles from freedom. It seemed almost impossible that we had come this far. I hugged Alex and said to him, 'We are free men! The whole world is open to us.' He nodded. 'I'm almost twenty years old, Alex,' I said to him. 'There's no limit to what we can accomplish. We're finally going to be free men. We can live; we can travel! We can go to England or Canada or . . . America.' "

"How long did it take to reach the American front after you got the message?" I ask.

"Well, as soon as we got the note we were all energized in a way we hadn't been before. We set out westward double-time, almost running along the road. We knew we were close, and we were trying to get there as quickly as we could. It was early evening when we finally reached a small river near Grimma."

"How far had you traveled at that point?"

"The sergeant said he thought we had traveled close to fifty miles. But when we got to that river and we could see the Americans camped on the other side, the memory of our long walk melted away as if it were a pleasant stroll. The Americans were all lined up on the other side and when they saw us arrive they all started cheering. 'Come on, guys!' they were shouting. 'Come on!'

"Immediately we splashed into the icy cold water. The river wasn't terribly deep, shallow enough to cross on foot, but we soon discovered that it had a very strong current, and the slippery rocks on the bottom were treacherous. I watched as one of our comrades tried to trudge across, carrying his suitcase over his head. He slipped on a rock and almost fell under water. We were all skin and bones, so we could be washed away pretty easily."

"Do you have any idea how much you weighed?" I ask.

"I believe I weighed around ninety pounds, not a lot considering I'm almost six feet tall."

"So, how then did you get across?"

"It was difficult to think clearly with our goal so close, but I knew that we had one more task to perform before we were free. I said to myself, 'I've waited almost six years to be liberated, I'm going to find a better way to do this.' I turned to Alex and said, 'We don't want to get swept away by this river. Let's find a safer way over.'

"We walked upstream a bit. I wasn't sure what I was looking for, but I knew there had to be an easier way to go about getting over the final hurdle between us and freedom. After just a little looking I found it: an old rowboat, just a short distance upstream. Alex and I pulled it along the shoreline, back to where our buddies were, and then we rowed across to the safety of the American line. Of the one hundred men in my original group, only sixty had made it this far."

"What was it like when you finally made it to the other side?" I ask.

"It was glorious. The Americans greeted us with open arms. We were all embracing, shaking hands, and we were saying 'Thank you, thank you for saving us!' They told us not to worry, that they were going to take care of us."

"And did they?"

"They did! They gave us so much food—more food than I'd seen in months and months. Chocolates, potatoes, milk, all of the things we had difficulty finding during the Uprising, all of the things we couldn't even dream of getting while we were in Stalag IV B. More than anything, I wanted to just stuff myself full of all this amazing food, but an old-timer from our group stopped me. 'Be careful with all of that food,' he said. 'Your system isn't up to it yet. Too much rich food and you'll get diarrhea like you've never seen in your life.' So I had to be very careful and stay disciplined—for the first few days I had to keep it simple."

"So, you had finally reached freedom. What were you thinking?" I ask him, feeling as if I've crossed some sort of finish line myself.

"For us, the war was essentially over," he answers. "The whole world was awaiting me." He smiles. "I was ready to start the life I always knew I should have."

"So, then what?" I ask him. "Why not go back to Poland?"

"No way," he says. "Those who went back to Poland after the war were retaliated against by the Russians, interrogated, or simply put up against a wall and shot. Russians hated Resistance fighters. Poles first were enemies of the Germans, but the Russians hated them, too. We got it from both sides. Poles were truly in a desperate situation."

"So, where did you go from there?" I ask. "How'd you decide what to do, where to go?"

"Well, after the initial joy of reaching freedom I was suddenly struck with the realization that all I had left in the world was the brown suede shoes I'd worn since Warsaw. They'd survived the Uprising, the sewer, and the camps. I finally took them off and proudly put on a pair of U.S. Army boots. Alex and I decided the smartest thing we could do was stick with the Americans now. We were in Germany for some time, then Austria, and finally in Italy."

"Italy?" I ask him. "What did you do there?"

"There were special Polish corps serving alongside the Allies at that point, and before too long we had enlisted with the famous Polish II Corps of the British army based in Italy." I'm amazed that my father wanted to join a fighting force again after all he had endured. "I decided I wanted to go to officer candidate school. I got promoted from corporal to the equivalent of sergeant, and the famous General Anders came over to me and shook my hand personally because I had something similar to three Purple Hearts. I was the only one with three, one for each injury. Most of the Poles who earned three Purple Hearts were dead."

"Did you see any more action?" I ask him.

"Not really," he answers. "Mostly they just moved us around. We stayed in Italy for almost a year. The British army eventually decided that most of the Polish soldiers stationed in Italy were to be transferred back to England. We landed in Glasgow, Scotland. Later, we were loaded onto a train and ended up near Gloucestershire, east of Bristol and west of London. This basically marked the end of our military careers—there wasn't much for soldiers to do in England.

We chased girls and took menial jobs, anything that would pay so we could enjoy life a little. I felt as if I was trying to make up for all of the years of youth I'd lost during the occupation.

"But eventually I'd had my fill of that life. I began studying English, sharpening my language skills, and eventually a notice came saying that the army was opening a mechanical trade school. If I passed the exam, I would be admitted. I studied and took the test and got in! I told Alex, 'I'm going to school. They're going to pay me a sergeant's salary, and they'll feed me and educate me. You should come, too!' Alex wasn't interested. Eventually he worked at a rubber factory and then in building construction in Bristol. I went to trade school, and when I finished there I took the entrance exam for the University of London. I passed and moved away. I graduated in 1954 as a civil engineer, and of course it was in London that I met your mother."

"Why did you pick America?" I ask.

"America is the land of opportunity," he says. "America means freedom to live and function any way you want. You become whatever you want to be in America if you work hard. My Polish cousins sent me a pamphlet that forty-one thousand new miles of superhighway were being built in the United States. So, we came to America on the *Queen Mary*. It took about a week back then. We left England in December 1955, and we landed in New York Harbor on January 3, 1956. I had five job offers my first week in the United States alone, and made four hundred dollars a month my first year. Soon after that we moved near Niagara Falls, and later to Brooklyn where you were born. And you know the rest of the story."

"So, what happened to Alex?"

"We drifted apart as sometimes friends do," he says. "We had different ideas about what we wanted life to be. We chose different paths. He got married to a nice English girl and settled in Bristol. And I met a nice Danish girl and came to America."

"But he was your best friend," I say.

"Friends stick together in bad times and often fall apart in good times." He sighs. "I wrote him a letter once, and he never answered. Or maybe it was vice versa."

"Do you think he's still alive?" I ask.

"I suppose that depends on what kind of life he's led," my father answers. "Here, let me show you a picture I have of him in my album." Dad pulls an old photo album out from a stack of books and papers. He puts it on the table and opens it. As he flips through the book, I notice there are photos missing.

"What were those photos?" I ask.

"Photos of your mother that she wanted back."

I sit quietly as the pages of my dad's life go flitting by. There are numerous empty spots where my mother used to be. "Here!" he says. "Alex!" My dad kisses his forefinger and touches the photo gently with it. "I love you, man!"

I look at the photo of a cute young man with wavy light brown hair, a boyish face, and a badly burned chin. Alex Chelmicki, my dad's best friend. "Dad, what would you do if you saw him now?" I ask.

"Oh, now I would embrace him, kiss him," my dad says, his eyes welling with tears. "Oh, if I met him again, I'd be so happy, so emotional. I'm sure I wouldn't be able to talk for five minutes."

I had a new mission.

18

FILLING IN THE BLANKS

I left my dad's house that week feeling positively charged. For the first time in my life I felt as if I was on the road to understanding, finally able to let go of a lifetime of unanswered questions. I felt empowered by so much new information, as if I had landed another exclusive news story. But there were still pieces of the puzzle to be filled in. Perhaps the most important thing I've learned from my journalism experience is that there is always one more thing to find out. On the train back to New York City, I kicked into high gear. I made a list of the names, dates, and locations my dad had mentioned, leads I could chase that could help add to his account.

I checked phone numbers and databases worldwide. I ordered history books. I stayed up all hours of the day and night surfing the net. I researched all of the places that might have records of events surrounding the Uprising and the POW camps in Germany. I called the Polish consulate in New York, the museums in Warsaw, and the now-decommissioned German POW camps, and then I made a serendipitous visit to an event at the Waldorf for the Kosciuszko Foundation, an organization dedicated to promoting Polish-American culture and education. I met several members of the Polish Army Veterans Association of America. I told them my father was in the Resistance and their eyes lit up. They told me I had to stop by their New York City headquarters "right away" and visit their museum.

Soon after, I joined them for an afternoon at their offices near Union Square. The roomful of elderly Polish veterans of World War II greeted me with open arms and said they were excited to learn about my father's past and my own personal interest in history. At one point in the conversation, one of them said, "It's a shame your father passed before being able to record his account for history." That's when I realized I hadn't made clear the most important part of all. "Oh, my father is still alive," I told them. This group of seasoned men turned to each other and cheered like young boys congratulating each other on a home run. "He's alive! He's alive!" they shouted in jubilation. I'll forever remember how those men, all in their eighties, celebrated my dad's being alive. Perhaps I had taken that fact for granted.

The veterans, none of whom had been in prison camps, explained that many prisoners of war had not lived long lives due to poor health and mental stress. "There are only a handful left," one of the veterans said. Many of those who had endured the hardship and atrocities of World War II never talked about it, just like my father. Only now, I was getting the chance to hear his story before it was too late. I felt I was suddenly sitting on a piece of history, and felt a duty to tell the story on behalf of those who could not.

The Polish veterans showed me their museum, which is small, but contains amazing World War II relics. I saw some of the patches and badges on Polish uniforms that mirrored the torn and tattered items I had discovered in the old tan leather suitcase. I spent hours there that afternoon, soaking up all the details that I could to help me on the journey with my father into his past.

I asked them about records. They told me that since most records were destroyed by the Germans or later by the communists, the chances were slim to none of there being any information specifically on my dad. We also had another strike against us. They said that since my dad had flown under the radar in the United States for all these years, it was improbable that we would be able to turn up any information about his past in Poland. On the way out, as I'm often apt to do, I asked Teofil Lachowicz, the group's historian, if he wouldn't mind doing a search anyway, "just for the heck of it." I never thought I'd hear from him again.

A few weeks later, I received a surprise e-mail from him with a paragraph that both amazed me and brought tears to my eyes. There is something powerful about seeing one's past in writing, in records that you thought had surely been burned or had never even existed to begin with. Despite the chaos of war, there was something on my father! A historian in Poland, who was assisting Mr. Lachowicz, not only located my dad's name in an archive, he found information about his injuries and key dates in his story.

The record was of "Ryszard Kossobudzki, son of Konstanty and Hanna Kossobudzki." He had been born August 4, 1925, and during the German occupation of Warsaw he served in the Polish Home Army. His conspiracy name was "Rys." In the Uprising he fought in Old Town in the Gozdawa group and was evacuated through the sewers. After an injury, he was admitted to the insurgent hospital at 23 Bracka Street on September 2, and after capitulation he was transported by train to the prisoner of war hospital in Zeithain, Germany. From there, on January 12, 1945, he was transferred to Stalag IV B. His POW number was 305147.

I was amazed and profoundly thankful. Having the historian find this brief biography was a revelation. All these years later, my dad's memories of these events had been almost exact. I was dumbfounded, and called him right away to tell him what I'd learned.

"That's not right," he said immediately. "They must be missing a number after the two for the date of my injury. I was admitted to that hospital after September 20. I know I'm right on that."

"Are you sure, Dad?" I asked.

"It's a typo, Rita," he said. "I'm sure."

I wanted to prove him right and see what else I could find, no matter how difficult the task. I kept hearing his voice in the back of my mind, as he'd challenged me so many times in childhood, "You can come up with something better than that." I had to admit though, unlike many other subjects I've interviewed, my eighty-four-year-old dad had been able to describe every scene from his teenage years with great specificity. We were talking about events that had taken place more than six decades ago, and yet he could remember every detail. Those who have worked with me know that when it comes to facts, my motto has always been "triple check." That was exactly what I was going to do with the most precious story of my life.

I located the 1956 *Queen Mary* manifest from when my parents made the journey to America. My dad's name was on it, listed as "stateless." I also obtained a record of my parents' applications to become American citizens. Though my mother had gone to the trouble of listing a tiny scar on her forehead that I never even knew she had, my dad hadn't bothered to list any of the scars scattered about his body. Perhaps he wanted to leave any suggestions of war back in Europe. He completely ignored the marks the war had left on him, the physical manifestations he would bear for the rest of his life. Even then, all those years ago, he had already decided to make his experiences in the war a thing of the past—to forget the scars, even if he couldn't forget the pain.

On his petition for naturalization, he signed his oath of allegiance to the United States with his new name, "Richard Roger Cosby." The year was 1961, and my dad said good-bye to Ryszard Kossobudzki. I hadn't given it much thought, but why had he changed his family name? I made one of my now-regular calls to him. "Dad," I asked, "How did you decide on the name Cosby?"

"Well," he said, "when your mother and I first came to the United States, I got a job working for an engineering company in Buffalo. At the time Buffalo was sort of a hot spot for Polish immigrants; for whatever reason a lot of us ended up there after the war. There were two or three Polish guys working at my company, and it didn't take long for them to find out that I was Polish, too. My name gave it away.

"At first I tried to embrace my Polish heritage, but eventually I started to feel very disenchanted. People always recognized me right away by my accent, and my coworkers constantly misspelled my name. It happened to your mother, too—at that point she was working in an office, dealing with customers over the phone, and everyone always forgot her name. It was frustrating for both of us.

"So, one day, I came home from work and said to your mother, 'You know, we're going to be in this country for the rest of our lives, probably. English is the language that people speak here. We don't have any relatives here—you and I are the only Kossobudzkis that we have to worry about! I think it would be helpful if we changed our name.' So, we sat down and decided on what name we wanted to take."

"How did you end up with Cosby?" I asked him.

"Well," he said, "I didn't want something artificial. There were lots of Polish surnames that sounded similar to mine—Kossobudski, Kossogovski, that sort of thing. I knew a lot of guys with names like that that just shortened it—they changed it to 'Koss.' But that seemed wrong to me—it was sort of a halfway name, not quite Polish but not quite Anglicized, either. I tried to think of American names that were close to that, and came up with Crosby."

"Crosby? Not Cosby?"

"Well, that was my first suggestion, but your mother thought it was pretentious. Bing Crosby was very famous at the time, and it seemed wrong to take the name of someone who was so well known. So, I suggested Cosby, and your mother liked it. She was Danish, of course, and a lot of Danish names end with 'by,' so she was happy that she could pretend it was a Danish name."

"So, one night you just sat down and decided on Cosby?"

"It didn't happen all at once," my dad says. "We looked at words in the dictionary some. I guess it took us a few days of deliberating, and eventually that's what we decided on. And then when we were naturalized we were asked if we wanted to keep our names, and we shouted 'No! We want to be Cosbys!' " He laughs. "And I decided that Richard was the closest American name to Ryszard. I always liked the name Roger, too, so I took that as my middle name. And from that point on I was Richard Roger Cosby. I was very happy with it."

I had no idea that my mother and father had chosen their name together. I picture the two of them as a young couple, staying up late in their apartment in Buffalo, going back and forth about names. It's not a scenario I had ever imagined before, but it's a pleasant one. I wonder how my life might have been different if the two of them had decided to keep my father's Polish name. I laugh to myself as I imagine my MSNBC show as *Rita Kossobudzki, Live & Direct* or *Fox News Live with Rita Kossobudzki.* Somehow it doesn't have the same ring.

I had decided that a good way to keep my dad involved in the fact-checking process, and to further test his memory, would be to give him assignments. When I finished reading any books I'd received, I sent them to his house in Virginia and asked him to read through them and compare his own memories with the accounts they presented. I was surprised at how quickly he always responded, and how game he was to take on the homework. He began sending me letters filled with extensive analyses of the books I'd sent, comparing his own recollections with those of the authors. Each of his letters was signed with the coolly formal, "Yours, Dad," as any correspondence from him always has been. He listed points he agreed and disagreed with, and explanations about why. He made notes of things that he wanted to know more about—his assignments for me.

I called the Polish consulate to see if they might provide assistance or point me to a contact in Poland. Marek Skulimowski, the very kind deputy consul general, quickly became fascinated with my father's story. "I thought I'd seen it all," he said. "I've helped research lots of war stories, but this is special." He began uncovering a surprising number of details in the history of Ryszard Kossobudzki. After he began looking into it, he called me and said, "Clearly your father was an amazing fighter. Finding out that he's still alive is like finding a rare coin."

My dad had indeed been a member of the Gozdawa Battalion,

a military group that had originated as the Association of Fighters for Independence in 1939. The AFI began working out of a printing house in the cellars of a church in Warsaw, printing propaganda against the Nazis—the propaganda my young dad and his friends had dispersed from trams into the streets of Warsaw. Eventually the AFI expanded into military action. In 1944 the battalion was moved to the City Center and began operating under the Gozdawa name. During the Uprising my father's battalion was instrumental in the defense of Old Town, and on August 31 they made an attempt to break through the Nazi lines into the City Center. After an unsuccessful attempt, they eventually made it into Warsaw's sewers and past the German fortifications to continue the fight.

I found an eighty-seven-year-old Polish Resistance fighter living in New Jersey who, incredibly, had been on the same Red Cross prisoner of war train as my dad. "How do you know he was on my train?" my dad quickly asked when I called to tell him.

"There were two transports, Dad," I was able to report. "Bill Biega and his wife, a medical student he married amidst the bombs and gunfire of the Uprising, were on your train. Each of the two trips carried about fourteen hundred wounded Polish Resistance fighters and nurses and doctors to Zeithain. One train stopped at Lodz, the other one didn't."

"He remembers the stop in Lodz?" my dad asked. "Did he say he thought we were all going to get shot in the head?"

"He thought the same thing," I told him. "That after the train was diverted, he was one of the ones who was taken with you into the deserted concentration camp. He said no one knew what was happening, but he, too, was afraid the Germans had gone back on what they promised. He says there was apparently a confrontation between the German army and the SS or Gestapo."

"We were lucky the German army won that argument!" my dad said enthusiastically. "I'm stunned you found someone living in America that was on my train and remembers that, too." It was nice to hear how happy my dad sounded to have confirmation of both his memory and his suspicions.

The real bombshell, however, came the following week when my contact at the Polish consulate called to tell me about a book he'd discovered by a young historian named Marek Galezowski. "You're not going to believe this," he told me, "but I've found a book written specifically about the Young Eagles." The book, *Orleta Warszawy*, which translates to *Warsaw's Eaglets*, had just been published a month before, and it is dedicated to Lieutenant Stan. He excitedly briefed me on parts of it.

It turns out that Stan was in fact his real name—my dad had just assumed that it was an alias. It moved me to learn that the young lieutenant had trusted my dad with his actual name. His full name was Stanislaw Srzednicki. He had been born on April 9, 1915, and died on August 20, 1944. During his life he had worked as a youth educator, instructor, and scout. He came from a patriotic family—the descendant of men who had participated in numerous Polish liberation movements over the long years of occupation. He was cofounder of the Young Eagles, and enlisted as a volunteer soldier when World War II began. Many of his trainees in the Young Eagles followed him into service, and for a time he was in command of a group of them in the Gozdawa Battalion. When he died he was awarded the Cross of Virtuti Militari, the highest honor the Polish military can give.

There are numerous references in the book to my dad, and his service commanding the Zula platoon of the Young Eagles, and his reconnaissance unit in the Uprising. On September 23, during the action of receiving arms parachuted by the Soviet forces, Tadeusz "Hart" Szymczak was killed and young corporal Ryszard Kossobudzki was seriously wounded. I asked the consul if he was sure it said the twenty-third. He was. It did. My dad's memory was absolutely spot-on. The consul then read to me, from page 285, my dad's bio, which contained a surprising revelation. In his application to award Ryszard Kossobudzki the Fighter's Cross, Captain Gozdawa said, "From the first days of the Uprising, he was a frontline soldier, fighting in the center of the city to defend the main post office. He showed a great courage and bravery. Corporal 'Rys' was an exemplary soldier . . ."

I couldn't call my dad fast enough. As I dialed, I wondered if he knew of the award and forgot to tell me, or if it wasn't a big deal to him, another fact he had tucked away. "Hi, Dad," I said. "I have a question for you. What's the Fighter's Cross?"

"Oh," he said, "that was one of the highest honors you could get, like a Bronze or Silver Star. That's a really big deal."

"Did you know you were supposed to get one?" I asked him. "Your leader filled out an application for you to get the Fighter's Cross."

He was silent for several seconds, clearly stunned by the news. He then blurted out, "You're kidding."

"Dad, you were supposed to get that award, according to some records I just found."

He was clearly choked up. "I didn't know," he murmured. "This is the first I've heard of this." And that was all he said. He quickly changed the topic to Lieutenant Stan and what a great man he was.

I said, "Dad, did you hear me? You were supposed to get that high honor!" I read him Captain Gozdawa's statement, choking back tears as I read, " 'He showed a great courage and bravery. Corporal "Rys" was an exemplary soldier.' Dad, he was talking about you. Not Lieutenant Stan or anyone else. He was talking about *you!*"

My father's reply quickly brought me back to the reality of what he went through. He didn't want recognition or attention on himself. "Rita," he said, "at the time we couldn't think about awards. I was thinking about making sure I survived, and more important, that my boys survived. As long as I didn't get a wooden cross, that was the only thing that mattered to me."

I was overwhelmed with emotion at being the one to discover and tell my own father of a major honor he was supposed to have received some sixty-five years earlier. I said, "Dad, I'm proud of you. You're a hero, Dad. This is a tremendous honor, and so well-deserved for what you had to endure."

He simply said, "I am proud of everyone in my unit who survived, and especially those who died. I will never accept being called a hero, but I guarantee you, I was never a coward."

Days later, Consul Skulimowski personally hand-delivered to me the *Orleta Warszawy* book. I excitedly and immediately searched the book's Polish text for any recognizable words from my dad's story. When I flipped to the back of the book, it included a list of profiles of notable members of the Young Eagles, and there, in the list, I discovered my father's name! There was a whole paragraph dedicated solely to him, but there was a blank square where his picture would have gone.

I overnighted the book to my dad. After he received it, he stayed up for several nights anxiously reading it. Though he said Polish was difficult for him to remember, the book brought his language back to life. He read it enthusiastically, excited by every page. He called me to say that he spotted himself in one of the group photos when he was a very young boy, but the author was missing a crucial piece of his story. "He doesn't know whether I'm dead or alive!" he told me. He took pride that he had concealed his identity and whereabouts. "See," he said. "See how well I camouflaged myself! This book never says I went to Italy, London, got married, came to the United States, got divorced."

He then translated a few of his favorite passages for me. The book says the unit of younger boys under Kossobudzki was great at putting all the graffiti on the walls. "Hitler is an asshole" and "Poland Fights, Poland Lives." He congratulated himself, "I guess we did a great job at thumbing our nose at the Germans." He also seemed pleased by his solid memory. "See, that's exactly what I told you," he said several times during our conversation about the book.

Where I might go through a school yearbook and point out people who were football stars, pranksters, or the beauty queen, my dad had gone through the book finding long lost friends and remarking, "That guy was easy to remember because his dad lost his right arm right before the war," or, "Oh, that's so and so, he was shot in the head." He told me, "The book made me feel like I was fifteen and back in Poland again. I slept next to these brave men and women, starved with them, bled with them. The great thing was to see some of them survived the hell."

Perhaps my dad's greatest shock was reading that Lieutenant Stan hadn't died in his arms. The book details that Stan received a shot to the head and binoculars on August 9, but didn't die until eleven days later on August 20. "All these years," my dad said to me, "all these years, I thought he died in my arms. I am stunned to learn he survived for eleven more days. He was a great leader."

The book also gave details of the booby-trapped tank explosion, and he was moved to read the profile of his girlfriend Henryka "Henia" Zylak that described her as courageous. "I never knew her last name until I read the book. Knowing her, she was riding that tank, and that was it." He said according to the book, the Germans had used almost a ton of explosives in that tank. Hundreds were killed, most instantly disintegrated. Fragments of bodies were later found even on third-floor balconies. "I saw a silhouette of blood on the wall," my dad told me again.

"Imagine the force it took to do that to a human body," I agreed. "It's horrifying."

He changed the subject. "Rita," he said, "did you know there is now a plaque in Warsaw dedicated to the bravery of the Young Eagles?" My dad's voice suddenly quavered as he translated the words inscribed on the plaque he saw on one of the pages: *Passersby note and declare to Poland, here rest your sons, faithful and obedient to the last hour.* My dad was choked up reading those words to me, barely able to continue our conversation that night.

I became more and more amazed by the accuracy of my dad's memory and overjoyed that I was helping fill in the blanks about these momentous events and the men and women my father lived and fought alongside. After a lifetime of miscommunication, we were finally talking regularly, having heartfelt conversations. I knew that this was the greatest gift I could give him—a chance to help him illuminate and bring into focus the details of his own past. Yet, in doing so, I was bringing wisdom and insight into my own life and fulfilling a deep desire to connect with a good and decent man who was always determined to press on, pursue the honorable path, and fight vigorously for what he believed in. Encouraged by the clarity and openness we were discovering between us, there was one important thing I had yet to share with him, a missing piece of his past that he'd never found.

"I have something to tell you, Dad," I told him one afternoon on the phone. "Something important."

"What is it, Rita?"

"I found out what happened to Alex."

19

FINDING ALEX

*Y*ou found him!" my dad says. There is a great, youthful joy in his voice. "Did you speak with him?" Ever since I left my dad's house in Virginia and continued my research, he'd been anxious to know if I'd turned up anything on Alex. Each time I spoke to him on the phone, he would always end the conversation with the same question: "Have you found Alex?" It had taken a good deal of searching, but I finally had, and I was unsure of how exactly to broach the subject with my father.

"Well, Dad," I tell him, "he never left England. He spent the rest of his life in Bristol." I clear my throat, sorry to have to tell my dad news that would disappoint him, but not wanting to mince words as he'd always taught me for so many years. I feel I need to muster the strength and just say what I know will break my father's heart. "He's passed away."

My dad falls silent. I can just hear his breathing on the other end of the line. After a few seconds, he asks in a low voice, "When?"

"December 2005," I say. "He was seventy-eight years old."

"How did he die?"

"He had cancer." I know the news must be breaking my dad's heart. Of all the things that happened during the war, I know that Alex had often been in his thoughts, even though many years had gone by. The bond the two of them had shared was extremely rare—without each other, neither of them would have likely survived the war. Even if they had become estranged in the years since their escape from Stalag IV B, it was palpable how hard it was for my dad to learn that his greatest friend was gone. Their bond was unbreakable.

"Tell me what you learned about him," my dad says. "Did you find out anything about his life?"

My quest for information on what had become of Alex had been illuminating, an incredibly emotional experience for me, too. The first thing I'd turned up in my hunt for Alex had been his obituary. I found the item in his hometown newspaper, the *Western Daily Press*, with the headline: "Polish Publican Who Was a City Character." The obituary featured a quotation from Matt Chelmicki, Alex's son, who said, "He was one of Bristol's characters. He was a great chap. I could go out with him for a drink as a friend as much as a father."

Alex became involved in the Resistance through his membership in the Scouts, and like my father, he got his start in a small Resistance cell distributing anti-Nazi literature.

After some preliminary searching, I was able to locate his daughter's phone number. Her name is Anna Sharpe, and she still lives in

Bristol, outside London. I was surprised at how nervous I felt when I actually picked up the phone to call her. I had prepared a list of questions, but this was unlike any research phone call I'd ever made. This was personal, much more than simply contacting a source for a story, a task I had performed countless times before. It was awkward yet exciting to call a person I'd never met, living in another country, and explain to her the unique bond we share.

I dialed the number, and when she said "Hello," my mind flooded with emotion. I searched desperately for the right words to begin our conversation, finally coming out with, "My name is Rita Cosby. You don't know me, but my father and your father saved each other's lives more than sixty years ago."

"I beg your pardon?" she replied.

"Our fathers were prisoners of war together during World War II," I explained, beginning to regain control of my emotions. "They became best friends. They helped each other survive."

For a moment she was silent, then, clearly moved and a bit shocked, she spoke. "Please," she said, excitedly, "tell me more." I told her about my dad and myself, about the lives we'd both led and about the book I was working on. Interestingly, she, too, is a writer. I told her about how my dad still spoke fondly of Alex, and about their story together. I asked her if she would do me the honor of telling me some things about her own father. She said she would tell me what she knew, but admitted that her father really didn't talk much at all about his war experiences with her.

"My whole life he always kept it inside," she said. "He only just started opening up about what had happened to him after he was diagnosed with cancer. He spoke to a family friend, a priest. I think he realized that he might not have much time left and wanted to get some of the things he'd gone through off his chest. Even then, though, we only really got bits and pieces." I think of my own dad, who had suddenly seemed older to me than he had before. I know that he, too, felt a need to tell his truths.

"My knowledge of his life before he came to England is patchy," Anna continued. "I'm sad that I didn't get a chance to talk with him about this before he died. I wish I'd had the chance to ask him more questions. I wish I'd had the chance that you have now."

"My dad said your father was a good friend to have in bad times," I said.

"Well," she told me, "he was always so lively. He always wanted to make the most of every single day. He lived life to the fullest, and spent a lot of time at the pub. He actually went out for drinks with my brother the night before he died. He treasured every moment. I think he must have felt lucky to have survived the things he went through." I thought of my own father's obsession with running and was struck by the divergent paths the two men took to escape their hidden pain. I know that my own dad's strictly regimented life is also a reaction to what he experienced during the war. It's interesting to think that he and Alex ended up living such opposite lives for the same reason.

One of my calls before Alex's daughter was with Dr. Mack Orsborn, examining physician of ex-POWs for the Veterans Administration and national expert on ex-POW issues. He's examined and interviewed more than six hundred American ex-POWs. Dr. Orsborn told me that ex-POWs have higher rates of disease than non-POWs, and many die early from medical conditions "and substance abuse problems." I think of Alex's drinking and cancer. Before it was called "post traumatic stress disorder" it was called "battle fatigue" or "shell shock." Sadly, so many soldiers suffer with PTSD and deal with it in different ways. The criteria are the same: a life-threatening event; reliving that event in flashbacks and nightmares; avoiding talking about it; and being generally overexcited.

"Ex-POWs often don't communicate well with family members," Dr. Orsborn told me. "They are not as emotional about things like deaths, major life experiences."

"Like divorce?" I asked.

"They have a hard time connecting with loved ones. Kids of POWs often live having a sense of not knowing who Dad really is. If a divorce is abrupt, you ask why did Dad behave this way? There's long-term numbness, emotional numbing because of what they went through. They avoid dealing with emotional issues."

"My dad was always disconnected emotionally," Anna Sharpe told me. "I think what my dad went through during the war made it difficult to engage with people for more than a short time. Long-term relationships were always difficult for him." She was quiet for a few seconds, then continued, her voice gripped with emotion. "But, boy, do I miss him," she said. "More than I ever thought I would." I thought of how much closer I felt like I'd gotten with my own dad as we worked on the details of his story, and realized how painful it would be if he were gone. Despite our differences and our disagreements, learning about his past has made me feel happier and more connected with him than I ever have before.

Dr. Orsborn told me it was probably good for my dad, too. "It's often a very positive experience for them to share their story finally." I realized that this book is a catharsis for my father . . . and for me. My conversation with Dr. Orsborn turned into a "house call" for me. I was glued to his every word. The call became very personal. I realized I was not alone in my experience, asking for and needing advice. "Many family members learn to live with boundaries and never break through," Dr. Orsborn said.

"Many kids of POWs don't understand POWs, they have a great misunderstanding of their father. His emotional withdrawal, lack of empathy and understanding, lack of connection with events. It's hurtful for the family and the family doesn't really understand. There is also a sense of avoidance in telling the story to protect loved ones from gory details. So, they wall off their experiences, especially from daughters and wives." Maybe my dad, Richard, and Anna's dad, Alex, were protecting their daughters from the horrors, shielding our minds as much as possible from pure evil.

Anna Sharpe also accentuated the positive. "I've realized lately how much my dad influences the way I think and act, even to this day," she said. "I always tell everyone I know to go and vote, to exercise their right. Without people like my dad and yours, we might not have that right. We can honor them just by exercising those rights—my father always told me that you have to fight for freedom.

"He was always truthful, too—sometimes to a fault. He never minced words and always spoke his mind. I guess he probably felt that life was too short not to say what you mean."

Her words stopped me. I told her, "That's almost exactly what my dad said when he got divorced. He said, 'Rita, life's too short not to be happy.' "

"My dad married twice, too," Anna continued. "He had three children, myself, Matt, and Gabby, and four grandchildren. In his later years he owned several pubs, and later a restaurant. He was always restless—he always wanted to achieve as much as he could every day, sometimes to a fault. He had a very short attention span, and never stuck with one thing for too long."

"Tell me more about his early life," I said. "How did he end up in the war?"

"He was born in 1927 to a well-to-do Polish family. His family owned a lot of land and had made his fortune as a composer. He wrote a famous Polish song called 'Grunt to rodzinka,' which translates loosely to 'Ode to the Family.' The song is still sung at Polish weddings to this day. When he was thirteen years old he was sent with his grandmother on a train toward the Russian border to escape the hardship of the German occupation. She passed away on the train en route, so he got off and had to make his way back to Warsaw all by himself. A thirteen-year-old boy, in the middle of the winter, traveling all the way back to Warsaw from the Russian border! It took him months, but he finally made his way back home. When he returned, he was too young to really fight in the Resistance, so he became a messenger. He finally became a soldier through the Scouts, just like your dad.

"Later on he advanced to sabotage missions, blowing up Nazi supply trains and things like that. During the Uprising he was injured, burned by a flamethrower I believe when he went to deliver a secret message to a Resistance cell in a basement. After he arrived, the Nazis blasted them with a flamethrower through the cellar window and set him on fire. He covered his face with his hands, and that probably saved his life.

"After he was injured, the Germans threw him into a mass grave. He climbed out and made it to a Resistance first-aid station. Later he was transferred to the German POW hospital where your dad was. He's had more treatment for his injuries since then—I know that he had a few different surgeries and skin grafts to correct the scarring on his face and hands, but he had the scars until the day he died."

"My dad still has scars, too," I told her. "From shrapnel wounds. He never wanted to talk about them until I began this book project."

"My father always kept pretty quiet about his scars, too," she replied. "I didn't know any of these stories until just before he died." I'm amazed by the parallels between my dad and Alex, and between Anna's life and my own. Even though they were separated by an ocean and hadn't seen each other in decades, these two men had lived their lives by very similar principles.

"The last time they saw each other was in 1950, in Bristol," I told her. "My dad wanted to invite your dad to the wedding, a year later, to my mother, but my grandmother decided it was going to be just the family. She didn't want to make it a big affair because she wasn't sure what kind of future my dad was going to offer her daughter as he had no steady job at that point. My dad sent Alex a letter, which said, 'I hope you congratulate me.'

"When I asked him why he lost touch with Alex, he told me, 'We didn't want to spread ourselves too thin. The past is the past. Alex got married and went on with his life.' I don't think they ever spoke again, but my father was hoping he could see Alex again, and told me if he could, he would be so happy, so emotional that he probably wouldn't be able to talk for five minutes. My dad never forgot your father, and the things they learned and experienced together."

I told her about my own father, about the man he had become, and about the life he went on to live in the United States after the war. I shared with her the pain I felt, growing up without really knowing my dad.

"Everyone has faults," she told me. "But for our fathers to have lived through the war, to have had the experiences they did, and to still turn out to be good, decent people despite it all is amazing. When I think about what they faced every day during the Uprising, and in the prisoner of war camp, I almost can't believe it. They saw the worst side of human nature and still managed to become honorable men. It's just amazing." She couldn't see them, but tears streamed down my face. "The thing is," she said, "I really did learn a lot from my father. Because of him, I know that there are ordinary people who sometimes do extraordinary things. It's really incredible."

I told her about how my dad had refused to acknowledge his heroism when we'd learned he was supposed to receive the Fighter's Cross. "My dad seems to think that what they went through was nothing compared to others and those who died," I told her. "That those were the 'real heroes.' "

When I had spoken to Kurt Vonnegut's son, Mark, he also said his dad "did not want to be seen as a hero. He said much of survival came down to luck." I said I thought it was more than luck. "I look at my dad as bigger than life," Mark told me. "Our fathers were lucky and remarkable people. They are beautiful stories of real-life heroes."

"My father was the same way," Anna said. "He was always modest. I think our dads were real heroes. The *real* heroes are the ones who don't brag about what they did. Years ago, I was out somewhere with my dad and we overheard a guy who was bragging about his role in the war. My dad turned to me and said, 'If he was really involved in the fight, he wouldn't be talking about it. Only the people who were on the fringes talk about it. Those who were in the thick of it don't talk.' "

Dr. Orsborn told me that more than three-quarters of ex-POWs have not talked about their experiences at all or have minimized them tremendously. "I've never met an ex-POW who exaggerates. They are always minimizing the experience, insisting that someone else had it worse than they did, no matter how horrific their ordeal was."

Anna and I spoke for a long time. No words can describe the amazing and instant bond we shared. It was so fulfilling to be able to tell her, "Your father saved my father's life. And my father repaid him by saving his." It felt good to reveal all of the incredible things I'd learned in the past few months to someone who felt as deeply moved as I did. She told me that all her life, she wanted to learn many of the secrets her father took to his grave, and was saddened that she hadn't asked more questions before he passed away. I was thrilled to help her fill in the holes in his history.

When our conversation ended, she said, "I am staggered. I never knew any of this, I never knew about this part of his life." She was both shocked and grateful that I had taken the time to call her.

When I related all of this to my father, he was overjoyed to learn what had become of Alex after the war, to know that he had children and lived a full and happy life. "Did you find out if Alex ever mentioned me? I wonder if he ever spoke of me—I considered him my best friend," he said, almost bashfully.

"Well," I replied, "Anna didn't say, but I actually spoke with Alex's son, Matt, as well. Matt told me that he didn't know you by name, but Alex definitely told him about the impact you had on his life. He told Matt that a friend had convinced him to leave the camp. That the friend had said, 'We have to get out of here.' Alex credited you with saving his life, Dad." I've never known my dad to let his emotions show, but I could tell how touched he was by this news.

Anna also said her dad only began talking about the Uprising in his later years. "I never knew he was even in a camp until about a year before he died when I found out he was getting an ex-POW pension from the British government. I was always screaming inside for him to talk about everything I wanted to know, but I knew his rule that he had to start the conversation." I told her I thought our dads came up with the "never ask about the past, only the future" rule in camp.

Alex's son, Matt, told me of a similar disconnect. "My dad was not good emotionally with me. Getting feedback from him was hard. Communicating with him was hard. There was always a dark period of his life that I could not break through." He said his dad did admit once, "I saw so many friends die. It could have been me." Matt ended our conversation by telling me that his dad didn't consider himself a hero, he considered himself one of life's lucky people. "That's why I live life to its fullest," he said. "I learned that from my dad."

Being able to find Alex's family and learn as much as I did made me realize that my search for the truth is affecting more lives than my own. Learning about my father's past hasn't just illuminated my own history—it's also touched the lives of another family, across the ocean. I hope others will read this story and pursue some of the stories of their own parents' lives.

After speaking with Alex's children I found myself eager to learn more about heroes and heroism, and the aftereffects of war. What was it that made men like Alex and my father do the things they did? How were they able to rise to the occasion, to bravely face the horrors of war? And how were they able to go on to live successful lives afterward?

I sought out Professor Samuel Oliner, emeritus professor of sociology at Humboldt State University in California, who at twelve years old had escaped Nazi execution himself and ended up being saved by a Polish Catholic family. He has spent two decades studying altruism and heroism. "Most people are bystanders," he told me. "Approximately 300 million people lived in Nazi-occupied Europe. Only about 5 percent of those were true heroes who risked their lives, 10 percent were killers or collaborators, and the bulk of them were bystanders." I told him my dad wouldn't let me call him heroic. "True heroes are humble," he told me. "They always assume everyone else would do the same thing in that situation. Your dad had an internalized moral code of justice, a righteousness, something he learned early on in his upbringing. He probably acquired good values from his parents or a role model." I thought of his mother. I thought of Lieutenant Stan. "Something in him said he could not walk away. Your father could not stand by like so many do."

Professor Robert Perloff, a former psychologist at the University of Pittsburgh and an army combat veteran of WWII, put it to me this way: "Courage is not the absence of fear. It's the presence of resolve, the presence of purpose."

Temple University professor Frank Farley is a psychologist, former president of the American Psychological Association, and a nationally recognized expert on heroism. After I told him my dad's story, he replied with some fascinating facts.

"Rita," he said, "you'll be interested to know that in studies I've conducted since the late 1980s in the Americas and Europe, people's parents always come out as their number-one heroes. Mom and Dad consistently outpoll everyone, no matter how old the survey participants are. This is universal, a constant. Parents top the list overwhelmingly." I was heartened to learn this fact. Working as I do in the media, where everyone seems to be obsessed with fame, I would have expected most people to idolize celebrities. It's heartening to know that most people think of their parents just as highly as I've come to.

When my dad told me he wasn't a hero, I asked him what then he considered a hero. "I would consider a hero a person who, number one, was willing to sacrifice himself for the benefit of somebody else, like saving his buddies. Number two, never expected a reward for it.

And number three, never boasted about it." How could he not realize that he'd just told me his résumé?

"Your father was truly heroic," Professor Farley told me. "Heroes can generally be broken down into three different categories. The first category is situational heroes, people who emerge from a crowd in a crisis to save someone while others stand by. Often they are only heroes for that moment, and it's often difficult to predict who will behave that way under duress.

"The second category is lifelong heroes, people for whom heroism is a defining quality. These people are often ideologically driven—men and women like Martin Luther King, Jr., Mother Teresa, and Gandhi. We call the third and final category '9-1-1 heroes,' who save people's lives in the course of their everyday jobs. They are people like firefighters, police officers, and medical personnel.

"Your father," he continued, "fits into all three categories. True heroes and risk-takers almost never admit to it. Narcissism is not a quality in true heroes. They often say, 'It was someone else who was the hero.' Your dad was unquestionably a hero, but he won't admit it. Our greatest heroes will never admit it—it goes against the grain of the generosity in their souls. Heroes are often quiet people.

"There's a lot we can learn from your father, including inspiration and dedication, heroic choices. We construct our lives by choices, and he made heroic choices. Your dad ran a high risk of death, doing it for a higher cause than himself. He had a way out—escape to Switzerland—but he didn't take it. It is such a profound motive—giving your life for someone you may not know. It is the most profound act a human can do. That is the ultimate, ultimate heroism. Your father was there. He stayed and fought for a greater cause. You don't get any more heroic than that."

20

YOURS

*I*t was impossible for me to talk with my father about his experiences during the war without the specter of his own mortality looming at the edge of the conversation. He has endured such unbelievable hardships and gone through so much to become the man he is today. His indomitable spirit and zeal for life and activity continually amazed me, but I couldn't escape the thought that his story was drawing to a close. My mother's death had been the catalyst for the journey we'd both taken together over the past few months. Surely her passing must have given him cause to consider the end of his own life. The subject came up accidentally one day when I called to tell him I was coming to Alexandria for a special visit. "We're going somewhere," I said. "Do you have a suit?"

"I have one, just one," he said. "I last wore it to my neighbor's wife's funeral."

My mind flashed to the sad conversation I'd had with my mom on her deathbed in which I delicately uncovered what she'd like for her funeral. Interestingly, my dad's next words were, "You know, Rita, I've been thinking . . . I wouldn't want to waste a good suit on my funeral." There was a long pause. "I would want to be cremated." I was a bit taken aback by his statement. Somehow this was not what I expected him to talk about, but it was familiar territory for me. Shortly before my mom died, I had asked her where she wanted to be buried. I slipped the grim question into pleasant conversation as I crouched by her bed during one of my last visits with her. "You know I've always loved to travel," I had told her, trying to sound casual, trying to hold it together, to keep my composure. "When I pass away, I think it would be kind of nice to be cremated and to have my ashes thrown out of a plane."

"Oh, I would definitely want to be cremated," my mother had agreed.

I had tried to keep a pleasant smile on my face and the tone of my voice bright. "Where would you want to have your ashes spread?" I asked her, pretending that this was a normal conversation for a mother and daughter to have, pretending my heart wasn't breaking.

"You know I love Todd's Point," she had said. "It would be beautiful if I could be sprinkled in the ocean near there." Todd's Point, in old Greenwich, Connecticut, was where she took her daily walks with her dog, Hippi, a beautiful beachside area that she loved dearly. I nodded, smiled, and tried to find the sense of closure I thought I should feel. I couldn't find it then, but when we scattered my mother's ashes in Connecticut on that beautiful fall day I knew we had done what she wanted.

Now that my dad had opened the door, I figured I'd walk in. "Have you given any thought to where you'd like your ashes spread?" I asked him, as I crooked the phone against my shoulder.

"Well," he answered, after a moment, "I guess I'd like for my ashes to be taken to Warsaw and dropped in the Vistula River, the river I used to swim in as a boy. But I suppose that's far too much to expect. The one thing I can say for sure is that I would hate to be buried among civilians. I never received very much recognition for my actions during the war, and that's the way I'd like to keep it. But it would mean a lot to me to be buried in a military cemetery—laid to rest alongside my brothers in arms. What I'd really love," he paused for a moment, "is to be snuck into Arlington Cemetery outside of Washington, D.C. I've been there before, and I know of a spot that would be the perfect place for my ashes. There's a garden, surrounded by monuments. There's a tree growing there—I'd like my ashes to be scattered beneath that tree."

The specificity of his vision let me know he'd given this a good deal of thought. "When did you see this place, Dad?" I asked him.

"At the funeral of my neighbor Joe's wife," he answered. "Joe was in the Air Force, so his wife got a burial at Arlington. I noticed a little plaza with raised flower pots, and I thought it would be a nice place to have my ashes laid to rest—a place where you could easily come to visit me. It's toward the Pentagon, at the end of Eisenhower Avenue."

I wanted to tell my father that I would be honored to grant his wish, but I knew what a difficult proposition this plan would be. "I like that idea," I told him, "but don't you think it would be pretty tricky to make it happen?"

"That's part of the appeal," he answered. "It would be a great final mission. Nobody would be watching or expecting something like that. All you'd have to do is mix the ashes into the soil around that tree. I would become a fertilizer for that nice tree. That way I could be useful, even after death. If the tree grows well, it would be nice that I helped a little bit." He told me these things matter-of-factly, simultaneously warming and breaking my heart. Even in death, my father was still committed to service, to doing good. "You could get away with it," he continued. "No one would have to know. Then, I could be among my brothers."

After that conversation, I couldn't get the thought of Arlington Cemetery out of my mind. I have been there many times as a journalist for ceremonies and visits to see the grave site of Tomaczek's father, who is buried on Quarter Master Hill. I still hadn't told my father I had found his mementos of war in my mother's things after her death, that she hadn't thrown them away as he suspected. I'd been waiting for the right moment to return his collection of relics from the past, the relics we'd spent months discussing. It had felt wonderful to give my dad the news that he had been recommended for the Fighter's Cross, that his heroism had been acknowledged even in his absence. I formulated a plan to give him the unexpected gift of his war relics in the way he deserved. I really wanted it to be a special moment . . . for both of us.

A few weeks later, I went to Virginia for another visit. He got dressed in his one nice suit, and I helped him trim his goatee and fix his hair. He looked dapper as we left his house and headed to Arlington Cemetery, the final resting spot of American heroes from prominent explorers and astronauts to John F. Kennedy, and the site of the Tomb of the Unknown Soldier. The cemetery is a poignant, visual chronicle of those Americans who made a difference.

It felt like a scene out of a movie as we arrived at the historic cemetery, my dad looking handsome in his suit, me excited about what was in store. It was a crisp fall day, the sky was blue, and the Stars and Stripes were proudly waving. I walked my dad into the Women in Military Service for America Memorial. WIMSA is located near the cemetery's beautiful, ornate gates.

As we meandered through the women's memorial, it was obvious how at home my father felt around the old military photographs and exhibits. He marveled at all of the pictures of women in the United States military. "You know," he said, after studying the pictures for a bit, "this reminds me how much guts the women in the Resistance had. The women were often in more dangerous situations than we were, delivering messages between units. If they were caught, that was it for them. Never forget that your namesake, Cousin Rita, was one brave lady." I smiled to myself and nodded. I wouldn't forget. Nor would I ever forget how important this experience was both for my dad and me. But the main event was yet to come.

I had spent a lot of time planning this day. I really wanted the moment we were about to share to be special. I've worked in television for over twenty years, and I have always felt confident ad-libbing live on the air for hours on end before millions of viewers. But this moment was different. I only had a few words that I needed to say to my dad, but I must have rehearsed them dozens of times. I wanted it to be perfect.

I walked my dad into a room draped in a magnificent regalia of American and military flags. There was a small table in the center of the room with a large item resting on it, covered in a dark blanket. My father glanced at me, a bit confused. "I know you thought all these years that your items from the war had been thrown out," I said to him.

"That's right," he replied.

"Well, Dad," I continued, "I have a surprise for you. Mom didn't throw your things away. She saved them. They were cherished. Alan and I found this in Mom's things." I pulled the blanket from the table to reveal the worn, tan leather suitcase that my mother had left behind. The suitcase of memories that had sent me on this journey. For several seconds he glanced back and forth between me and the suitcase, not saying a word, and then he walked over and moved his hands hesitantly over the scuffed leather. In one quick motion he undid the metal clasps and raised the lid.

As he looked into the suitcase, I could see the memories rushing back into his mind. He switched into engineer mode, surveying the contents of the case from one corner to the other in one quick, analytical sweep. His eyes widened as he recognized each of the items. After a moment, he zeroed in on a small piece of red and white fabric that was poking out of a dilapidated brown leather wallet. Almost breathlessly, he pulled the wallet from the case and opened it to get at the fabric. It was only once he'd pulled it out that I realized what it was—his red and white Polish armband, the one he'd worn during the war. Just as he had survived the conflict, so, too, had this badge of courage, this mark of resistance.

He unfolded it carefully, gently rubbing his fingers across the fabric. He held on to it for a long time, almost as if he didn't want to let it go to search through the rest of the suitcase's contents. "This band represented my band of brothers," he said softly. "I never washed it. This is dirt from Warsaw." He slipped it onto his arm, just as he had done when he had risen up against the Nazis. "The last time I wore this," he said, "I was stumbling to that boxcar on my way to Germany. Had it been on my right arm, where I'd been hit by the shrapnel, it would have been ripped to shreds and drenched in blood."

He stood there for a moment, deep in thought, and then resumed going through the case's contents. I watched as he picked up each item, studying it and feeling the weight of its memory. His hands were shaking as he fumbled with the tattered remains of his past, almost as if he couldn't believe what he was touching. Every time he reached into that suitcase he was reaching back into history, and a flood of emotion was pouring down on him. Every so often he seemed to be searching for words, but none came. He was dumbfounded.

The next thing he pulled out was an old metal cigarette box. It was so old and covered in rust and patina that it nearly blended into the suitcase's lining. "Oh, my goodness," he said, "my little metal box! This is it!"

He opened the box and pulled out his old prisoner tag from Stalag IV B. It was a small bit of metal with a perforation in its center so that it could be easily broken in half and used for identification purposes in the event of the prisoner's death. Each half was printed with my dad's prisoner number: 305147. No names, no other type of identification.

"It's made out of cheap steel," he said, quietly. "The Germans made us wear them. It was always around my neck, or in my pocket." He read the number to himself and shook his head gently. "You see," he said, "we were just numbers to them. Not even human beings— just numbers."

Suddenly, we both noticed a tiny silver pendant attached to the heavy Stalag IV B chain. It was a trinket of the Virgin Mary, which intrigued me, because I had never known my father to be an overtly religious man. "Dad," I said softly, "can you tell me about that pendant? Where did it come from?"

He smiled. "My mother gave me this," he said. "Right before the Uprising began. I wore it on a piece of string around my neck every day I fought. She gave it to me to protect me from the bullets during the Uprising. She said, 'This will be watching over you and keeping you safe.' I wore it every day, because when we went out on a mission I never knew if I would come back. I wanted all the protection I could get. The pendant is from Czestochowa, a very sacred Catholic place in Poland. It took a miracle for me to get out of there alive," he said. "It must have worked. It hung around my neck against my chest, which it turns out is the one part of my body that escaped injury. I was a lucky guy. I got out—a lot of my pals died." He said he made sure he brought it to the POW camp and attached it to the upper part of the chain closest to his neck, so it would be with him protecting him in his darkest hour.

It was the most profound treasure in his little metal box, and said more about him than all the words I could write. I knew for certain his mother would be happy to know he had it back.

Then, he delicately picked up a small piece of fabric with stars affixed to it. It was something I hadn't paid very much attention to, three small gold stars like the stars a child would get on a nicely done paper. They were crooked on the fabric, hastily placed. He lifted the piece of fabric and held it against his chest, next to his heart. It was so small it barely stood out at all, but I could see how much it meant to my dad. "These are my 'Purple Hearts,'" he said. "I think they must have made them so small because so many people were seriously injured during the war. They're not as big a deal as American Purple Hearts." It seemed fitting that the stars were so understated, just like the courageous people who fought in that war. Just like my dad himself. "So many of us were wounded that we couldn't worry about awards or recognition," he said. "I always think about those who didn't survive. They, and their families, are the ones who really deserve the fanfare."

Accompanying the stars was the handwritten letter he'd sent to apply for the awards after Alex encouraged him to do so in Italy.

My research had validated many of my father's memories, but it was fascinating to see this firsthand source, marked with the exact details. There they were, written in his neatly lettered handwriting: the exact dates of his injuries, and where they occurred. In order to be awarded the stars he had to describe each one, and list witnesses and commanders. The dates were all there: "August 22, 1944—Aerial bombing." "August 26, 1944—Grenade explosion, injured near the eyes." And finally, "September 23, 1944—Mortar shell explosion, shrapnel wounds in legs and arms."

He returned to the old wallet that had held his armband. Inside it were the few personal belongings he'd been able to keep with him while imprisoned in Stalag IV B, including some faded, crumpled letters from his mother. They were small, folded postcards, each with a circular stamp dated 1944 or 1945. The cards were all post-marked "Deutschland" and "Zeithain" or "Stammlager IV B Muhl-berg." Beneath these addresses were his name and POW number. "I remember this," he said, almost more to himself than to me. He unfolded the first of the letters and read it out loud in his newly re-gained Polish.

"I was so thrilled to receive these letters," he said once he'd finished. "I was one of the first in my group in the hospital to re-ceive a letter from a loved one. It made me kind of famous there. It confirmed what I had hoped through the entire Uprising: that my parents had survived the fighting in Warsaw and escaped to their country house. Remember when I saw those lights from the train, wondering where they were and if it could have been them?" He smiled. "When I got this letter, everyone in the hospital cheered. If I could get this letter, it meant that there was hope for all of the other soldiers' missing loved ones, too. It gave them hope."

"What does the letter from your mom say?" I asked him.

"Well, we had to keep it brief," he said. "Mostly it just says, 'Be careful of your health, and try not to catch a cold.' "

"Catch a cold?" I said, quite surprised. It seemed like such a strange thing to say. There he was, in a POW camp in terrible conditions, and his mother was saying what any mother would say under totally mundane circumstances. A cold would have been the least of his worries! "Could you write back to her?" I asked.

"Oh, yes," he said. "But I had to write everything in code, so as not to put her in jeopardy. I was always afraid to include personal details, or even to reveal through my writing that she was my mother. I was afraid that if the censors got too much information about her from my letters, they would go after her. I didn't want that to happen. I also didn't have the heart to tell her I was lying on a bed dying at that point, starving. I wanted her to think I was okay. She was my mother." His voice cracked and he started to weep softly. He fingered the edges of his armband once again, and then added, "I didn't want her to worry about me."

He then pulled from the case a photo of himself from his time as a student in London. I looked over his shoulder at the handsome young man in the old photograph, smiling at the camera with the world ahead of him. It was a photograph that he'd sent to his mother, and there was a short note to her scribbled on the back. It was signed, "Yours, Richard." This was always the way he signed letters to me, too. My entire life it had always seemed distant and impersonal. I wanted him to write "Love, Dad," instead, reflecting a normal child's need for affirmation. As I stood there watching him study this picture, thinking about his mother, the person he had loved more than anyone in the world, I finally realized that his closing line to me all these years was not a symptom of the distance between us, it was yet another leftover from his time during the war—a safety mechanism he'd acquired and never given up. During the war, he signed letters to his loved ones "Yours" to keep the details of their relationships vague; to keep them safe from harm. When I saw the depth of love he had for his mother, still to this day mourning her loss, I suddenly knew the significance and profound love behind "Yours, Richard." It was his highest blessing, his way of wishing me safe.

My dad spent a long time going through the items in that case, and when he finished, he neatly repacked it and carried it out cradled in his arms like an infant. I guess in a way it was: We had just brought to life his past. Outside, it was a spectacular sunny day and we could see the Lincoln Memorial towering in the distance. Filled with memories from a great afternoon, we drove back to his house in Alexandria and stayed up until the wee hours of the morning, just the two of us, sitting at the kitchen table, going through each slip of paper my mother had packed away for him. He told me the stories behind all of them, his eyes lighting up with every discovery.

For the first time in years, perhaps ever, I finally felt at home with my dad.

The next morning we talked more about the suitcase and how shocked he was to see it again after all these years. I wanted to stay longer, but work called me back to New York. Dad drove me to the train station and we sat waiting together for its arrival, both appreciating that it had been delayed so that we could spend some more time together. A bright, colorful calico of autumn leaves drifted across the tracks, swirling gently in the breeze.

"I had a really nice time with you the past few months, Rita," he tells me. "I'm so grateful to you for helping me fill in the blanks in my past."

"It was my pleasure, Dad," I tell him.

He was silent for a moment, and then said, "I think it's important you finally know your family history. You finally know who you are."

21

Homecoming

*M*y time with my dad had shone a light into the dark corners of his life and lit up my own. The many months spent working with him on his story have given me a stronger sense of self, a deeper understanding, and a fulfillment in my being that has made me feel more alive than I've ever felt before. Though at times the effort was painful, I felt as if we'd both taken an important journey together. As the leaves fell from the trees and fall crept closer and closer to winter, I had the unique opportunity to invite my dad on an adventure so profound it changed both of our lives forever.

I called him one evening in early November to pose the offer. "Hi, Dad," I said when he answered the phone. "How would you like to spend Thanksgiving together this year?"

"That would be great, Rita," he replied sincerely, a notable warmth in his voice. The newfound closeness we'd established while working on this project was still something of a pleasant novelty for me. I pressed on.

"How would you feel," I asked, pausing, out of nervousness more than for effect, "about Thanksgiving . . . in Warsaw?"

He was silent for a moment. I knew what a big question this was for him. He'd always sworn he would never go back to Poland.

"Poland?" he eventually replied, with definite surprise in his voice.

"The Ministry of Foreign Affairs and the Office of the President have arranged some special meetings for us," I said.

"The president of what?" he asked, puzzled.

"The President of Poland, Dad."

There was a long pause.

"I don't know, Rita," he said. "I've spent a lifetime away from Poland. I haven't been there since the war, since the Nazis took me out of there at gunpoint. That would be very difficult for me."

"I know," I said, "but don't you think it's time you finally went home? Don't you want to see your homeland free of Nazis and communism?"

"I'm really not sure, Rita. There are still a lot of bad memories for me there. After sixty-five years I'm not sure I'd even recognize it or could handle my emotions."

"Dad," I continued, determined to convince him, "I think if you were ever planning on going back, now is the time. I promise I'll be with you through it all. Alex went back. I think it's time that you go back, too." As soon as I brought up Alex I knew that I'd made an impression. My dad was silent for a bit, and then said, "I'll go. Let's do this together." I was thrilled. I hung up the phone overcome with excitement. This was the first Thanksgiving we would be sharing in thirty years. And we'd be in Warsaw.

I had never been to Poland, but had always dreamed that I might someday visit the country with my dad. Given the distance between us for most of my life, the idea of visiting Poland with him had been little more than a fantasy. I couldn't believe that moment when we were sitting on the plane together and the captain announced the weather in Warsaw over the intercom system. My dad was visibly nervous, even joking that in addition to his new suit, shirt, and ties, which he excitedly spent hours shopping for, he had packed plenty of tummy medicine. That was understandable. After all, the last time he'd seen the country of his birth it was lying in ruins, reduced to smoldering rubble and filled with bodies of his dead comrades. Neither of us had any idea what to expect. I think he worried that he would not understand any of the language or, worse, that he might not be well received since it took so long for him to return.

I was curious about what my father's first impressions were, and peppered him with questions throughout the trip. When we stood at the top of the stairway together and looked out of the entrance of the plane, we knew the importance of the moment, sixty-five years in the making.

Dad turned to me and asked, "Well, should I go, or should you go first?"

I said, "You, Dad." So, he took a deep breath, and squeezed my hand gently, then nervously made his way down the stairs . . . and together we took our first steps on Polish soil.

When we reached the center of town we were pleasantly surprised by the city that greeted us. As we walked into Old Town, the part of

Warsaw where my father had grown up and mainly fought, he was amazed at how the city had been completely rebuilt, exactly as it was, using actual bricks and stones recovered from the rubble. After all these years, it was exactly as he remembered it as a young boy, before the war ravaged his country. City Center, where he made his way out of the sewers to fight his last few weeks, was also now vibrant and bustling with activity. I had become so immersed in my father's war stories and in that moment in time that I was half-expecting the city to be just as war-torn as he'd described.

As I was checking us into the hotel, there was a momentary glitch; they only had one room under "Cosby," so while I tried to figure it out with the concierge, my dad wandered over to see what was going on in the park across from the hotel. He spotted Warsaw's Tomb of the Unknown, which he was seeing for the first time, a monument bearing an eternal flame dedicated to all the unidentified soldiers who had given their lives during Poland's battles. He watched a small ceremony happening there, a changing of the guards. Several young Scouts, no more than teenagers, were gathered around the monument, and within minutes he was chatting and taking pictures with the young men, who were thrilled to meet someone who survived the Uprising. I was amazed. The man I saw with those young Scouts was not the same man who'd been so resistant to opening up about his past just a few months earlier. And I knew I was not the same daughter looking at him.

When he finished talking to them he walked back across the street, beaming. "It's wonderful to be here and see the reverence people still have for soldiers," he said.

"Guess why check-in was confusing?" I asked as I handed him his room key. He looked at me puzzled. I smiled broadly and said, "The hotel has you listed as 'Kossobudzki. Ryszard Kossobudzki.'"

The reservations had been made by Poland's Foreign Ministry. The last time he was referred to as Kossobudzki was right before he became an American citizen in the 1960s.

As we embarked on our first day, my dad announced he was not on a "tourist trip," but rather "a pilgrimage." Each day, as our van drove through the city, it was readily apparent that Poland still bore the scars it had received during the war—but just as Poland is recovering, so is my dad. The scars of war run deep. In many ways, Warsaw is a city of ghosts, a place where the painful past is both readily acknowledged and honored. Despite the sheen of modernism that the city has acquired, powerful reminders of the war and of what happened there are ever present. After the fall of communism in 1989, Poland was at long last able to begin erecting monuments and remembrances to those who had fought so valiantly during the Uprising. It seemed everywhere we looked there was a beautiful plaque or a monument to a significant event that had taken place there, many listing the names of men and women I'd been hearing about for months. To see them honored at every turn in the city was overwhelming and profound. Even the local Starbucks bore a historical marker, a bronze plaque stating that two hundred people had died near that spot fighting for freedom.

The city of Warsaw has opened a spectacular museum dedicated exclusively to those who fought in the Uprising. Visiting it and seeing my dad look at artifacts of long ago was deeply moving for the two of us, as we both discovered pieces of his past together. I was shocked to see a piece of bread just like the horrible rationed bread that was served at Stalag IV B. This bread, now some sixty-five years old, didn't have a spot of mold on it. Obviously my father had been right—it was composed of sawdust.

Touring the Warsaw Rising Museum was an incredible experience, and a special opportunity to have a revealing and amazingly detailed glimpse into my father's past, learning details I had never known before. I even had the opportunity to walk through a model of the sewer canals. Though only about one hundred feet of sheer darkness and clean, the tunnel was still terrifyingly claustrophobic and disorienting when I hit a fork and had to choose which path to take. All I could think about was how horrifying my father's ordeal must have been years ago. When I asked him if he was also going to try the model sewer in the museum, he said, "I did it once in 1944—that was enough for me." At that moment, I put my hand on his back and watched as he stared into the darkness of the sewer. Little did he know that, in just a matter of hours, he'd be staring into the eyes of other men who had also experienced that same darkness and same terror on that devastating night.

For while I was there, I had secretly arranged to surprise my dad by reintroducing him to three members of his elite Eaglet unit: Feliks "Felek" Jeziorek, Marian "Grom" Elgas, and Stanislaw "Beniaminek" Iwanczak. Yes! They were alive! We had used every journalistic skill in the book to track them down.

All handsome men in their eighties, they were acting like teenagers, excitedly waiting with big, eager smiles to utter their first words to my father after all these years. Felek touched my face with his hand and sweetly said, "You look like your father, Rys. You know, he was one of the bravest fighters we had."

When I brought the three heroes in and announced their code-names to my dad, he was shocked speechless. These incredibly honorable men, who had survived Hitler's onslaught and given their all to fight in the Uprising, were in fact now standing in front of him to talk and reminisce about the years of sacrifice and hardship. Now, these men who had fought alongside my dad and were the last alive who were able to talk of the war firsthand, were suddenly a part of my extended family because of my father's eternal bond with them.

Each of them had brought something to share, including photos and a diary that mentioned my dad several times, as well as the location of his near-fatal injury by the mortar shell. From quips to old jokes to harrowingly close calls, they quickly caught up, recounting stories of the battlefield and of the decades they were apart. It was beautiful watching them together. My dad had always told me that he was sure his friends and his country must have forgotten about him. It was incredibly moving to see that they had not. Felek wore a mini-version of his Fighter's Cross, the Polish equivalent of a Bronze or Silver Star, and showed my dad the paperwork he had saying my dad was supposed to get one, too.

In museum records, there was also the filing for my dad's award from his command. Despite months of exhaustive grilling from me, there was still a story my dad had yet to tell me, about an event that some viewed as one of the Eaglets' greatest triumphs. My dad captured three SS men without firing the only bullet he had. He and his three men, with one gun and one bullet among them, pulled a trick and drew all the Nazis' bullets out by making them think they were surrounded. By raising a helmet on a stick at various spots around the wall, they fooled the Germans into believing that there were many more than just the four meagerly armed Resistance fighters. The Nazis fell for the ruse, and before long they had fired all their bullets. They popped up, threw their arms in the air, and yelled, "Nicht schiessen!" (Don't shoot!).

"They surrendered like a jack-in-the-box and I felt like the king of Poland," my dad said, laughing at the memory with his buddies. "I got the idea for the helmet trick from an American western starring

Gary Cooper." I laughed along with my dad and was impressed how clever he was at such a young age and in such dire circumstances.

When it was time for us to leave his comrades, my dad warmly embraced each of his friends. It was clear he was fighting to hold back tears. I heard him murmur, "I only cry when nobody's looking. Eaglets don't cry, remember." Felek patted his shoulder, put his arms around my father's neck, and spoke in a whisper as if his heart was broken. "Cry, cry," he said. "It's okay to cry." My dad had told me weeks ago that a man named Felek had been with him that night the German machine guns lit up the night sky, and was sure they both had saved each other's lives. I've learned since that it was Felek who trudged through the sewers right in front of my dad, carrying the machine gun that left its mark on my dad's forehead so many years ago. As the two men hugged, the tears streaming down my dad's face matched my own. After spending more than six decades feeling that a soldier couldn't cry, he suddenly realized it was okay. I was crying because he was finally able to release his feelings. He told me he felt he had lost his youth way too soon and wished he'd been back earlier to see those who survived. It was one of many times my dad openly wept during our stay in Poland.

The next days in Warsaw were a whirlwind. We spent cherished time with Ewa Junczyk-Ziomecka, Secretary of State in the Polish President's Chancellery, who compared her father to mine. The parallels between the lives of the two men were amazing.

"My father didn't talk about the Warsaw Uprising for many years because of the communists. The Soviet censors deleted that chapter of history. Your father kept silent for so many years for a different reason. He was his own censor. They didn't talk about it, but this was the most important point in their lives. They were young and ready to die for their values, for Warsaw. Sometimes during the conversations with my father, I had a strange feeling that the war, the Uprising, and the participation in the underground was the best thing that happened in his life. I know it sounds very strange, but he felt he made a difference. Of course the price was incredible. The price was death, or a camp, or being shot on the street."

As my dad had told me his story, I, too, had been struck by the realization that he talked about his time during the war as if it was his greatest moment. At first it seemed odd to me, but now, talking to Ewa, I finally understood. During the Uprising my dad suffered immeasurably, but he felt significant and emboldened by the camaraderie of his fellow fighters. He felt that he had been called to do something so essential that he would have given his life for it.

My dad's inspirational story had made its way up from the consulate to the highest tiers of the Polish government, and we had a meeting with the president himself. President Lech Kaczynski sat privately with my dad and me for an hour. He greeted us warmly, as his father had briefly been in the same Resistance unit as my dad, and spoke about how his own father was one of very few Resistance fighters who actually had a gun during the fighting. He praised my father for his bravery, calling his generation "true patriots," and presented him with a beautiful, personally inscribed plaque, honoring his achievements during the Uprising. My dad was at first speechless. Looking splendid in his new blue suit, he accepted the honor on behalf of himself and his fellow Eaglets. Incredibly proud, I was moved to tears as I watched the moment unfold. For here was a man, forced out of his homeland long ago at gunpoint with nothing but a suitcase of cigarettes to his name. And now, all these years later, he'd returned to stand alongside the president, in what amounted to a hero's welcome in the Presidential Palace. It was an amazing sight. He was clearly humbled by all the attention, and I couldn't help but recall the man who had remained silent to his little girl about his war wounds . . . and now his being honored in Warsaw by a democratically elected president, what seems an entire lifetime later, was absolutely one of the proudest and most emotional moments of my life.

We also spent a morning with Andrzej Wajda, the award-winning Polish filmmaker whose movies about the Resistance are known around the world, and, in part, are the very reason why he received an honorary Oscar in 2000 at the Academy Awards. He seemed awed by my dad and treated him with great interest and reverence. "When I first went to Hollywood," he said, "I told them about what had happened in Warsaw's sewers, and they didn't believe me that it was a real story." Mr. Wajda could truly appreciate my father's past, as his own father, an officer in the Polish infantry, was murdered at the Katyn Forest massacre. His recent film *Katyn* is about the mass murder of thousands of Polish soldiers and members of the intelligentsia by the Soviets in the early part of World War II. My dad in turn told Mr. Wajda how his own uncle was also killed at Katyn.

Mr. Wajda listened to my father's Uprising story with fascination. "To meet anyone who survived to this day," he said, "is a very moving, very emotional experience because so few are left." Before we departed, he told my dad that he was glad he had named one of the brave fighters "Kossobudzki" in his famous Resistance film, *Ashes and Diamonds*. He said he was happy to put the face of a real fighter with the name.

The next stop on our trip was the entrance to the sewers where my dad and his comrades desperately evacuated after being overwhelmed by the Nazis. As we walked in my father's old neighborhood, he described the sewer below us as a "luxury sewer," because they only had to crouch at certain points. He went on to describe that where the tunnels intersected, their hands and fingers pressed hard along the cold, slimy brick to help them find their way in the darkness.

A few blocks further, we spotted what is now a series of beautiful and imposing bronze statues in Old Town created to honor those who fought in the Uprising. One showed a man scrambling down into the sewer, causing my dad to remember the name Major Barry. He was the towering figure in the night sky who stood with a long whip atop a pile of backpacks at the entrance, forcing everyone going in to drop their precious bags for fear they'd clog the tunnel. He remembered the major whipping the legs of a pleading man in front of him, forcing him to obey.

I was surprised to see that one of the sculptures was of a woman holding a small child. There were no children allowed in the sewers, as it was too dangerous if they cried or screamed. But we learned from our guide that one woman drugged her two-year-old daughter and carried her in front, covered by her large coat so Major Barry didn't see her. The child survived and is now a woman in her late sixties, a miraculous, living piece of history.

Eventually we found the now-famous manhole that covered the actual entrance to my dad's escape, but it was in the middle of what had become a busy intersection! I stood there in dismay, watching as traffic rushed back and forth over the landmark we'd come so far to see. Undeterred, we stopped morning traffic, including buses and even a police car, as my dad purposefully made his way toward the manhole cover in the center of the street. Incredibly, every driver seemed to immediately understand and showed utmost respect; not a single horn honked. Drivers nodded and smiled, realizing that this was an old fighter returning to his harrowing past.

The hardest stop for my dad was the site of the infamous tank explosion, in which his beloved girlfriend Henryka was instantly vaporized. But today there were more tragic surprises for him. He learned that an astonishing five hundred people had died and eight hundred others had been injured in that square when his buddies commandeered what was really a Nazi armored personnel carrier. What he also didn't know, until that moment, was that the tragedy was devastating in another shocking way. The historian who was helping us explained that an explosives expert from the Uprising recently revealed that he had warned those fighters that the German carrier was actually filled with mines. But this group of excited young men and women ignored his words and drove the vehicle to show it off to the leader of all the Polish Resistance, whose office was across from the square.

What happened next may forever remain in question—whether it was booby-trapped or an accident—but it's believed a lever within the carrier was pulled to ignite the massive explosion. When we were told this, my dad slammed his umbrella on the ground and shouted, "No! No! No!" It was sadness relived, almost impossible to bear. He wept uncontrollably and walked away to gather his thoughts in the face of what he had just learned. The historian had no idea of the impact and weight of the words he had just shared. He soon realized this was no routine historical tour. He later explained that so little was left of all those people near the explosion, military and many civilian, that they could only shovel up their remains into a few baskets and bury them all together in a mass grave.

My dad said that after that explosion decades ago, nothing could ever shock him in his life, that he lost all emotions, that it's the reason that nothing else ever affected him. He said that his "soul exploded" with that tank, rendering him forever numb. I understand now that that moment was the turning point in his emotional state, and also how incredible it was for my dad to go on. It is nothing short of remarkable that he was able to live his life as well as he had. I only wish I had known earlier about what he'd seen in those bullet-riddled streets and the anguish he had endured in that blood-drenched square. It would have helped me to understand him a lot better throughout the years.

We finally made it to 23 Bracka Street, the makeshift field "hospital" where he'd been taken after he was severely injured by mortar shrapnel. Many of the buildings in Warsaw had been reduced to rubble during the fighting, but amazingly, much of this old apartment complex, full of courtyards and backdoor entrances, was still standing. The day the Nazis wanted to torch it, it was raining heavily. The hospital area, ironically, has now been converted into a plush spa. Luxurious beds now line the rooms where wounded Resistance fighters once fought for their lives. My dad's eyes widened as he gazed up at the high ceilings. "I remember lying on my stiff bed, staring up at that ceiling, and wondering if I would survive," he said to me as we stood inside. "This hospital saved my life." In the courtyard right outside the hospital door stood a solemn reminder of those who did not survive, a beautiful statue of the Virgin Mary with an eternal light flickering over the mass grave of more than thirty fighters. Flowers were strewn everywhere; it was clear it had become hallowed ground.

While there, we met an unusual, very elderly-looking woman in disheveled clothes who was living on the top floor of the former hospital. We walked into her dark and filthy one-bedroom apartment where a small table was covered with Uprising medals, which she clearly looked at every day. We assumed they were her husband's or another relative's, but it turned out she was once a feisty and beautiful sixteen-year-old Resistance fighter, forever locked in the memories of her past. My father was so moved by this sight, he offered her some money as a gift. She refused, a proud Resistance fighter to the end.

From Bracka Street we retraced my dad's hobbled steps to the railroad tracks where he had been loaded onto the train to Germany. At the time it had been a temporary depot, but it has since been converted into a permanent, busy train station. My dad immediately recognized the sloping hill that led to the train and somberly said, "The last time I was here, I took my last steps in Poland." I tried to imagine the chaotic scene all those years ago, my dad and his wounded brothers-in-arms being pushed, dragged, and carried onto the waiting trains at gunpoint, with no idea what their futures held. Looking at the tracks now, you'd never know how much pain and fear had passed over them—and how much courage.

When Thanksgiving itself finally rolled around, Poland's secretary of state and her friends arranged a full Thanksgiving feast for us at the one restaurant in Warsaw that served turkey with all the trimmings. My dad got his glass of victory vodka, and as we sat down to the first Thanksgiving dinner we'd shared in years, he made a toast. "To my boys who survived and those who did not," he said, solemnly raising his glass. As he sipped and sat down again, I could see the tears in his eyes. He then added, barely able to speak, "In my whole life, Poland will forever be my finest hour."

Before the end of the week, we paid our respects at the grave of his mentor, Lieutenant Stan. My dad had a quiet conversation with his long-lost lieutenant, reprimanding him for "dying too soon," and told me that he'd love to have some of his ashes buried in the military cemetery near Lieutenant Stan. Then, we made an emotional visit to the grave of my dad's mother.

Reaching the grave site, he immediately knelt upon the ivy-covered rock and ran his fingers over the cold marble, tenderly flicking a bit of debris away so as to read his mother's name more clearly. The pain rushing through his body was immediately etched on his face. He laid a bouquet of yellow roses, her favorite, by her headstone. My dad had great reverence and admiration for his mother. As I watched him there, head bowed in thought and love for her, it was clear that not seeing his own mother since the beginning of the Uprising was his greatest regret.

"I called my father 'Father,'" he said as he looked down at the grave, "but I called my mother 'Sweetheart.' She was the most courageous woman I have ever known. When everything seemed to be falling apart around us, she kept our family together."

"I wish I'd gotten a chance to meet her," I told him as we hugged. For my entire life, my dad had never even mentioned her name, but in the past few months I had learned all about her bravery and resourcefulness, and his profound love for her. Though I never met Grandmother Hanna, I had a newfound admiration for her strength. "You know, Dad," I told him, "I think she'd be very proud of you. You survived the Uprising, you survived the POW camps. You came to America with no money, got married, and created a whole new life."

"I do have a lot to be proud of," he replied. "I have you."

Words are sometimes breathtaking. I had never heard these words from my father before.

Words were few and far between when, days later, we visited Auschwitz-Birkenau, the horrific, still-standing concentration camp memorial located just a few hours from Warsaw. When it first opened in World War II, it housed Resistance fighters and Polish political prisoners. That included the journalist, a family friend, who returned from Auschwitz a vegetable, and comrades of my dad, some as young as seventeen when they perished after enduring a brutal Gestapo grilling. It's believed more than one million people, overwhelmingly Jews, died in Auschwitz's gas chambers. When my dad and I saw the train tracks that dead-end inside the camp, literally right next to the crematorium, he observed the abomination of it all, and remarked, "This was truly Hell on Earth." He paused, shook his head, and commented how lucky he had been during the war. For this veteran journalist, who's seen the hand of death and destruction in many distant regions of the world, this was utterly shocking and difficult to even begin to comprehend.

We continued our quiet and contemplative walk as the museum's curator told us of the staggering number of helpless victims whose voices were silenced forever here. She also gave us an emotional private tour upon hearing of my father's tragic connection to the massive complex, where several hundred buildings once stood. My dad immediately recognized the guard towers and barbed wire, eerily similar to what he saw in his own camp, and the triple wooden bunk beds were the same generic ones he barely could sleep on in Stalag IV B with Alex on the top bunk, him in the middle.

The last person we arranged to meet with in Poland was someone I had learned was in the Zeithain camp at the same time as my dad—but this final meeting had a surprising twist. Eighty-seven-year-old Tadeusz Goralski brought with him a small letter he got from a loved one while in the camp, and since it listed the barracks, we were able to determine from his camp map that my dad's barracks was only about ten yards away. The bespectacled five-foot-seven-inch Goralski beamed when he then pulled out his tarnished, now-familiar

POW tag, and my father suddenly realized the numbers were so close that Mr. Goralski had to have been registered only minutes before him. They didn't remember each other from their days in the midst of war and starvation, but will remember their meeting in that air-conditioned hotel room the rest of their lives.

On the morning we were leaving Poland, my dad went out early for the last of his daily, solitary walks. He climbed a hill to a beautiful Polish cathedral as the sun rose over the city. The guard at the door stopped him on the way in, saying, "No tourists until 11:00 A.M. Only people who are praying are allowed now." My dad replied, "I'm here to pray." My dad made his way inside to a small pew.

At breakfast, as he told this story, I asked him, "Did you pray?"

"I did," he said. "For the first time in more than seventy years, I knelt and prayed."

"What did you pray for?" I asked.

"I asked God why he dealt Poles such a bad hand in history. And I prayed for the people of Poland, hoping they can be free from their dark past, as I am now." I pictured my dad quietly kneeling in that cathedral and praying not for himself, but for others.

A few hours later we were on the plane, watching as Poland receded into the distance. My dad watched with tears in his eyes. "Bye-bye, my dear Poland," he said softly. "I hope to see you again."

Many people accept relationships with parents or other loved ones as just being the way they are, distant or complicated, and feel the wall between them is too high to climb. I've always been an optimist, but my relationship with my father was one challenge I was always pessimistic about. I am glad I faced the challenge, quelled my own fears, and took the leap of faith to get to finally know him. I now see I would have been incomplete without trying. Who wants to live with wondering what could've been? I now realize I learned that from my dad. In fact, many of the determined and positive maxims I live by, and shared with my friends through the years, I heard my dad say while we were in Poland. Indeed, as the saying goes, the apple doesn't fall far from the tree.

Dad always insisted our gifts not be store-bought, but rather be something we wrote or made or did. I hope this book is the most special gift I could ever give. I hope I have given him the gift of a daughter's love and the ability to release painful memories. After all these years, he was finally able to let go of all those pent-up feelings and weep. He was finally able to mourn the loss of his mother, whom he never saw again after the Uprising; mourn the loss of Lieutenant Stan, whom he always believed had died in his arms; and mourn the loss of his comrades, to whom he had no time to say good-bye because he was dodging bullets.

In a way, the war punched a hole in his heart. He wasn't able to bury his friends or his family. Instead, he buried his emotions. It was a heavy burden to keep his life and emotions secret, locked away tightly but not forgotten. I hope in opening this suitcase of his memories, those painful chapters are now behind him, and for the rest of his life, he can live more fully and deeply with those who love and admire him. We now have a deeper relationship than I ever thought possible. I know he regrets not being there more for my brother and me when we were growing up and is saddened by all the missed opportunities, but I believe he finally understands the loss he gave us . . . because he bravely undertook the challenge to understand and mourn his own. Whatever time is left for us, we will embrace our present. We no longer need to run from the past.

• • •

As a television journalist, I know that time is precious. In broadcasting, with constant deadlines to file stories and the need to be on the air anchoring exactly at the top of the hour, I cannot waste a second. Deadlines in journalism are unrelenting and unbending. So it has been in my quest to uncover and discover my dad's story, to celebrate this period of our lives and not waste this precious time together. The burning desire to know of one's past is as meaningful to our existence as our DNA. Indeed, as deep as any other facet of my life, these precious months shared with my dad have become the very oxygen of my being, allowing me to learn, embrace, and love all that I possibly can about my father and our rich Resistance heritage.

Keep in mind that in the "discovery" of family, most often there will be both good and bad. That is, after all, what being a family is all about. Yet, perhaps you too might be inspired to earnestly attempt to know those you love. Since beginning this journey, I have overcome my feelings of abandonment, developed wonderfully meaningful feelings for my dad, and refused to let past negative feelings retain a place in my life. I see what the missing piece in my life has always been and now understand why that had to be. I have forgiven him, and I hope he's forgiven me for not understanding all these years what he went through.

I walked the streets and back alleyways with my father, took the same footsteps he took, and shared the split-second decisions he had made to save his life and those of his comrades. I know now what a brave man my father is. He doesn't need to run anymore. He faced down the Nazis during the Warsaw Uprising and fought for his life at Zeithain and Stalag IV B. But I believe that taking the trip back to Poland may be considered his most courageous act. He faced the demons of his past and came out victorious. "Thank you for bringing me here," he said as we made our way to the airport. "We should come back sometime."

"I'll come back with you anytime." I smiled at him and took his hand.

"I'm so happy you are here," he said. "I'm crying because I'm happy."

As we sat together on the plane, making our way back across the ocean to the United States, he turned to me and said, "I didn't know what to expect, but I am not the same man I was when I came to Poland. This visit has changed me. My outlook is better, and I'm going to participate in life more. I didn't think anyone knew I existed, that anyone cared. Now that I've seen Warsaw again, I realize that they cared about Ryszard 'Rys' Kossobudzki—and they still care about Richard Cosby."

During our first phone call after he returned home, my dad said he was very grateful to have taken this journey with me, and the call ended with him saying, "I love you so much." I will remember the sheer joy in his voice the rest of my life. This was a "joint assignment" in which we both learned how much we have to be thankful for. My dad is thankful for having the chance to return to his homeland and to revisit the powerful memories of his no-longer-secret past. As for me, I am thankful to have been able to give him the key that unlocked his heart and finally gave him closure. My Thanksgiving toast, which I offered that memorable evening in Warsaw, is what I am truly most thankful for . . . I am glad to have my father, my quiet hero, finally home.

AFTERMATH

For more than forty years after World War II, the communist regime in Poland refused to allow most books, movies, or monuments dedicated to the Uprising, but things changed in 1989 with the culmination of the immense contributions and years of tireless efforts by Pope John Paul II, Ronald Reagan, and Lech Walesa's Solidarity movement. They helped bring down the Iron Curtain, creating freedom in Poland in June 1989, five months before the Berlin Wall fell in Germany. After 1989, Poles could resurrect monuments and finally school kids in Poland could learn of the heroism of their ancestors. It's only in the last twenty years that survivors could tell their story and say "I was there." This is why so little is still known, and why more facts and people are emerging. And sadly, that generation is fading quickly. There are fewer and fewer alive to tell what really happened.

WARSAW

Warsaw was the only occupied city to rise up against the Germans on such a large scale. During the Uprising, two hundred thousand Poles were killed, mainly civilians, and twenty thousand German troops were killed or wounded. Before September 1939, Warsaw was called the "Paris of the North," with cabarets, parks, and lots of culture. By the end of the Uprising, virtually all of the city had been leveled. Today, Warsaw is a lively, lovely European city once again.

JEWISH GHETTO

Prewar Poland had 3.5 million Jews, the biggest Jewish population in Europe. The Warsaw Ghetto was the largest in Europe, with 450,000 people living there. Three million Jews were killed in Poland during the war. In 1939, a third of Warsaw's population was Jewish. Today, only a small percentage of Jews live in all of Poland.

STALAG IV B

Today, there are mass graves at the end of the camp, where more than six thousand bodies are buried. After the Russians arrived to "liberate" the camp, my dad's ominous prediction to Alex came true: They ran a brutal Soviet camp there for several years. The Russians turned the tables on the Germans and gave vicious payback to them and others they deemed enemies of their communist regime.

The main road through the massive camp is now used by locals. An old gravel road leads up to it, and there are memorials along the camp road honoring those who died and those who survived. Part of the massive community latrine is still there, made of concrete, so sturdy that even the Russians couldn't destroy it when they tried to hide remnants of the camp. Also, the foundations of some of the barracks still exist. When it was being used as a POW camp by the Germans, they mowed the land on the immediate perimeter of the massive facility, so if an inmate tried to escape, he could easily be seen and shot from the guard towers. Birch trees now grow there, making a silver forest around it.

Walking through it today, it feels huge, hauntingly quiet. It wasn't until the Iron Curtain fell in 1989 that they started to think about preserving the camp.

ZEITHAIN

Zeithain today looks like one big cemetery, surrounded by mass graves of all nationalities. It's estimated that thirty thousand Soviet POWs alone died in this enormous camp, many from starvation or severe tuberculosis. Today, it's meadow and woodland. There is a small two-storied museum and a reconstructed barracks, as well as a large stone entranceway at the front of the camp. At one point, thirty-two thousand POWs were housed at Zeithain, with between one hundred and two hundred people living in each small wooden barracks.

WORLD WAR II CASUALTIES

World War II statistics vary greatly. What's undisputed is that it was the deadliest conflict in human history. The war resulted in the deaths of one-fifth of the Polish population, three million of the Polish Jewry and three million Polish Gentiles. Estimates of total dead worldwide range from fifty million to well over seventy million. There were between forty and fifty-two million civilian deaths.

The estimates of total military dead range from twenty to twenty-five million, including deaths in captivity of about five million prisoners of war.

POWS

There were more than 130,000 Americans captured in World War II, 7,140 Americans captured in the Korean War, and 725 Americans captured in Vietnam. According to latest estimates (2010) by Dr. Charles Stenger of the American Ex-Prisoners of War, there are approximately 16,000 U.S. ex-POWs still alive today:

- No living World War I ex-POWs
- World War II—14,000
- Korean War—1,200
- Vietnam War—500
- Gulf War—21
- Somalia—1
- Kosovo—3
- Iraq—8
- Afghanistan—1

POLAND–UNITED STATES RELATIONS

In 2000, there were almost ten million people of Polish descent in the United States, a million in New York State alone. Poland is one of the United States' staunchest allies, and it is as firmly rooted in America's beginnings as any nation on earth.

It was, after all, Polish nobleman Casimir Pulaski who served as a general-officer in George Washington's army. He was killed after leading a charge against British forces in the Battle of Savannah and is considered to be "the father of the American cavalry." Also, the great Polish warrior and U.S. general Thaddeus Kosciuszko, another hero of our American Revolution, said to be "the best engineer" in Washington's army. He designed the plans for West Point.

More than two centuries later—and because of her close ties to the United States—Poland was one of the first countries to help the U.S. in Iraq, and there are Polish soldiers now in Afghanistan helping American forces.

In 1791, Poland had the first constitution in Europe, the second in the world, only after the United States of America. For 123 years in its history, Poland was not even on the map of Europe, because it had been swallowed up by three dominant spheres of influence, namely, Austria, Prussia, and Russia. Its people are used to fighting for their freedom. Or as Poles are fond of saying, "For our freedom and yours!"

ALEX

Alex returned to Poland in the 1980s during the Solidarity movement, when the communist government declared martial law. He and his son, Matt, who was seventeen at the time, drove across Europe to bring supplies to the country's embattled citizens. Alex wanted to show support for his former countrymen, to show Poles that the rest of the world had not forgotten them. When I spoke with Matt, he told me his father had said, "You're free because people died for you. Don't ever forget that."

MY DAD

At eighty-four, my dad is walking five miles a day, calling me regularly just to say "hello," and still doesn't eat turnips.

ACKNOWLEDGMENTS

This story has been a true labor of love and an extraordinary journey, which I did not take alone. For all those who helped my dear father and me, I am eternally grateful.

Special thanks go to Bruce Littlefield, who has been my "Alex," a lifesaver throughout this project and my full partner in writing this book. I am forever appreciative of his boundless talent, professionalism, and friendship since we met in journalism class at USC.

Thanks to my friends at Simon & Schuster—Louise Burke, Anthony Ziccardi, and Jean Anne Rose—whose passion drew me to Threshold Editions. What a privilege it has been working with them. Editor Abby Zidle's thoughtful advice, keen eye, and profound optimism for this project kept me seeking excellence, and Kristin Dwyer and Kerrie Loyd have made sure you heard about it. I'm grateful to my agent, David Vigliano, who immediately said this was a story that needed to be told.

I salute my distinguished military experts Lt. Colonel W. Thomas Smith, Jr., and Lt. Colonel Rick Kiernan, who provided incredible guidance and support, along with friends Dr. Munir Kazmir, Dr. Judy Kuriansky, Leela Hatfield, Lisa Wexler, Scott Stewart, Claire O'Connor, James Edstrom, Marvin Scott, and the ever-energized

Lorri Scott, whose 4 a.m. e-mails were like blasts of caffeine after a long workfest.

Thanks to all who helped with the meticulous research in three languages, and to editorial assistant Elias Primoff for sharing his talents and helping us connect the dots. Commissioner Brian Andersson with the N.Y. Department of Records located my father's first steps on U.S. soil, the *Queen Mary* manifest, and his naturalization papers. Tom Bernheim and Nan O'Brien, my "German team," visited what remains of Stalag IV B and the Zeithain camp, and tirelessly scoured historic records, including finding my father's name on their POW registry. They received major assistance from the Society for the Preservation of Camp Muhlberg (Stalag IV B), especially its wonderful director Angelika Stamm, the Saxon Memorials Foundation, and the staff of Memorial Zeithain. Additionally, I was blessed to have Frank Idzikowski, who shared the experiences he's had with his father-in-law, who also survived Stalag IV B.

The U.S. Holocaust Memorial Museum helped with their extensive archives, and I received wonderful support from Carolyn Hessel at the Jewish Book Council, the curators at the Memorial Auschwitz-Birkenau Memorial and State Museum, and Iwona Hoffman and others with the Museum of the History of Polish Jews, which is being built where the Warsaw Ghetto once stood, to make sure the world never forgets.

From the beginning, Alex Storozynski, President of the Kosciuszko Foundation, has graciously guided me and served as a touchstone for this project. The foundation is a remarkable resource for Polish history and culture. I spent many hours there talking to their experts, seeing footage and photos, and I was fortunate to meet Wanda Lorenc and Mieczyslaw Madejski, two courageous Resistance fighters who, like my father, also bore the scars of war.

I am deeply indebted to the Polish Army Veterans Association of America and Teofil Lachowicz, a walking history book on World War II Poland, who, along with historian Andrzej Toczewski, sent me the life-altering e-mail with the first details of my father's war records, which surprisingly survived the Nazi inferno and opened the floodgates for this book.

The staff at the Women in Military Service for America Memorial at Arlington National Cemetery provided the perfect setting for me to give my dad back his suitcase of memories, which jump-started his desire to finally return home. Ewa Zadrzynska, with the help of Malwina Antoniszczak, organized an unforgettable adventure for us back to my father's beloved Poland.

I will be forever grateful to Ewa Junczyk-Ziomecka, Secretary of State, Chancellery of the President of Poland, whose instant respect and admiration for my father made for the best welcome home we could have ever imagined. The Honorable President of the Republic of Poland Lech Kaczynski and First Lady Maria Kaczynska were incredibly gracious during our visit. The moments we spent in the Presidential Palace, where my dad was finally honored for his accomplishments in the war, will, for this father and daughter, forever be one of the greatest days of our lives.

Jan Oldakowski, director of the Warsaw Rising Museum, and archivist Jan Radziukiewicz generously opened their doors and hearts and shared the extraordinary resources of one of the most unique and compelling museums I have ever seen.

Author Marek Galezowski with the National Institute of Remembrance inspired us with his book on the Eaglets and helped my dad bring closure to sixty-five years of lingering questions about his brave comrades in arms. Academy Award recipient and director Andrzej Wajda showed admiration and reverence for my father's survival on the battlefield and in the sewers, scenes similar to what Wajda himself captured so poignantly in his brilliant films.

Thanks to the World Union of the Home Army Veterans, the group of "Orleta," who, though their numbers are quickly dwindling, remain steadfastly dedicated to keeping the memory of the Eaglets alive. I'm also grateful to Polish historians Andrzej and Zofia Kunert, and Małgorzata Koszarek from the Polish Home Army Museum in Krakow, for sharing their immeasurable knowledge and resources.

This book would not have been possible without the tremendous cooperation of the Ministry of Foreign Affairs of the Republic of Poland, the Polish Cultural Institute, and the Consulate General of the Republic of Poland in New York, especially deputy consul general Marek Skulimowski. He gave invaluable support to the "Kossobudzkis," treating my father like a gallant warrior as he returned to the homeland he was willing to give his life for.

I would like to thank my beautiful mother; I know she is smiling down on me now and happy over my newly established relationship with the handsome young man she met in London, who convinced her to follow the American dream.

Words cannot express my thanks to my phenomenal brother, Alan, and my dear friend and sister-in-law, Katie, who have blessed me with the gift of love and family.

To Tomaczek, my partner and soulmate—your creative genius, your thoughtful and caring comments, and your endless encouragement have made this journey an exquisite treasure to my heart.

Lastly, to my father and his indomitable spirit, and to all those, past, present and future, who like the Eaglets, are "faithful and obedient to the last hour"—you and your families will always have this proud daughter's love and utmost respect.